Ghostly & Creepy Experiences

Anything GHOST
Volume One

Lex Wahl
with paranormal insights by
Al Rauber

Copyright ©2016 by Lex Wahl

All rights reserved.
The personal stories, photographs and illustrations contained in this book belong to those who shared them with Anything Ghost. However, all the written content in this book has been edited, so use of the content as it is presented in this book may not be reproduced or transmitted in any form or by any means, electronic or mechanical, including photocopying, recording, or by an information storage and retrieval system—except by a reviewer who may quote brief passages in a review to be printed in a magazine or newspaper—without permission in writing from the publisher.

ISBN: 978-0-9968408-3-5

Cover: edited work of public domain art by Peter Newell (1862-1924). From the book, "The Hunting of the Snark" by Lewis Carroll, 1903.

Photographs and illustrations included in this book are from artists (as attributed below each work), and from those who submitted photos with their stories. No photos or illustrations in this book may be reproduced in anyway without consent of the artists or from those who submitted work for this book, except for those noted as "public domain" (not including the book's cover art).

10 9 8 7 6 5 4 3 2 1

Preface

The idea behind Anything Ghost was simple: create a podcast (audio show) where people could send their paranormal experiences, and read those stories on the podcast. It was the first ghost story podcast of its kind—and it worked. Ever since the release of episode #1 in late January of 2006, the stories have never stopped coming in.

Over the years, the listeners have asked me to compile some of the stories into a book format, and I have finally done it.

I sifted through countless emails, reached out to those who sent in their stories, and put together this collection of true paranormal experiences—from all around our world. I have made edits to the stories, but what I've included in this book is pretty much what I read when the story was sent to me. For those who are interested in hearing the original recordings, there is an episode number and release date after each story.

While compiling the book (rummaging through archived email; dusting off old Word documents; sifting through archives of audio of files), I remembered that some people sent photographs along with their stories. So, with their approval, I began adding some of those photos to the book. When news got out that I was adding photos to the book, some went back to the place of their experience and took fresh pictures—one contributor even created a drawing of her experience.

Over the life of the Anything Ghost, listeners have asked me to talk about my own paranormal experiences. I thought this book would be an ideal place for that, so I've shared several of my own experiences in the book. My stories are peppered throughout, but can be found quickly going to the index at the end.

January 29, 2016 marked the tenth anniversary of Anything Ghost. In the early days of the podcast, Anything Ghost was the only one of its kind. But things have changed since then, and there are now countless true ghost story podcasts out there. And even though someone would have eventually come up with the idea of a ghost story sharing podcast, it makes me proud to know that I created Anything Ghost, and it was the pioneer of true ghost story podcasts.

You can find out more information about Anything Ghost by visiting the website: www.anythingghost.com.

I'd like to thank Al Rauber (renowned and respected paranormal investigator) for his support of Anything Ghost when it was first starting out (and since), and for allowing me to share some of his knowledge of ghosts in the book—found at the beginning of each chapter.

Anything Ghost is all about the stories, and it wouldn't be anything without those who shared their experiences: thanks to everyone who has shared stories on the podcast (I am grateful for their support over the past ten years); and a special thanks to those who allowed me to share their experiences and pictures in this book!

My hope is that "Anything Ghost Volume One" will be a great source of "ghostly and creepy" entertainment, as well as an insightful look into what may be going on all around us.

Enjoy the ghost stories!
Lex

Table of Contents

Preface III

Types of Phenomenon - The Crisis Apparition 9

Chapter - 1 11

    A Haunted Paris, France Apartment 13

    Old Village Manor House 15

    The Weeping Lady 18

    Apartment 530 19

    A Voice Off the Side of the Road 21

    Paper Route Orb 22

    Similar Dreams 23

    The Oakleigh House 24

    Swollen Tongue 25

    Cigarette Break 26

    The Girl and the Bouncing Ball 27

        Funeral Parlor Home 28

        My Grandparents' House 29

    Voices of a Hundred Ancient Tongues 32

    Birthday Ghost Children 35

    Soft Footsteps 37

    Beginnings of a Medium 39

    My Visiting Uncle 40

    The Shaman 41

Types of Phenomenon - A Place Memory or Residual Haunting 43

Chapter - 2 45

    The Shadow Person in My Attic 47

    Hospital Ghost 49

    Ghostly Good-bye 50

    Bangkok, Thailand Ghost Experiences 52

    Fifth House to the Left 54

    The House Next Door to Grandma's .56

    An Archaeologist's Experience with Ancestral Ghosts 59

    The Two-Story House on Lafayette 61

    The Shadow Visitors 64

Sidewalk Ghost ... 66
The Knocking Ghost ... 68
Electric People ... 70
New England Ghost Story ... 72
The Man Upstairs ... 75
Jealous Ghost ... 79
The Ghost in Apartment 9 ... 81
Ghostly Ship Stories ... 82

Types of Phenomenon - Transient Spirits ... 85

Chapter - 3 ... 87

My Stay at the Myrtles Plantation ... 89
The Earthquake Ghost ... 94
Devil Dog of New Zealand ... 95
The Doorknob Jiggler ... 96
The Sleep and Snore Ernie Doll ... 97
Philadelphia Haunting ... 98
The Gift of Cows ... 99
"I am the Boogie Man" ... 100
Haunted Colonial Home in the Woods ... 101
The Old Part of the House ... 105
A Walk at Bethany Lake Park ... 108
Emergency Call from the Dead ... 109
The Vietnam Veteran Spirit ... 111
Apparition in My Room ... 114
The Sinclair Library ... 116
Ghost Scars ... 117
A Dark Image in the Hall ... 120

Types of Phenomenon - Poltergeist Activity ... 123

Chapter - 4 ... 125

Louisiana Library Ghost ... 127
Las Luces Fantasmas ... 130
Haunted Office Space ... 131
The Museum Stories ... 134
The Children's Tea Set ... 136
Oriskany Battlefield ... 138

Basement Shadow Person	140
Home for Troubled Teens	142
Mr. Keen's Halloween Promise	144
Haunted Stockton Apartment	146
Haunted Birmingham Home	148
Ghostly Rail Sounds	150
Haunted Arkansas Mobile Home	152
The Haunted Victorian Home	156
Room 212 in the Stanley Hotel	160
Peek-a-Boo, I See You!	162
Is Emily a Ghost?	166

Types of Phenomenon - A Purpose Haunting 169

Chapter - 5 171

Dog Keeps an Eye on an Apparition	173
Fourteen Floors Up	175
Dan's Run in Henryville	177
"Sing and Snore Ernie"	178
Golden Gate Park Experience	179
Waverly Hills Experience	180
Noises in the Kentucky Woodlands	181
The Tuxedo Man	182
Haunted Home for the Elderly	184
Haunted Auto Parts Store	185
The Old Lady Who Lived Here	186
The Little Yellow House in Redlands	188
A Haunted Childhood Home	189
Bronx, New York Ghost Stories	190
The Haunted Evelyn Apartments	192
Funeral Home Ghost	194
A Small Boy Ghost in Fallujah, Iraq	196
The Cobbler's Ghost in Merseyside	197
The Notting Hill Flat	199
The Forgotten Lodger	200

Types of Phenomenon - A True Haunting 203

Chapter - 6 205
    The Ghost of Llanrumney Hall 207
    Haunted Club 210
    The Ghosts of 39 Gordon Street 211
    The World War II Ghost 215
    The Haunted Projection Room 216
    A Hospital Ghost 219
    Mystery Man in a Hong Kong Hotel 222
    Red Hill Hotel 224
    A Ghost at Uncle's House 227
    Haunting at Silverwater Prison 229
    Unexplained Experiences 231
    The Shadow Man at Grandpa's House 232
    Haunted Family Summer Cottage 234
        The Breathing Dead 235
    A Haunted House in Nebraska 236
    Uncle Makes One Last Visit 237
    The Walking Lady of Auburn 238
    Loyola Marymount University 239
    She Followed Us Down from the Attic 241

Chapter - 7 247
    Index of Names 247

Chapter - 8 249
    Index of Extra Material 249

Types of Phenomenon Commonly Referred to as a Haunting

The Crisis Apparition
This is the most common type of "haunting". In this situation, an apparition will appear to a friend or a loved one during a time of great stress or trauma.
- Always a purpose or reason for this occurrence such as a request for help, reassurance, to say goodbye, etc.
- Always a one time situation.
- Parapsychologists believe this is just a telepathic communication from a person under stress to another living being and NOT a true "haunting."

Courtesy of Al Rauber. All rights reserved. Copyright 2016.

The stories that follow in Chapter 1 are not intended to be examples of the above described phenomenon.

Public Domain.
Newell, Peter. 1862-1924.

1 | Chapter One

- A Haunted Paris, France Apartment
- Old Village Manor House
- The Weeping Lady
- Apartment 530
- A Voice Off the Side of the Road
- Paper Route Orb
- Similar Dreams
- The Oakleigh House
- Swollen Tongue
- Cigarette Break
- The Girl and the Bouncing Ball
- Funeral Parlor Home
- My Grandparents' House
- Voices of a Hundred Ancient Tongues
- Birthday Ghost Children
- Soft Footsteps
- Beginnings of a Medium
- My Visiting Uncle
- The Shaman

A Haunted Paris, France Apartment
Juliette (Paris, France)

This is the story of events that took place a little over ten years ago in Paris, France.

I had recently moved into a new apartment near the Canal Saint Martin and had just had twins. When the twins were still small, but old enough to eat their dinner in high chairs, I would often notice them looking and laughing at the same part of the wall (next to a walk-in closet). It was very hard to distract them whenever it happened, and it only happened in that one part of the apartment.

Once they were old enough to talk, my son would tell me that he "liked the little boy that came to see him in his room at night; but he didn't like it when he got teased."

He went on to tell me that some nights he would see a boy's hand appear above his feet at the end of his bed—and the hand would wave at him. If he was awake, the boy and him would play a waving game for a few minutes; but if he ignored it, the hand would tug at the blankets.

I did feel uneasy, because I thought of all the movies where kids saw things and the parents didn't believe them; but I also kept in mind that my kids would tell me completely outrageous things; so I put it down to kiddy stuff, and didn't question him too much. I did stay watchful, though.

Later, I moved the two of them into a bigger room. After this move, my daughter began tell me about a lady in white that she would see walking outside the bedroom window at night. The lady wore a funny hat and would carry a tray of food in her hands. As we lived three flights up, I put it down to a strange dream.

The kids then told me about a boy who would come out to look at them, and then run through the wall—in the exact spot they used to stare and giggle when they were babies. I had never told them about this. Gradually, they grew older and the stories stopped.

And then there was a fire.

It was a small fire; upstairs in a blocked chimney, and it was taken care of immediately by the fire brigade. They came again the next day to check behind some of the walls in the building for faulty wiring; it was then that I discovered that behind the part of the wall (where the kids said they saw the little boy run) was a service staircase that had been walled up.

I started investigating the building's history, and found that some Jewish children had been hidden there during the Second World War. They were eventually found and taken away to Nazi concentration camps.

Even stranger was seeing an old photograph from the turn of the century showing that a wooden staircase and ramps had covered part of the building. These were from a much earlier time when craftsmen (such as shoemakers and the like), would have little workrooms in the courtyards and shops on the pavement out front.

Many extra wooden structures like this linked buildings together, or served as very bad living quarters for the very poor. They were terrible fire hazards and rat havens, and were torn down long ago.

During the First World War, part of our building had been used to house the wounded. Nurses would use the outside staircases and ramps to visit the patients and bring them trays of food. These particular nurses were from a religious order and wore white outfits with "funny hats."

I have since left that apartment and the kids have never seen anything weird since then; but my son occasionally tells me that a little boy really did use to wave at him from the end of his bed. My daughter also recalls being scared of a lady in white—whom she saw a few times out her window three floors up.

I felt very moved by this experience, and I hope that in some way we gave comfort to the little boy and any other children who may also have been there.

Anything Ghost Episode #223
May 21, 2016

Haunted Apartments

In 2007, there was a popular story on Anything Ghost about a haunted apartment. It was a long, self-narrated story sent to me by Laura in San Francisco.

In her story, Laura talked about a time in her life when—after having roommate issues—she decided to move out on her own. She found an apartment in New York, and began her new life.

Shortly after moving in, Laura began to notice a strange odor when she entered the apartment; she also began to see a strange mold on the walls; then a neighborhood girl told Laura she looked like the woman who had lived there before—and other neighbors were giving Laura strange side-glances.

Soon, Laura began to feel depressed and became reclusive—not answering the phone, and staying in bed. Then she began to hear someone talking to her: the voice asked if it could use Laura as a way to get out of the apartment. Laura agreed—but strangely, she soon found herself thinking about taking her own life. However, with help from a suicide hotline, Laura was able to stave off the darkness.

After doing some investigative work, Laura found that the previous tenant had the same first name and last initial as Laura, and looked very similar to her. She also found that this woman had recently taken her own life in that same apartment.

The story is still very popular, so I replay it from time-to-time on Anything Ghost.

Old Village Manor House
Robb (U.K.)

This happened to me sixteen years ago in England. At that time, I was working for a company that made sure when someone rented out a house, that it was fully furnished and that everything was in place—all the bedding, cutlery, etc.

The company sent me down to an old village in England. It was an old manor house that was split into two units. One half of the unit was owned, but I was to furnish the other unit. In this particular unit all I had to do was set up the bedding and the cutlery.

So I went to the house at first call of the morning. I walked around the back to get the key and opened the door. As soon as I shut the old oak door behind me, all the hairs on the back of my neck went up. This seemed strange to me at the moment, but I didn't really think anything of it, and I just cracked on.

I continued upstairs, and on the landing at the top of the stairs I saw all the beds. The beds were in wrappings for storage. It was my job to cut off the wrappings and wheel the beds into the bedrooms.

As I walked down the hall, I noticed a small bedroom on the left side of the hall that contained a bed that was already made up. It had a sort of maroon scratchy Hessian wool blanket. So I thought to myself, "Okay. That room is already made up."

I then looked in the room that was a little to the left, and saw that it contained two beds that were also made up. I walked further down the hallway, and I saw a bedroom on the left that needed bedding. Lastly, I came to the master bedroom that had a door with a glass panel in it. I entered the master bedroom and noticed it too needed bedding.

By this time, I began to feel uneasy—as if someone else was there—and I went to see if maybe the agent was in the house. So I called out. No one answered.

I continued up the stairs from the first floor to make sure nobody was in the house. At the top of the stairs I found an attic. I entered the attic. It was dusty and weird. Inside, amongst other things, I saw an old rocking horse and wooden carved toys—and the wallpaper appeared to be hand drawn with pictures of rocking horses and clown faces. After looking around, I thought it looked very strange, and having reached the conclusion that no one was in the house, I headed back downstairs (figuring I would get my work done and get out as soon as possible).

I went back into the bedroom that needed bedding, threw my keys and newspaper on the couch, and set out to unwrap the bed. I soon became fixated on an old dial-up phone that was on the bedside. I just could not stop looking at it. For some reason, I had this feeling that it was about to ring—I was so certain, that I could almost hear it ringing in my head.

Then, just beyond the wall behind the phone, I began to hear footsteps… very slowly. The footsteps were making there way down the hallway towards the wall. I was frozen in place. Somehow, in my mind's eye, I knew what the person coming down the hall looked like: a man in his late 40's or early 50's, slick black hair, mustache with a pointy goatee beard, with a red smoking jacket on. And, he was looking at me through the wall as he was walking down the corridor. Again, this was just something I pictured—I don't know where that image came from.

Suddenly, it felt like someone was pushing my face: it felt like pins and needles digging into my face in the shape of fingers and was pushing in on me.

Just as the footsteps reached the end of the hallway (at which point the person should have appeared in front of the glass panel in the door), I turned to look behind me and saw the bay window.

At this point, I thought to myself, "I'm going to jump. I'm going to jump through the bay window. And when I land on the deck below, I'll probably break an arm or leg—but I need to get out now!"

But I waited a few more seconds.

The footsteps seemed to stop.

I then turned to grab my keys and newspaper from the sofa with the intention of getting out of there…but they were gone. I grabbed a pillow and lifted it up to see if they were underneath. But instead, on the underside of the pillow I saw blood. I threw the pillow down, and ran down the hallway. I quickly came upon the room at the end of the hallway and peered inside. There I saw my keys and newspaper lying neatly on middle of the bed. I jumped in the room and grabbed my keys and newspaper, and headed down the old spiral staircase. As I was heading down the staircase, something took my knees out: it felt like a strong wind, but very focused on the back of my knees. This nearly caused me to trip down the stairs, but I got my footing and continued my way down.

Near the bottom of the stairs was a very large, long mirror. As I was heading down, I thought to myself, "Don't look in the mirror!"

I went down the stairs, ran out the door, shut the door, and never went back. I went back to the office and told the company something very weird happened and I am not going back there.

The company sent in the agent who rented the place out. He reported that there was a partially made bedding in the main bedroom, the bedding was made in the far bedroom, and as for the two remaining bedrooms there was neither a bed in the room or beddings on the beds. And he said there was no maroon wool blanket on any of the beds in the house.

Photo by Robb (U.K.)
The tall window is where the spiral staircase was; the window on the lower left was the room where Robb left his keys and paper; the trees obscure the attic window on the right.

As I said, that was 16 years ago, and it's still a very vivid memory. I now live two streets away from that house, and have been back to visit since. Whenever I look at the house, it certainly does seem to be looking back at me.

Anything Ghost Episode #223
May 21, 2016

The Weeping Lady
Kel (Seattle, US)

I worked on a Christmas tree lot at a supermarket in Seattle a couple of years ago. I had to walk about twenty minutes up a steep hill to get home. Each night, I would pass a large, boarded-up building. The building had a window at the ground level through which I could see a hollowed-out basement. The light from the other side of the street would shine through just enough to make out the remains of boxes, chairs and tables left behind when the building was condemned.

One night, after clocking out at the tree lot, I happened to glance again through that window and was startled to see an elderly Asian woman with her head in her hands weeping hysterically; she was sitting in a chair near the middle of the room. As I passed, she lifted her head, and dried her eyes with a cloth. I looked away quickly—half as not to embarrass her, and half because it scared me!

Then I stopped in my tracks for a moment and, after thinking about what I had just seen, decided to walk back to the window and have another look. There was nobody there...just a couple of chairs and overturned tables surrounded by graffiti-covered walls.

Anything Ghost Episode #127
January 22, 2011

The Great Mausoleum - Lex Wahl

When I was in my early 20's, I got a much-needed job: it was at the Forest Lawn Glendale flower shop. The main part of my job was delivering flowers to graves. The cemetery had a seven-floor mausoleum called the Great Mausoleum—and at holidays we had large stacks of orders to be placed there. I would grab an old 1920's flower cart, fill its tank with water and flowers, and then set off to work. To fill orders, I would look at the name on the order and match it with the room's name and deceased's name; I would then grab the vases, fill them with water and cut flowers to match the order, and replace the vases. Tedious work.

My first Christmas there, I had to go in early to get a head start on the never-ending placements in the Great Mausoleum. After letting myself in the locked door, I grabbed a flower cart and began my seven-floor trek—which entailed a couple weeks of work.

It was a Saturday at 7 a.m. The sun was just coming up, and I was peering out the stained-glass windows at the empty cemetery grounds. I was on the 4th floor (Freesia). By myself. The mausoleum was closed. Then—echoing through the marble halls a couple of floors below me—I heard the sound of a chain moving (each room was cordoned off by brass chains). I froze. Then, it sounded again. I grabbed the van keys, fled up the marble stairs, out the door, and sped back to the flower shop.

Once I got to the shop, I tried to calm my self down; I sauntered into the shop and acted as if I'd forgot something (I was actually stalling, so I could go back to the mausoleum after it was opened to the public).

One of the florists looked at me as I walked in, laughed and said, "You look like you just saw a ghost."

Apartment 530
Joevanny (Puerto Rico)

I grew up in my grandmother's three-bedroom apartment, and being that I'm the eldest of her grandkids, I grew up with most of my uncles still living there. My mother had to work so I spent years in my grandma's house clueless of what was going on through the years.

About two weeks ago, I visited my oldest uncle—whom I regard as a father figure, and for whom I have the utmost respect. He approaches life with a logical explanation to everything; a very smart person who, through the years, I'd always believed was an atheist—saying everything in life has a logical explanation. That was the case until the film Paranormal Activity was given to him by his youngest brother. The elder uncle became furious about it—but quite frankly, I have never seen my uncle so spooked from what I believe was a not so good or even that scary of a movie.

He did not tell me everything but did mention that the events that were presented in that movie were similar to his experiences in the apartment—the apartment that I grew up to call home.

I did not pry for information, but it did not take long for my mother to tell me what was going on in apartment 530.

When my uncles were younger, they slept in the same room (two of them on a bunk bed and my oldest uncle on his own bed). My uncle always told tales of seeing shadows and faces coming from the bedroom door; he and his brothers would often hear voices coming from his closet. The brothers would often complain in the middle of the night, saying that someone had just kicked their beds from underneath.

My grandmother once burned candles and asked for guidance. My grandfather, who did not believe in such things, woke up in the middle of the night and blew out the candles. Just after blowing them out, the apartment began shaking.

I have kept my own experiences in the apartment to myself all these years. I'd always assumed it was an over-active imagination, but now I know it was not.

I have always to slept covered head to toe—completely buried in my blankets. This one evening was no exception, however, I decided to peek over the covers, and as I peered into the dark room, I saw the shadow of eerie hands approaching me. They appeared as if they were trying to choke me. I pulled the covers back over my head.

Two weeks ago, when the most serious and respectable of my uncles told me that the incidents in Paranormal Activity reminded him of events in his childhood—and, that they took place in the same room, in the same apartment #530—I knew that I had not imagined those eerie hands that approached me that one evening.

Anything Ghost Episode #112
April 17, 2010

Milo Says Goodbye - Lex Wahl

The first dog we rescued was a 65-pound mixed breed. We got him when he less than a year old, and named him Milo. He and our other dog had very active lives of hiking, beaches, mountains, parks, restaurants, road trips, three to four walks a day...but he finally passed away at the age of 18. It was a very sad few days that followed. We retrieved his ashes and placed them in the family room.

A week after he passed, we were getting ready for bed; it was 11 p.m. We began to notice the faint sound of music, but could not tell where it was coming from. Thinking it was a neighbor, I stepped outside...but the music stopped; so, it had to be coming from indoors. We looked around for what was probably five minutes, when I finally found the source: it was a clock radio in the bathroom. The alarm was not set (never used), and neither of us had touched it; so we had no idea why it turned on. It never did that again.

The next night, again at 11 p.m., we were settled in bed when one of the smoke alarms began making random beeping noises. I got up to take a look, and it stopped. It never did that again.

Then on the third night, again at 11 p.m., and again we were bedded down to sleep, the bedside landline phone rang. I got up angry at who would call at 11 p.m. (because our landline was basically a "spam" phone line); but when I looked at the caller-ID, it listed my wife's mobile phone as the caller. Her mobile phone was downstairs, and we were the only two home (other than our other dog, who was at our bedside).

I began to recognize the pattern of electronic devices being used to get our attention three nights in a row—and always at the same time. The first thought that came to my mind (probably because I missed him so much) was that it was Milo. And although I felt silly doing so, I went downstairs, grabbed a couple of dog biscuits from the cupboard, put them on his box of ashes, and told him I missed him a lot. There were no more disturbances.

A Voice Off the Side of the Road
Angel (Paramount, California)

In July of 2006, my brother and I went to visit some family in Mexico. At the time this story occurred we were in a small village where my aunt and her family lived.

One night, my aunt's aunt called her to inform her that she was getting rid of some couches and asked if she wanted them. My aunt really liked them, so she accepted. Afterwards, my uncle, brother, cousin and I went to go get them. Her aunt did not live that far away from them. In fact, they were practically neighbors—she lived a quarter of a mile away. However, we had to take a longer route to get to her house because there were crops in between.

It was around 9 p.m. when we arrived. My brother and cousin took one couch, and my uncle and I took the other. Midway to getting to my uncle's house, the couches got too heavy for my brother and cousin, so my uncle asked me if I could wait where I was while he helped my brother and cousin. He would then come back and help me. I accepted, and as such was left alone on the road.

The area where I was left at was a long dirt road with very dim street lamps and was in between some woods and crops—I was practically in the darkness with no homes in sight.

After being alone for a few minutes, I started to hear some movement in the woods. At first I thought it was an animal, so I ignored it. A few seconds later, I heard someone say in Spanish, "Hey you!"

I began to get scared and could not believe what I was hearing. After that, the same voice said, "Hey you! Yeah you! Angel! Come over here."

I was scared out of my mind: someone—or something—called me by name. I wanted to run but at the same time, I didn't want to leave the couch in the middle of the road. I don't know if it was the adrenaline or the fact that I was scared but I picked up the couch and ran with it all the way back to my uncle's home.

When I arrived at the house, my uncles, brother, and cousin were in shock that I made it all the way to the house with the couch by myself. They saw my face and noticed I was pale and frightened. For several minutes they all tried to get my attention but I was zoned out. I was obviously in shock because of what I'd heard. After a few minutes my uncle gave me a slight slap to bring me out of it, and then offered me a cigarette to relax.

After awhile, I relaxed and I began to cry and told them of my experience. While I was telling my uncles the story, they both looked at each other with scared faces. When I was done they asked me where the incident occurred. After I told them, they proceeded to tell me that two weeks ago, in those woods where I heard the voice, the body of a male who had died two day's prior was discovered. I was shocked and could not believe what I was hearing. After the news sunk in, it started to make sense why I heard a voice. But I still couldn't understand how the ghost knew my name.

I went back to that area the next night to confront the thing, but nothing ever happened. It's been seven years since that incident, and to this day it frightens me to even pass by that area.

Anything Ghost Episode #188
March 8, 2014

Paper Route Orb
Michael (Queretaro, Mexico)

I was about twelve years old when I used to have an evening paper route after school.

I usually planned my route so I could finish on the top of the hill right by the graveyard—this was so I could just dash straight down the hill to my house when I was done.

One night, I finished my route (since it was winter it was already dark by 5 p.m.), and I was standing on the top of the hill looking at the stars. There was one star that caught my attention—since it was the brightest of them all. After a couple of minutes, I headed down the hill quite fast and noticed that the star appeared to be moving. I thought it was the illusion when objects far away seem to be moving beside you. The surprise came when I got to the house where I stopped, and that star just carried on.

It was really weird because I swear it was the same star and it started moving exactly at the same time I started moving—only, it did not stop and just carried on until I could no longer see it.

Anything Ghost Episode #86
March 29, 2009

Similar Dreams

Helena (Stockholm, Sweden)

My best friend used to live in a big, very old house in my hometown. It was a rectory (since her dad was the priest in our little township at the time). My best friend and I used to play and hang out there a lot after school, and she would often tell me about how she was scared of certain parts of the house—the attic, for example. There were so many rooms in the house, and it was just my friend and her parents living there. So the house almost felt abandoned because of how big it was. She never told me about specific things happening, but I too felt uncomfortable whenever visiting. The house felt strange and very, very unwelcoming.

About two years ago, I had a very vivid dream about that house. I was standing in the kitchen with my friend. She handed me a set of keys, and told me the house was mine. She then walked out and left me alone. It was dark. All of the sudden, I became aware of something going on outside. I walked up to the window, looked out, and saw a bunch of people standing there looking in at me: men, women and children—all looking like they were from a couple of centuries back in time. They came closer and closer until they where pressing their hands on the window, banging. They didn't say anything but they conveyed the feeling of wanting to come inside—in a threatening way. I felt extremely frightened and stressed. I also felt like maybe they where already in the house, since the front door wasn't the only way in. Then I woke up. It was the kind of dream that makes you want to turn on the night light. I couldn't go back to sleep for a long time after that.

About a week later, I was hanging out with my best friend, and told her about the dream. What she told me next gave me the chills. She said that she had almost exact same dream a couple of years ago when she still lived in that house—everything was the same, except the part when she gave me the keys. In the dream she stood in the kitchen, then walked up to the window and saw people pressing their hands and banging on the glass, demanding to come inside. All the tiny hair on my arms stood up when she told me this. We discussed it for a long time, but we couldn't explain it. What are the odds of this happening? And what does it mean? I'm very interested in the paranormal, and I think that maybe something in that house (or the house itself), came to both me and my friend through these dreams.

I've never had the same dream since then, and neither has my friend.

Anything Ghost Episode #210
August 16, 2015

The Oakleigh House
Rita (Queensland, Australia)

The house I lived in for a while when I was growing up was in Oakleigh, in the outer suburbs of Melbourne. At the time, the home was approximately 60 years old and was a large Californian bungalow style home. I lived in it with my parents and a younger sister. The house itself was nothing remarkable, in the sense that it had no sinister history that we knew of. However, I never really liked the house as a child. I always had the impression I was never quite alone—even when I was the sole occupant (the rest of the family was out). I would always see glimpses of shadows or movement; objects such as sewing scissors, jewelry and other articles would go missing and be located in different parts of the house. Many incidents happened in the house that frightened me. I was not very keen on speaking to my parents about the occurrences, as I was fearful they would ridicule me as having an over-active imagination.

There was one incident when my younger sister (seven years old) and I (eleven years old) were watching TV in the dining room. I was sitting in a chair and my sister was sitting across from me. To the left of me, approximately two to three feet, was a wall, and against the wall there was a telephone table with the house phone. It was an older phone that had a dial wheel and cords. The coiled cord went from side of the phone to the bottom of the ear and mouthpiece and the other straight cord went from the back of the phone to the connection wall socket.

Our mother was in the kitchen preparing the evening meal and father was at work. My sister and I were engrossed in the television program. Then, unexpectedly from my peripheral vision, I noticed movement. The cord that ran from the back of the phone to the wall socket was slowly dragging up the wall as if someone had looped the cable over their index finger and was steadily inching it upwards along the wall. I turned to look at it; by this time it had reached approximately three and a half feet up the wall and then it suddenly dropped—as if whatever or whoever was manipulating the cord was caught and had let go. The only evidence that the cord had been disturbed was that it was swinging back and forth limply.

I could feel a cold chill run up my spine and the hairs the back of my neck stick up with fear and disbelief. I looked at my sister who had the same expression of shock and fear on her face. We both said at the same time, "Did you see that?"

Without waiting for each other's response we both raced into the kitchen and alerted our mother. After inspecting the cable, our mother could not give us an explanation.

After that incident, I felt comfortable in sharing with our mother some of the other paranormal experiences I'd had at the house. She tried to appease me with some possible logical answers to the happenings. I gathered she wanted to end the topic so that it would not terrify my younger sister. Therefore, I let the conversation go. I will tell you though, that I was comforted with the reality that my younger sister had also witnessed the incident with the phone. It reassured me that the events I had seen in the past were not the works of an over-active child's imagination.

There have been many more occurrences in that house. I would be happy to share with you and your audience later and if you are interested.

Anything Ghost Episode #129
February 26, 2011

Swollen Tongue
Vicki (Bulacan, Philippines)

My friend lives with her parents in a bungalow house in rural Bulacan. Their house was located at the end of a forest, and the next-door neighbor was about a ten-minute walk away. As a side note, the Philippines has a rich culture that also includes supernatural beings. It is told that these beings usually live in the forest and some of them are quite territorial, and will wreak havoc on a person who dares cross them.

Ever since my friend hit puberty, she always felt that someone was with her in the room—especially if she was left alone at home. This presence didn't bother the family though, and nothing bad happened until the day she became serious with a boyfriend.

This guy became close to the family, so he usually visited on weekends. One night, my friend had the strangest dream. She was talking to someone who was trying to convince her to leave her boyfriend for him; he said that if she went with him, he would give her everything, and that she would never have the need for anything again. In the dream, she was aware that he loved her and somehow had been a part of her life for a while. However, she strongly refused him and told him to go away.

When she woke up, she turned to her sister who is sleeping at the bed next to her to say something, but she couldn't. She then found that her tongue had swollen overnight to the point that she could not even speak or make a sound. Crying uncontrollably, she let her family know what happened by texting it on her phone. They then decided to take her to the hospital. But the moment they stepped out of the house, she was able to speak again. They still had her checked up by a doctor, who, after several medical tests, told them that there was absolutely nothing wrong.

She told us this story for the first and last time that day. Since then, she has absolutely refused to talk about it, and will change the topic or walk away whenever the topic comes up.

Anything Ghost Episode #183
November 13, 2013

Cigarette Break
Steve (Manchester, UK)

Although I have been investigating the paranormal since I was about 16 (I'm now 44), I thought I'd relay a personal experience that really caught me off guard.

About nine years ago I moved in with my current partner (after deciding to give up my own home). I seem to have a bit of a knack for being able to feel atmospheres in buildings—be they homes or commercial premises. On a few occasions I have noticed a bit of an atmosphere in the house that sometimes felt like what I can only describe as thick and heavy. I thought that it was just due to it being a new building to me and never really paid it much attention.

One early morning, after we had lived there for about six months, I came downstairs for a cigarette. It was about 3:00 a.m. I walked through to the kitchen and opened the back door. I lit a cigarette and sat down at the kitchen table, trying to relax so I'd be able to sleep when I returned upstairs. I never turned on the lights, as the street lighting from outside was always sufficient for me to see what I needed.

As I was thinking about things and trying to get my mind to wind down, I realized that I could no longer see any lighting coming through the front room window. At first, I thought that maybe some of the street lights had broken. But as I began to pay attention, I noticed a very large black, human-shaped figure was filling the whole the doorway—and it was this object that was blocking out most of the light.

I began to feel very cold, and I slowly rose from my chair. I was starting to think I had a very large intruder in the house, and I was preparing to defend myself. As I rose up to my full height, the figure began to shrink in on itself. It grew smaller and smaller before my very eyes, until it transformed into a dense black ball that hung in the centre of the doorway. As I pulled back, completely caught unaware and feeling a little unsure of what I was witnessing, the ball faded away. All at once the street lighting came flooding back into the kitchen.

Needless to say, the cigarette didn't hold that much appeal anymore, and although I'm used to investigating other peoples problems, finding one on my own doorstep was a little disconcerting to say the least. This was the start of many more experiences for my family and me at that place, before we eventually moved out.

Anything Ghost Episode #115
June 6, 2010

The Girl and the Bouncing Ball
Tracey (Mountain Grove, Missouri)

My family and I are no strangers to the paranormal. It seems that we are bonded to spirits and they like to make themselves known. It all started with my family in California.

My grandparents lived in an ordinary house, in and ordinary city and we did ordinary things. Nothing really special or unusual ever happened—except for one day.

We were all sitting watching TV in the living room. Everything was quiet except for the noise radiating from the receiver. Then we heard a noise above us that was coming from the second floor. The noise went from one end of the living room ceiling, all the way to the other end. There was no room above where we were sitting, only the attic. As we listened, we realized that it sounded like something was bouncing. When the noise got to the end of the room, it would pause and then come back the other way. I'd pictured the noise to be that of a little girl bouncing a ball outside on the sidewalk. Except, this noise was not outside.

We never felt afraid as we followed the noise with our eyes. My grandfather seemed more annoyed with the sound than afraid—my grandmother, too. One of them would shout, "Quit bouncing that ball!"

Then, just like that, the noise would stop.

The "little girl" (as I pictured her) would bounce her ball from one end of the ceiling to the other; and each time she did we would ask her to stop, and she would.

My Aunt, who lived in the house with my grandparents at that time, would see a girl peeking up from the foot of her bed—like she was either curious or playing a game. My sister saw her, as well: one time she saw her walking past the door in the hall; and other times she saw her sitting in a room (and appeared to be combing her hair).

We never felt threatened in that house. In fact, we all felt very welcomed. But due to the fact that the area was becoming more and more unsafe, we decided to move.

Many people tried living in that house—a few businesses even tried setting up shop there. But no one ever stayed long. As of now it still sets empty and abandoned—except for the little girl we had to leave behind.

Funeral Parlor Home
(Story 2)

Fast-forward. We'd been living in our new house for a few years. It was in a little town in southern Missouri. My great aunt owned a video arcade. She was moving her business to another location, so my parents and her decided to turn the building into apartments for herself, my parents, me and my older sister (who was expecting).

When the place was finished there were three rooms in one building (all connected by doors). The layout made it very easy for us to visit one another.

After living there for a few months peculiar things started to happen. None of my parents smoked but sometimes we would smell cigar and cigarette smoke as if it were being blown in directly in our faces. Our bathroom was through the kitchen and my room was across the kitchen and down the hall. My mother would occasionally see a small figure walk into the bathroom. Thinking it was me, she would ask if I was okay (I guess due to the fact that I hadn't emerged out the restroom). She would watch the bathroom door for a response, and I would soon come out of my bedroom to answer my mother. My mother would just look at me. There was no way I could have gotten by her without her knowing—especially since she was watching the only bathroom door. Once in a while we would feel a touch, a cold chill, or hear a noise. Although, nothing that we ever experienced made us feel unwelcome.

One night, I got out of bed and proceeded to cross the hall to use the restroom. Everyone was asleep, so the hall was pitch dark—except for two little night lights lighting the path to the bathroom. For some reason, I stopped in the middle of the hall and turned to look down the hall to the living room area. There, standing looking right at me, was a tall figure in what looked like a mid-running stance. He looked like he had something in his hand, although I could not see what. Even though it was dark all around, I could see this "man" standing there and staring at me. It seemed like forever! Then I made a move back to my room and the figure moved as well—it took off running! I ran into my room and then, for some reason, I ran back to the living room. I looked in the direction in which he ran, but there was nothing but wall. Needless to say, I ran right to my parents' room at that point.

After that experience, my mother and father began fighting—a lot. My mother began acting strange. She wouldn't want to do anything but become a recluse.

Somehow, the subject of all the strange occurrences came up with my great aunt. She then disclosed the origin of the building that she had bought (and where we lived). Apparently, it used to be a funeral parlor. My aunt's section was where the bodies were embalmed, and our section was where they were viewed.

In addition to living in the "funeral parlor," as we came to call it, there were many other things that happened to my mother and I. For some reason, my father never experienced anything, and if he did he never made it known—at least not to us.

My mother would often be lying in bed (due to the increased depression of being in the house). One day, she was lying in bed with her hand dangling off the bed. Just as she was getting relaxed she felt what she described as a bone hand wrapping around her arm and pulling. To this day neither my mother or I will sleep with our hands or feet hanging off the bed. There were also times when she was lying in bed watching TV, and sometimes when she looked at the pillow next to her, she noticed an indent—like someone was lying next to her.

You could not breathe in that house! When you left you felt the world in it's vastness, but when you stepped in that house it was like the world became a vacuum: consuming every breath from your lungs.

My sister, as I mentioned, lived in another area of the building. Her kitchen was part of the original part of the building. There was something about that area: my sister would try her hardest to avoid going in there. If she could get a meal somewhere else, she would. She always said she felt like she was being watched in that kitchen. Needless to say, she ate many meals at our apartment or at my grandparents' place.

Well, it looked like we were moving again.

My Grandparents' House

(Story 3)

Fast-forward…again.

At this point, my family all lived in the same town again. We would go visit my grandparents at their house quite often. Nothing ever bothered us at our house, but we always felt more comfortable at my grandparents' home. I don't know why.

My grandma was diagnosed with Stage IV Melanoma cancer, and so my mother, aunt, and I would take turns taking care of her and my grandfather (who was wheelchair bound). My grandmother was bedridden by that point, so we placed a baby monitor by her bed to monitor her needs. One time, my grandmother was sleeping, so we went into the living room to take a little bit of time for ourselves—to decompress, if you will.

Then we heard grandma talking...but not to us.

Over the monitor we could hear her having what sounded like a conversation. My grandma was talking as clear as day; and sometimes we heard a faint muffled noise—as if in response. My mother and my aunt just stared at each other, and then at me. I took it upon my self to go see who was in there with her.

When I got into the room the air was a little heavy. I don't know if it was because there was someone or something in there, or if it was because I was nervous. I asked grandma, "Who are you talking to?"

She replied, "That man. Over there."

I looked over. "Grandma, there is no man."

She scuffed, and in a stern voice said, "Yes! There is! He is standing right there smiling at me!"

At that point I just thought it best to agree with grandma. I mean who knows, there may be a man there. I asked her, "Do you want me to tell him to leave"?

Then she replied, "No. You don't see that man there?"

I said, "No Grandma, I don't, but if you see him than that is okay."

Weeks after that grandma died in her bed the way she wanted to: in her sleep. The only pain that was left to feel in the house was with us missing her terribly. We promised my grandmother and grandfather that we would not put grandpa in a nursing home. He was, like I said, wheelchair bound (having only one leg and in very poor health himself). So my mom, aunt, and I took turns caring for grandpa.

After a doctor's visit, we were told that grandpa had cancer everywhere: lungs, throat and bones. He must have had it for a long time but somehow we never knew it. Grandpa liked to watch his TV in the dining room, so we watched our shows in the living room. He would come into the living room to wish us goodnight and then would go off to bed. We still had the monitors hooked up from grandma in case grandpa needed us.

We soon began to hear him talking, too. But not to us: it sounded like he was chatting with an old friend. Telling whoever or whatever about things that had happened in the family. The next morning grandpa had a stroke in his bed, and in 3 weeks he died.

In their will my grandparents left my family their house.

I miss them a lot. They were the only grandparents I ever got to know. I was so very close to them.

My husband and I sleep in the room that both of my grandparents died in, and our bed is in the same spot theirs was. It is the only way it will fit into the bedroom. I feel no fear in the house, but my grandparents do make themselves known.

I will be getting into bed late at night and will hear a loud crash—like the sound of glass shattering. I will get up thinking the cat knocked something over, but after checking the whole house….nothing. Sometimes lights will flicker; at times I see something pass by out of the corner of my eye. I do not feel threatened. I am not scared. Rather, their presence makes me feel like I am safe. I know they are watching over us.

My grandmother would often tell us stories of this house and the things she would see. You see, when we moved to Missouri from California, my grandparents bought this house from a couple that had lost their son in a bad car accident. Understanding that there were too many memories for them there, my grandparents got it at a good price. There were times that my grandmother would awaken during the night and at the foot of the bed, she would see a figure of what looked like a man in a white button up shirt…just staring at her from the end of the bed. Obviously being terribly afraid, my grandmother would scream and proceed to kick at the figure. The figure would then just stare and then go away. We think it was the spirit of the son that the previous owners lost, coming back home to look for his mother. After a while he stopped coming around.

There was one time when I had to get up to get a drink of water. Looking down the hallway from the kitchen, I saw what looked like a figure in a white gown. The figure was standing at the end the hallway. Then, after staring for what seemed like forever, she would walk into the direction of my bedroom. I do feel deep down, that was my grandma.

Anything Ghost Episode #221
April 6, 2016

Voices of a Hundred Ancient Tongues
Donna (Plymouth, Michigan)

I was 18 years old and was living at my uncle's house with my father, as well. I had been sleeping on the couch in those days, as I had no bedroom. One evening, my boyfriend and I decided to take a walk to Riverside Cemetery in Plymouth. The cemetery sits behind the courthouse, and up on the hill above Hines Park (which is a public wooded forest with the occasional playground).

We had just begun dating and were happy to be out together alone that night. Nothing out of the usual had been happening, nor had we been discussing anything frightening or supernatural. I was a young Pagan, still learning ancient religions and practices, and he had been a few years ahead of me. This was the underlining attraction between us.

We had reached the entrance to the cemetery and began walking along the cement-walking path into the right entrance. Again, no jitters or anything, this was normal for us. We were holding hands and talking about something, I don't remember what, most likely the nightclub we both attended regularly at the time. As we continued walking he stopped short and stood very still gripping my hand very tightly. I asked what was the matter, and he motioned for me to be quiet. He just stood there next to me staring right into the middle of the cemetery. It was dark but I could still see the fear on his face. When you see real fear on someone's face, it makes them look very unnatural. It's a look you do not have to question.

"Nick, what is wrong? What are you looking at?" I asked quietly—now nervous myself.

He looked at me very sharply with eyes of complete seriousness. "You need to turn around slowly and get out of here now," he said.

I was really scared then, and found it hard to move.

"What's going on Nick!?" I asked again, this time much more sternly and desperately.

"You need to turn around, get behind me and start walking back to the entrance...right now! They don't want you here. I can see them jumping towards us and they don't want you here! Go now!" He was yelling at me at this point.

I began to run as fast as I could and stopped at the line where the street met the cemetery entrance. I looked back and Nick was still standing there looking into the cemetery. I wanted to go back and grab him for fear that he was in real danger. I yelled for him to come back. He just stood there, motionless.

Finally, after what seemed an eternity, he turned around and walked very slowly back to me. As soon as he crossed the threshold of the cemetery entrance he was back to his usual self. I was crying and I pleaded with him to tell me what was going on.

He looked at me with sadness on his face and said, "I think I just gave you the worst thing a human could ever get from another person. I fear you may be in some trouble now."

I was scared, confused and tired. I wanted to get home and forget what had just happened. I wanted him to be more clear with me about what he was saying, but he was done. He wasn't going to give me anymore information than that.

I finally made it home around 3 a.m. or so, and laid down on the couch. By then I was calm and collected and even convinced myself that it was all just a bunch of hooey.

I was facing the back of the couch and almost asleep when I heard the most horrific sound in the universe. It was a voice…a voice that had a million other voices in it at the same time. It was baritone, very deep and loud. It scolded me in a language I had never heard before. I don't know what it said, but it was threatening me, that much I do know. I was so scared that I actually went fire hot. I didn't get a chill or get cold; my entire body felt like it was on fire in one fell swoop. I couldn't move and I remember my heart actually hurt—like I was having a heart attack. It felt like something heavy sat on my chest and I couldn't breathe.

Then, the voice was gone. Nothing had been moved or altered in the room, nor did I see anything. I think I may have passed out from fear, because I woke the next morning not remembering what happened after I felt the hot flash.

I spent the next week trying to forget what happened, too afraid to tell anyone anything—including Nick.

The next Saturday I went to see another friend, Joe, in his one room apartment. When he let me in the door he pulled me frantically to the phone answering machine in his living space. He had the same fear look on his face that Nick did that night a week earlier.

"You have to listen to this, please!" He said, panting.

He pushed play on the answering machine, and the same voice boomed in the recording. Again, there were many languages in many voices all in one—and very dark and with a low tone. They had the same threatening sound. I sat down on his sofa, and my hands began to shake in my lap.

"What the hell is this on my answering machine? Have you ever heard anything like this before? I came home this afternoon from work and it was on my machine!" He said.

"Yes, I heard the same voice in my living room one week ago." I said.

He looked at me for a few moments, and then asked me to leave. I knew he was afraid of me at that point. I can't explain to you why, but I knew he was right to fear me.

Nothing else had ever happened again after that next Saturday. I have never found out exactly what it was that followed me home from that cemetery, how it knew me, why it was angry with me or what it was trying to say to me.

Thirteen years later, I happened to run into a mutual friend of Nick's on Facebook, and somehow we ended up talking about that night. I told him what happened just as I am telling you, and he knew what it was that followed me. He let me know that Nick had done something years ago that had "created" something evil. It wasn't devil worship or some such nonsense, it was something else entirely. Something I know nothing about. It seems Nick is still plagued by that thing. The theory that our mutual friend had was that it was angry with me for being with Nick, and for having his attention. It wanted to scare me away from Nick. We eventually did break up.

For the last thirteen years it's all been a mystery that feels like it happened just moments ago. The fear is still very real and I do my best not to speak of it out loud for fear of attracting it again. There is something in Riverside Cemetery, and I will not be paying it a visit again.

Anything Ghost Episode #180
September 3, 2013

Booms in the Basement - Lex Wahl

My father grew up in Michigan. He was 8 to 10 years old at the time of this story. One winter morning, just before sunrise, his mother sent him to the basement to fetch something. He opened the door to the basement, turned on the light and walked down the steps into the freezing basement air. Suddenly, he began to hear an ominous low booming sound: "boom...boom....boom....boom." Then it stopped. But soon, it began again: "boom...boom...boom..."

My father froze in his tracks. The banging seemed to engulf the whole basement. His first thought was that it was a ghost pining for his attention. Scared, he grabbed what he needed, scrambled up the stairs, and slammed the door behind him.

The next morning, his mother once again asked my dad to retrieve something from the basement. Again, it was just before sunrise. When he opened the door and turned on the light, he recalled the scary moment from the day before. Apprehensive, he slowly walked down the stairs; then..."boom...boom...boom...boom." He scrambled across the basement to complete his errand, and ran back up to the house.

The following morning his mother again asked him to go back to the basement. Fear beset him, and he explained that there was a ghost in the basement. She stopped what she was doing, and went to investigate. She walked down into the basement, and my father remained at the top of the stairs. The sound began, and my father's eyes grew large. His mother looked around. She then walked over to the window in the basement and peered outside. There she saw the source: a neighbor cutting firewood on the frozen ground.

Birthday Ghost Children
Carro (Stockholm, Sweden)

This story is about something that happened in the house where I grew up. Before I begin, I would like to tell you a little about my parents' house. It was built in the 1920's outside the city of Gävle. From the beginning, it was a two-family house, but that changed over the years. When my parents bought it in the 80's, they were the only ones to live there (together with my older sister). I don't know much about the previous owners, but I can imagine how much life and energy that has flown through the house since it was built. How many memories, tears and laughter were stuck in walls of the house?

In the beginning of the 1990's, I was about to turn six or seven years old. I was tossing and turning in bed, waiting for my parents and my sister to come to my room. It was tradition in my family, to enter the room and sing "Happy birthday" to the one whose birthday it was. Now it was my turn. The night felt like an eternity. The long wait was tiring, but I could not sleep. I think everyone who has been waiting for Christmas day or birthday presents knows how it feels. I was about to get breakfast served in bed as well—and presents! I am pretty sure I had wished for toys: dinosaurs, or probably an Ariel doll. "The Little Mermaid" was my favorite!

The sun was rising and the light was finding its way through my curtains. I was waiting and waiting, tossing and turning, and waiting. That was when I saw them: a boy and a girl. They were standing beside my bed. I thought to myself, "They are my first birthday visitors!"

Yes, I was sure of it. They had come to wish me a happy birthday. At my age, I found nothing weird about it. But now I have trouble explaining why their presence was so natural to me: maybe I had more visitors like them, and I can't remember that today. Either way, I hadn't seen these children before.

They were not scaring me in any way, and they did not say anything. They were just standing there, looking at me. The clothes they wore reminded me of the ones from a Swedish children's book—a book I know took place in the early 1900's. The boy wore a round hat, a shirt and a vest. The girl wore a dress. Her hair was in two long braids that were hanging down on her shoulders. I didn't say anything to either child. I was just looking at them, knowing they would go away soon, and that my family would come in and celebrate my birthday, soon.

I closed my eyes, and tried to sleep. When I looked again, the children had disappeared.

When at last my family came, I didn't think about telling them about my visitors. Deep down inside, I think I understood that the children did not belong to this world.

Photo by Carro (Stockholm, Sweden)
Carro's parents' house where she saw the children.

It took many years, before I began to think about what I had experienced as a child. The children beside my bed was just one of many things that happened in that house. But like I said, I did not think of it as anything paranormal at first, because when it happened, it was the opposite of supernatural – it was completely natural.

Anything Ghost Episode #218
January 30, 2016

Soft Footsteps
Valerie (Bakersfield, California)

Ever since we moved into a brand new home that my husband and I purchased, we have heard noises in our home. The builders blamed it on the settling of the house and it being newly built. We disregarded the noises and also blamed it on the "settling" of the house.

I've suffered from insomnia since I can remember, so I am a light sleeper. One night, about a year into us living at our home, my mother called me. She said she had something to do and couldn't watch my elderly, and slow moving grandma (who at the time was very sick with some type of virus). I of course, agreed.

Being that my daughter and son were at my in-laws house that weekend, I gave my grandma my daughter's bedroom. I set my grandma up and got her comfortable. I told her I'd check up on her in the middle of the night, and that if she needed anything from me, she could just call out for me.

My daughter's bedroom was on the other side of the house toward the front, and my bedroom was towards the back. It wasn't a very large house, but there was a little walk between the rooms because the kitchen, laundry room and two small living rooms were in the center.

The first night, my husband was asleep on the bed and I was doing some late night online shopping. I was wide awake sitting on the floor on the side of the bed near the wall, when I heard soft slow-moving footsteps on the carpet. The footsteps were heading from the door to the other side of my bed. I looked over and saw what appeared to be a short figure in a white long gown who looked like a little old lady. I automatically thought my grandma had come to my room looking for me. I asked in Spanish, "Grandma? Are you okay? Do you need anything?"

No answer. The footsteps stopped.

I pointed the light of my phone to the area where I thought my grandma was and I saw absolutely nothing. I was confused. I heard and saw it perfectly. But grandma was too old and slow to disappear so quickly, and she is not one to joke in that way—especially at 2 a.m. I then became very afraid and tried to wake up my husband. When I told him my experience, he didn't believe me and went back to sleep.

Instead of going to sleep, I got up and used my phone to light my way to the light-switch and turned on the lights. I then ran to my daughter's room to check up on my grandma. She was sound asleep. I had no logical explanation as to what happened. It was so real. I then turned the lights off, went to bed with my husband, and I pulled the covers all the way to my face. I eventually fell asleep.

Since that night, my husband began to work away for weeks at a time, and I had to stay at home alone with my kids. I have since heard the footsteps, and on one occasion even felt as if someone lightly sat at the bottom part of my bed. Thinking it was one of my kids, I called out their names. I then looked to my side, and saw them asleep.

On another occasion, I woke up to the feeling of being watched by a little girl—I thought maybe my daughter was looking at me from the doorway of my bedroom. When I looked at the clock it was 3 a.m. Just like before, my daughter was asleep next to me.

As I said before, since the first time it happened when my grandma came over, it has happened repeatedly and always between the hours of two or three in the morning. It has grown to the point that I now sleep in fear with the light on, and with my kids in my bed.

I am not familiar with the land or anything of concern in the area, but plan on looking into it to see if maybe something was disturbed with the construction of my neighborhood.

Anything Ghost Episode #220
March 19, 2016

Haunted Guest House - Lex Wahl

In 2001, we rented a newly built guest house in Pasadena, California. Only one person had lived there before us, and that was only for a few months. The house was 450 square feet (we were way ahead of the "tiny house" fad in that respect), but it had some valuable amenities such as a yard for the pups, washer and dryer, a garage and air conditioning. I don't know the history of the land, but while we lived there I had strange experiences. In fact, those experiences were what eventually lead me to begin Anything Ghost.

The first odd thing I recall were knocks in the wall. These knocks happened at the same time most mornings, and never at any other time—and they were always at the head of the bed. One morning the bang was so loud it caused us to jump out of bed.

Early one weekend morning, about the same time as the knocks, I was asleep and lying on my stomach. I slowly awoke to a tapping on my back. It was two quick taps that went from my left upper-back, then to the adjacent far right side; then down a few inches on the left, then back over to the far right. When the two taps went lower for the fifth time, I jumped out of bed. The tapping felt like when a doctor taps on your back while he/she is checking your lungs.

Another thing that happened was a cold breeze would pass over my face. I was up late one night (it was winter and cold in Pasadena so all the windows were closed), and as I sat working on the computer, I felt a cold breeze pass over my face. This had happened a few times before, so I focused on communicating after feeling the breeze, and immediately heard that familiar knock on the wall coming from the bedroom.

Beginnings of a Medium
Karli (Boise, Idaho)

These are just a few experiences I had with my daughter when she was young.

The first one I can remember she was around two-and-a-half and she was sitting on my bed facing the bathroom door. I was folding the laundry and she said, "I'm folding clothes with Mama."

When I asked her who she was talking to she said, "The Lady in the bathroom."

I turned to look at the doorway but nothing was there. I didn't want to scare her so I just acted like it was nothing and moved on.

A few weeks later she came into the room I was in and really wanted to make sure all the doors and windows were locked. When I asked her why she said, "There's a man outside the window in a brown bicycle helmet."

I thought it was odd and assured her house was locked up tight.

A few days later, my husband was going though his Marine pictures and she pointed to a picture of a solider and said, "That's the man in the bike helmet, outside the window!"

It was not a bike helmet, it was a military helmet; and the man in the picture had passed away.

The last experience really stayed with me. It's the only one that really scared me.

I was pregnant with my second daughter. My husband was working nights, so my oldest daughter (who was three by then), was sleeping with me. That night, she suddenly woke me up. She was scared and told me, "The little boy at the end of the bed would not leave me alone."

She went on to tell me that he was lost and could not find his mom. She finally called out to him and said, "Leave me alone! I don't want to play with you!"

She then she fell back to sleep. But I did not. I sat there terrified with all the lights on, hoping he did not think I was HIS mother.

My daughter is a teenager now and does not talk much about spirits anymore. When I ask her, she says she would rather not talk about it.

Anything Ghost Episode #220
March 19, 2016

My Visiting Uncle
Lauren (Ventura, California)

My brother and I were really close to my uncle. When we lived in New Mexico, he would take us out for breakfast and drive us in his car with the music blasting (while he sang at the top of his lungs), making us laugh nonstop. After we moved to California, he would sometimes come out for a visit and spoil us just as much as he did in New Mexico. So when we got the news he had passed away in his sleep, we could not believe it. Due to my absence at his funeral in New Mexico, I took the news of his passing pretty hard.

My mom's house in California had big windows in the living rooms that overlooked a deck with a nice view of the city. My niece, who was four at the time (and is my brother's only child), would often fall asleep in one of the living rooms with the big windows.

One morning, my niece told my mom about a man outside of the windows who kept bothering her all night. My mom asked her what man she was talking about.

My niece said, "The man outside last night. His name is Junior. He was nice and really funny, but I was trying to sleep and he kept waking me up."

My mom told my brother about it and they couldn't believe it. Since he was a baby, my uncle's favorite spot to hang out when he came to visit, was out on the deck enjoying the view and—he always went by "Junior."

I'm glad my niece got the chance to meet him, and it's nice to know that he continues to make others laugh.

My other story involves my uncle as well. I was folding my laundry in my mom's laundry room. Between the laundry room to the foyer and main hallway was a swinging door. Over the years, the door had become stiff and didn't swing easily unless it was pushed with excessive force.

I was folding laundry and the door was left open. As I was finishing up, the door started to move and then closed really fast. I just stood frozen in place. I opened the door to ask my mom (who was down the hall), if she had closed the door. She told me she had not.

At first I was a little freaked out, but then I began to feel a comforting feeling come over me as I realized who it may have been. I said out loud, "Hi Uncle. I miss you, and I love you."

Anything Ghost Episode #220
March 19, 2016

The Shaman
Christine (San Francisco, California)

This story takes place in Seoul, South Korea. When I was 7 years old, my family took me to Seoul for the first time. I met my maternal grandmother, aunts, uncles, and several cousins.

My grandmother's apartment building was a massive building. It was 30 stories, and she lived near the top. It was unnerving because of the time it took the elevators to move up that high. The hallway to each unit was exposed to the outdoors. A cement and metal guardrail was all that stood between you and the dizzying drop below. I was too small to look over the edge, but an adult could rest their elbows over the ledge and look down. My uncles often stood their smoking in the evenings.

One early evening, after returning from a water park, something truly disturbing happened. A group of us were laughing and talking outside the entrance to my grandmother's apartment, and enjoying the last rays of sunlight before we turned in. One of my cousins, a teenager, suddenly picked up my 2 year old cousin, still a toddler in training diapers, and dangled him by the torso over the ledge. The adults pleaded quietly with my cousin to pull the toddler to safety. They were afraid to move or raise their voices. Eventually, one of my uncles snatched the toddler back from the ledge, and my older cousin was severely scolded. When pressed to explain himself, he was unable to give any excuse. His mother was perplexed and ashamed, and said he had never behaved like this in his life.

When my grandmother heard the story later that evening, she blamed it on the "shaman woman." It wasn't until I was much older, and when she eventually immigrated to the United States herself, that she told me the story.

My grandmother had a neighbor in the apartment complex. He was a young man who had recently married, but my grandmother had never been able to catch a glimpse of his wife. He was always kind and polite to her, so my grandmother didn't think much of it—that is, not until the screaming, shouting, and loud bangs started. After a few days of the noise, my grandmother asked the young man what was going on.

He apologized to her, but he seemed troubled. He explained that his wife was ill and he would be taking her to the hospital. Mental illness is stigmatized in Korea, and isn't openly talked about. In order to be polite, my grandmother didn't ask any further, and wished them well.

Things were peaceful for a few weeks. Eventually, the man and his wife returned, and things seemed to calm down for a bit. My grandmother even glimpsed the young man's wife a few times. She didn't seem to leave the house, but she did stroll down the corridor—probably to get some fresh air. She looked frail and thin. My grandmother would smile at her, but she never seemed to acknowledge her or any of the other neighbors.

Then the screaming started up again. It was louder this time, and in a few days, my grandmother heard (along with the screaming), crying, crashing, and the distinct sound of bells. She was horrified because she finally understood what was going on: the bells she heard were Shaman bells. My grandmother realized the woman was being exorcised.

Koreans don't have the same idea of spirits and of possession as a Christian or Catholic view. They don't believe in demons, but rather in spirits and gods that live around them that are neither good or evil. Possession is also something that doesn't happen randomly. From my grandmother's explanation, possession happened to those who were destined to be Shamans. Gods and spirits spoke to those who were chosen to be a link to normal people and the world of spirits, and if the chosen refused their gifts, they would be tormented to death.

I don't know if I buy into this idea. Mental illness has often been confused with "possession" in many cultures. But thinking about my grandmother, (awake at night, listening to the sound of chanting, screams, and ringing bells), I couldn't blame her for thinking there was a supernatural element to this story.

But what happened next is what truly troubles me. Early one morning, my grandmother was looking out her front door. The sounds from the neighbors had finally died down. She was watching the sunrise and contemplating her day, when she heard the door to the neighbors creak open. Before her eyes could register who it was, there was a flash of black and white. And shortly after, a deafening crash.

Some days later, she found out from a different neighbor that the young man and the "caregiver" had fallen asleep. His wife had slipped away from them and fallen to her death. They moved away after that. But my grandmother felt that spot was haunted by the young woman who escaped her destiny as a shaman by ending her life.

Anything Ghost Episode #220
March 19, 2016

Types of Phenomenon Commonly Referred to as a Haunting

A Place Memory or Residual Haunting

Also known as a Psychic Impression. An event from the past or a residue of a past event imprints itself into the atmosphere and replays itself from time to time.

- No apparent purpose or reason for this occurrence.
- The actors in this scene are there only in energy form.
- Sometimes portrays a very emotional event but can also be just a dull, common practice like walking up and down a staircase.
- The energy will stay even if the building is knocked down or the area changes appearance
- A Place Memory is NOT a true "haunting."

Courtesy of Al Rauber. All rights reserved. Copyright 2016.

The stories that follow in Chapter 2 are not intended to be examples of the above described phenomenon.

Public Domain.
Cruikshank, George. 1792-1878.

2 | Chapter Two

- The Shadow Person in My Attic
- Hospital Ghost
- Ghostly Good-bye
- Bangkok, Thailand Ghost Experiences
- Fifth House to the Left
- The House Next Door to Grandma's
- An Archaeologist's Experience with Ancestral Ghosts
- The Two-Story House on Lafayette

- The Shadow Visitors
- Sidewalk Ghost
- The Knocking Ghost
- Electric People
- New England Ghost Story
- The Man Upstairs
- Jealous Ghost
- The Ghost in Apartment 9
- Ghostly Ship Stories

The Shadow Person in My Attic
George (South Wales, Swansea)

This experience happened around ten years ago. I am an only child and lived very far from my friend; my nearest neighbor was around five minutes walking distance from my house—being that I lived on a large field surrounded by woodland.

When I was 17 years old, and still living in my parents' house in Swansea, I was often left home alone: my dad worked the night shift, and my mom was almost always staying at my grandmother's house (since my grandmother had Alzheimer's and needed constant supervision). Nevertheless, being home alone was always exciting and it never bothered me. That was until one particular night.

It started at around 7 p.m. I was in my bedroom messaging friends and listening to music. But then I started hearing a strange rhythmic tapping noise coming from directly above me. My bedroom was on the second floor, so I knew something was making a noise in the attic. I quickly passed it off as something in the piping. After about five minutes the sounds stopped completely, so I figured I was correct in my deduction, and I went back to listening to music.

At around 9 p.m., I was in my upstairs bathroom getting ready to take a shower when I heard the exact same noises tapping in the same sequence as before. Although, this time they were much louder and sounded more like thumps—as if something were constantly being dropped onto the attic floor. This started to scare me; especially considering how late it was, the fact that I was home alone, and in a house that was surrounded by forests.

I called my dad at his work informing him on what I was hearing. Then I began to realize that while I was talking to my dad on the phone, the thumping noises had stopped. I said goodbye to my dad, and decided to go back to my bedroom. I shut the door and went to sleep.

In the middle of the night I was awoken by the sound of water running from above my bedroom. This made me very nervous, as I thought a pipe had burst, and that soon the upstairs of the house was going to flood. But then noticed that my bedroom door was wide open—and I was sure that I closed it before I went to sleep.

The attic was only accessible by pulling down a ladder and climbing up. I do not know what I was thinking, but I decided to climb out of bed, pull down the ladder and see if I could find where the water noise was coming from.

I opened the attic hatch, pulled down the ladder and climbed up to the attic. When I got to the top of the ladder, I smelled something putrid that is not describable—even though I can still smell it sometimes to this day. I reached for my flashlight and scanned the attic with the beam. Through the light I could only see cobwebs and boxes. But then noticed that the audible sound of water pouring had stopped. I froze into complete silence, and began walking back towards the ladder.

As I did so, I walked into a patch of warm air (the rest of my attic was ice cold). In my fear, I remember feeling as though I had walked into something and disturbed it.

Then, I heard the same thumping noise, but this time it was coming from directly behind me. The noise was so loud that the sound was vibrating the attic floor. I turned around quickly and positioned my flashlight beam into the bottom corner of the attic (where I believed the sound was emanating from). What I saw next was the most horrific and haunting thing I have ever seen. It was a shadow person, and it was hunched over—looking directly up at me. It was darker than the rest of the room, and appeared to have white eyes that were just staring at me. I froze as I stared for what felt like minutes, but was most likely just a few seconds. I then screamed louder than I ever have, jumped down the attic hatch, ran down my stairs, scurried through the garden, and made it down to the front driveway—I screamed the whole way.

As I was standing on the driveway, bent over and trying to catch my breath, I glanced back up at the house (that was now about 50 yards away.) There in my bedroom window, looking down at me, was that same dark figure. The figure slowly moved away and out of sight.

At that point, I quickly ran to my nearest neighbor's house and called my parents. I told my parents everything, and they came home as quickly as they could. We moved to another house shorty after that incident.

I now live with university friends in England. I never saw anything after that, and so I have concluded that the shadow person was linked to that house.

But at night, I sometimes see that shadow person when I close my eyes, and remember back to that day, and how scary it really was.

Anything Ghost Episode #220
March 19, 2016

Hospital Ghost
Emily (North East of England)

I have had many run ins with the paranormal but I would say this one makes the best story.

I was new to work in the hospital where I live as an auxiliary nurse. One day a patient had requested to move rooms (we had private rooms for some patients), and I was not told why, but was asked to go and clean down the room and change the sheets. While I was doing this I was startled by an elderly man standing by the door. As I looked up he said, "Oh. I must have the wrong room," and left in a dash.

I quickly ran out to apologize to the man (thinking I'd given him a shock, and figuring I'd help direct him to where he was trying to go), but once I got out into the corridor, no one was there.

I then saw a co-worker and asked if she had seen the man who came out room 35. She said no, and looked confused (considering that she was standing right outside the room). I described what he looked like (his suit, his walking stick and glasses). Her face turned white, and I asked what's wrong? She told me that a very large number of patients have requested to move from that side room because they see an old man by the door. He just stands there watching them while they sleep. Sometimes he has been seen just appearing during the day and then disappearing. She said my description of the man was exactly what other nursing staff and patients had seen.

After thinking about it for a while, I realized that the nursing alarm button goes off when nobody is in there and the toilet flushes, as well.

Anything Ghost Episode #221
April 6, 2016

Ghostly Good-bye
Cari (Willington, Connecticut)

My husband and I were high school sweethearts, as were a good number of our childhood friends. Together, we cheerfully egged each other on toward adulthood, one couple reaching a milestone first (career, first baby, what have you), and the rest of us sheepishly raising our game so as not be left behind.

One couple, Tom and Sarah, early emerged as the leaders of our little pack: The first to get married, first to snag grown up jobs, and first to leave behind the apartments of our youth and buy an actual house.

It was this last part that particularly delighted our circle of friends. As real live home owners, Tom and Sarah became the de facto hosts of every Memorial Day, 4th of July, and Labor Day party we threw together, because their quarter acre of land (a kingly plot to our minds) meant that no pesky neighbors would be banging on the walls and calling the police when we get a little too loud.

The house was impressive. A sprawling old farmhouse, it had the honor of being one of the last stops on the Underground Railroad: a final pause between the Detroit area and the freedom offered by Canadian soil. It was looming and ancient, with drafty bits and unfinished crawl ways and hardwood floors that creaked if you even thought about stepping on them.

We all rolled our eyes when Tom and Sarah declared it haunted. Of course it was haunted. How could it not be? The stories of the couple's two Huskies growling and snarling into empty corners, just made us snicker; and Sarah's insistence that rocking chairs would rock violently, untouched and in empty rooms, just made us chuckle.

Even the couple's most famous story elicited nothing more than polite interest when it was told at parties: one day, in the week Tom and Sarah were moving in, the two of them decided to take a brief nap before the arrival of a friend (who was due to come help with some heavy lifting). The couple flopped down on their bed, exhausted from unpacking. They soon heard the front door open and shut. That was followed by the unmistakable sounds of someone stomping up the stairs, and then running down the hall. Tom looked at Sarah and said, "Here comes John."

Sarah nodded, knowing that the sounds were their friend who was always loved to make an exuberant entrance. The couple started to get up, expecting John to fling the door open to the bedroom...but nothing happened.

Puzzled, Tom stuck his head into the hallway, calling for John. No answer. Chalking it up to one of John's pranks (let's make mysterious noises in the allegedly haunted house), Tom walked downstairs and then outside, still calling for John.

John wasn't there. In fact, when Tom irritably called him a few moments later, John was flustered and apologetic for being late because he was stuck in traffic. Clearly, Tom and Sarah insisted that this was proof that they were living with a ghost.

But no matter how insistent our friends were that their house was haunted, none of us really cared. After all, whatever spectral residents rubbed elbows with the couple during quiet moments, they left us alone during our house parties.

Several years later, when Tom and Sarah sold that old house and upgraded to new construction out in the 'burbs, my husband and I offered to help with the moving process. Sarah and I took the new house station: unpacking and finding new places for everything; while Tom and my husband Ken were on the old house end of things: doing a final walk-through and one last vacuuming session before handing over the keys to the Realtor.

It was a bright and sunny afternoon. Sarah and I were in the kitchen surrounded by half unpacked boxes of glasses and bowls in need of new homes, when the phone rang. Sarah picked it up and said little beyond hello, and she listened intently to the caller. Then she laughed a knowing sort of laugh and said, "It was checking us out at the end—just like it did at the beginning!"

She put the phone back in the cradle and said to me, "The ghost said its farewells to Ken," and as I looked at her, uncomprehending, she explained:

Tom and the two Huskies went to return the moving truck, while my husband stayed behind to vacuum one last time. While upstairs, over the noise of the vacuum cleaner, my husband heard the unmistakable sounds of something running up the stairs. Figuring it meant Tom had returned with the dogs, and that the dogs were bounding upstairs to greet him, he moved to the side of the hallway to make room for the two Huskies—clearing barreling toward him.

He then felt the rush of bodies past his legs, looked up from vacuuming and saw...nothing. The hallway was empty. A brief tour revealed that the whole house was empty. No dogs. No explanation for the noise or the physical sensation of something rushing past him.

Tom says he rounded the corner onto his street, and saw my husband sitting on the porch—his hand gripping the vacuum cleaner, tightly. "It's a good thing you've moved, Tom," my husband said, "Because I'm not ever going back in that house again."

And as a man of his word, he never has.

Anything Ghost Episode #216
December 19, 2015

Bangkok, Thailand Ghost Experiences
Anonymous (Minneapolis, Minnesota)

December of 2009 my husband and I went on a vacation with my parents to Thailand. We had a great time. We spent the night in a Bangkok hotel before getting up early the next morning to catch the flight back home. The hotel that we stayed at was the same hotel my sister had stayed at a few years prior. I found out later, while talking with my mom, that my sister had a ghostly experience while staying at the hotel.

We were out late and returned to the hotel about 11 p.m. It was around midnight by the time we were getting ready for bed.

The layout of the hotel was just like hotels here in the US. The entry was located on my left when I was in bed and the window was to my right. We were on the 6th floor towards the front of the hotel, and there were lights beaming back up, lighting the room from the window leaving a light reflection on the ceiling. My husband needed to use the bathroom, and I decided to get to bed. All the lights were off because the light from outside was illuminating the room already. As I was lying in bed I saw the shadow of a figure on the ceiling. It moved from left to right as if moving across the foot of my bed. If it was a shadow from outside (though we were on the 6th floor, it may have been possible) it should have been moving from the foot of my bed towards my head or vice versa, but instead the shadow figure moved from my left to my right—as if it was in the room. I yelled out to my husband but the shadow disappeared before I could get his attention. I quickly turned on all the lights and left them on all night. Of course I didn't sleep all night and couldn't wait until 4 a.m. to go to the airport.

A few years prior to my experience, my three sisters and parents were on vacation together in Bangkok, Thailand. The last few days before they were to return home they booked side-by-side hotel rooms with connecting internal entry doors (this was at the same hotel that I had stayed at). The first day nothing remarkable happened. On the second evening they all met downstairs in the lobby with the intention of going out. All three sisters made it downstairs just in time to meet with my parents, but my baby sister needed to go back to my parents' room because she forgot something. Everyone waited in the lobby as she went back upstairs. As she was in the room looking for her item, she heard quiet sobbing from their room next door. When she called out, the sobbing stopped and no one answered. The minute she stopped calling out the quiet sobbing continued. She unlocked the door between the two rooms, and went in to look. She called out again and no one answered. She couldn't find anyone inside. By this time, she became frightened and took off running without grabbing her item.

When she got back downstairs in the lobby, she asked everyone if anyone was upstairs. Everyone looked at her confused. She proceeded to tell them her encounter and everyone became scared.

My parents went to the front desk to ask about the room; the receptionist didn't say anything but offered a different room. My parents persisted about the incident and she refused to comment. They eventually ended up switching rooms and spent a few more nights there without incident.

Anything Ghost Episode #200
December 19, 2015

Haunted Hotels

Anything Ghost has shared many haunted hotel experiences over the years. Aside from the Bangkok, Thailand experience (previous page), here are some others that are included in this book:

- **Sidewalk Ghost**
    Roderick (Pas, Manitoba, Canada) - *Chapter 2*
- **Room 212 in the Stanley Hotel**
    Jenna (Toledo, Ohio) - *Chapter 4*
- **Mystery Man in a Hong Kong Hotel**
    Nick (Toronto, Canada) - *Chapter 6*
- **Red Hill Hotel**
    Alice (Bendigo, Victoria, Australia) - *Chapter 6*

Fifth House to the Left
Marco (San Jose, California)

My family and I grew up in the 90's in east San Jose, California. This was a time when it was much safer for children to play together on the streets, or take a bike ride or roller skate alone in the daytime. When alone on our bikes and skates, we would only stroll as far as the fifth house to the left, where our childhood friend Amy lived; or to the right, five houses to the corner of the block. I remember one afternoon in the summer I was at home reading in the living room, my mother was gardening in the backyard, and my little sister Em was outside roller-skating (she was ten and I was twelve). As I was reading my book, I suddenly heard my sister's skates pounding and skating at a fast pace. I looked out the window and saw my little sister racing to skate from the sidewalk from the left, into our driveway—as if being chased. My protective brother instinct kicked in, and I ran to the front door where she immediately opened it, stormed in, and shut the door behind her, staring at me with fear in her eyes. "What happened, Em?!", I asked, now scared myself that someone was chasing her.

She wouldn't speak.

"What happened?! Are you okay? Was someone chasing you?! You look like you just saw a ghost!"

After about 30 seconds of staring at me with wide eyes and fear in her face, she calmed her lungs from the fast return home and started to tell me about what had happened to her. She said to me:

She had gone outside to skate because she was bored, and wanted to go see if Amy was home to join her in skating. She started to skate past the other houses, and when she got to the sidewalk near Amy's house, she headed up her driveway. She then began to skate to the right (because a garage stuck out into the driveway). But, as she skated around the corner to the front door, she saw something: it was in a long dress that looked like shreds of a dirty white ragged dress. It had the face of a lady, not old, but not young either: the skin on her face looked decomposed, scratched and dirty. Her hair was black, long and messy, tangled, and dirty. Her eyes were the very disturbing: they were super wide—my sister could only see the whites—and were glaring at her. The woman was floating off the ground smoothly and heading towards my sister very fast. She was a few feet from my sister and approaching her fast. She said the lady was kind of see-through; and even though she only saw her for about two seconds before turning around to sprinting back home, she noticed that her hands were up as if she wanted to grab her. But what scared her the most was her huge grin: it stretched unnaturally wide.

My sister quickly turned around in fear and sprinted back to the sidewalk. She felt as if the woman was chasing her, and she was too scared to look back. But once my sister was halfway home, she did look back and saw the woman up in Amy's tree. She was sitting on a huge tree limb, with one hand reaching out at her. She was moving her fingers open and closed as if saying bye to her—with that huge grin on her face, and huge eyes that looked just as wide from three houses away.

My sister finished telling me what happened. She took off her skates, and I looked outside the window to the left over to the large tree down the street. "That tree?" I asked Em.

My sister walked into her room without answering.

Amy's house. This is the tree where Marco's sister saw the lady figure "waving."

Photo by Marco (San Jose, California)
A photo of Amy's house, where Marco's sister saw a strange woman.

Anytime I ask her about it, she refuses to talk about it—even to this day. I told my other siblings about the story, and none of us ever went to Amy's house again.

As we grew older, we'd frequently walk or drive past the house. For me, a chill would go down my spine when I wondered if I should even dare to even look towards the front door.

Anything Ghost Episode #216
December 19, 2015

The House Next Door to Grandma's
Kristina (New Jersey, US)

Throughout my life I have had many paranormal encounters. I've come to believe that I'm sort of sensitive to the supernatural.

When I was very young, my family (mom, dad, two older brothers) lived at my grandma's house. It was a small house where my two brothers and I shared a bedroom. In our bedroom there was a door to the attic. Some of my earliest memories are of being terrified of that door. I would never be able to fall asleep in my own bed. I would fall asleep in my mom's bedroom with her, and my father would carry me to my room whenever he came up to bed. I remember waking up in the middle of the night, so terrified that I would run and jump into the bottom bunk of my brother's bed and put myself in between him and the wall. I could always see someone standing in the middle of the room by the light of the streetlight that came in through the window. I couldn't make out the face, just the outline of a shadowed figure leaning down to look at me.

I would never want to be in the upstairs of the house by myself, even as I got older (after we no longer lived there). When we would visit my grandma's house, I would still feel so uneasy about the upstairs of the house. I can remember always seeing shadowy figures out of the corner of my eye in that house.

When I was five, we moved to the house next door where grandma lived (we owned both houses, and stayed with grandma while the other house was being renovated). In grandma's house I had my very own room, but I still hated to sleep alone. I remember begging to sleep on the floor of my brother's room so I wouldn't be alone. I also remember, on more than one occasion, waking up in the middle of the night to the feeling of being shaken or touched. Also, things would often be moved or go missing. These paranormal experiences would come and go, but they were usually small things like that.

However, when I was about 17 my older cousin moved into my house with her two-year-old son. At that point, things began to get much more active.

Having grown up with my older cousin (as her and I were the only two girls in the family), we sometimes experienced paranormal things together—perhaps we are both sensitive and thus the activity increased—but we usually brushed the experiences we had off, and tried to ignore them.

When my cousin moved in, things got steadily more active. It started off as just hearing someone walk around upstairs when no one else was home—my cousin, my mom and I all experienced this. My mom even told us about one time when she had walked out into the kitchen and saw a figure standing in the back hall by the door. She described him as a tall, shadowy man. She told us that he was there for a few seconds and then just vanished.

We all came to believe there were a few different spirits in my house. There were a few reasons for this: the first being that I had a Rottweiler. She was the sweetest, most loving dog you could ever meet. She just loved to cuddle. When sitting in my living room there was a clear view of the stairs that lead to the second story. There were times when I was sitting in that living room with my cousin or other family members, that my dog would sit and appear to watch someone going up and down the stairs. Sometimes she watched in a calm, indifferent manner; but other times she sat in front of me (and whoever else was in the room) and growled protectively.

The second reason we believe there were a few different spirits in the house was that others in the family saw the same shadow man that my mom had seen, and so we were certain it was a man. But that theory changed when my cousin and I set up a recorder in our bedroom when no one else was home. We made sure everything else was silent and sat on the floor with the recorder between us. We started asking questions.

"Is anyone or anything in here with us?"

"Who are you?"

"Are you connected to the house or someone here?"

"Are you male or female?"

When we played the recording back, none of our questions were answered, except one: very clearly after we asked the gender of the spirit, we heard a female voice say, "female."

One night my cousin and I were about to go to sleep (we shared bunk beds in the room and her son had his own bed on the other side of the room), and we heard and felt a loud bang, as if someone had hit the footboard of our bed very hard. When I leaned down to look at her she looked as shocked as I felt, and I asked, "Was that you?"

She said no.

Well, it wasn't me either. I was on Skype with my then boyfriend, who also heard the bang. She and I tried to recreate the bang. I even kicked the bed as hard as I could, and we couldn't get it to make the same loud bang—it wasn't even close to how loud it had been.

The activity began to escalate even more after that.

One night, I was up late in bed doing homework and studying. The room was dark except my baby cousin's night-light and the light from my laptop. The baby was asleep, and so was my cousin. I heard a shuffling sound coming from by my baby cousin's bed. At first I didn't pay it much attention as I thought he was just moving around in his sleep. But out of the corner of my eye, I noticed that he wasn't moving at all. It was the blanket that was over the baby, and it was sliding downward. It looked like someone was standing at the side of his bed and tugging it slowly off of him—except, there was nobody there. I watched, wondering if my eyes were playing tricks on me. That was when his leg, now completely uncovered by the blanket, began to lift in the air and he began to slowly slide off his bed. I didn't take my eyes off of him as I called my cousin's name loudly to wake her up. As soon as I did, my baby cousin's leg dropped, and whatever was pulling him seemed to stop. My cousin did not wake up, and I waited for a little while longer, and nothing else happened. I went back to sleep.

The next day I told my cousin about it and she was very upset. She did not want anything touching or harming her son. From then on she had him sleep in the bed with her, just in case.

One night, my cousin decided to leave her phone recording all night. We listened to it the next day. For a long time it was silent, and then the door could be heard opening, and then someone pacing and back and forth next to our bed.

We would also hear someone walking around in the attic or hear loud bangs coming from up there.

Other strange things would happen, such as if ever we had candles lit, they would flicker and go out shortly after they were lit with no real explanation.

My cousin lived with us for a while, but soon found a place with her boyfriend and moved out. Activity continued for a while after she was gone—and I was glad to have moved away to college by the time she was getting ready to leave.

I now live back at home while I'm finishing up my last year of college. While the paranormal activity seems to have calmed down, I can still sometimes hear people walking around upstairs—even when I am alone.

Anything Ghost Episode #216
December 19, 2015

An Archaeologist's Experience with Ancestral Ghosts
Bekah (California, US)

I'll start with the fact that I'm an archaeologist. At this point, I've had many different types of archaeology jobs and none of them are as glamorous or adventuresome as Indiana Jones leads on. Much of our work consists of watching a machine move soil, or doing a pedestrian survey (basically getting paid to hike while looking at the ground). However, the very first job I had after graduating with my B.A. was not the typical archaeology job. Due to an unfortunate series of poor choices by a construction company, a Native American graveyard was uncovered and many of the remains were moved. Since this was a very culturally and politically sensitive incident, I will not share where it happened or which tribe claimed these individuals as their ancestors, but I will share the experiences I had when I entered the project as an archaeologist assisting in the repatriation and reburial of these ancestral remains.

I was relieved when I got this job because my first workday happened to line up perfectly with graduation. As I spoke with my new boss about the daily tasks and responsibilities, she also explained that we'd be working with a tribal crew and they would conduct ceremonies every week as a way of cleansing ourselves from ancestors who might want to follow us home. As much as I didn't want to believe that ancestor spirits could follow me home, I was admittedly nervous about this potential... let's call it "work hazard."

The night before starting my new job, I had a nightmare that I was in a longhouse with white skeletal figures and we were sitting in a circle around the fire. They were speaking a language I didn't understand, but I could tell they were very angry. I was uneasy when I woke up and decided to tell the tribal elder about the dream when I got into work. Within the first hour of my first day, I was already getting a private ceremony to remove the ancestors. I like to think they were playfully hazing the newbie, but I doubt it. I experienced several strange things at the site, but I was the only one who witnessed them, so I kept telling myself that I was being paranoid. That is, until my neighbor informed me of my visitors.

I had been working on this project for about 3 or 4 months and lived a few miles away from the site. Every time I came home, I had a routine of taking off the dirty outer layer of clothes while I greeted and made small talk with my downstairs neighbor. One day, as I was going through this routine, she asked how I was and I mentioned I was really tired because I'd slept poorly the night before—it was just one of those nights where you wake up immediately after falling back to sleep. When I told her this, she looked confused. She said, "Ya, I wouldn't sleep well either if I had ten guests over all night, stomping around."

I froze. I lived in a studio apartment. Alone. No guests. Just me. And I didn't get up once that night. I told her that I didn't have anyone over, but she didn't believe me and simply asked me to be quieter next time.

Photo by Bekah (California, US)
Bekah was sent to work at a Native American graveyard.

I went to the tribal elder and he thought it best to permanently install the ceremonial cleansing relics in my car so the ancestors would get the, "I respect you, but you're not invited" hint. The experiences continued until the reburial a year later. I would hear out-of-place noises and see movements out of the corner of my eye, all of which was explained by the tribal members as signs that the ancestors were uneasy. One time, I was driving back to my apartment late at night and heard movement in my trunk. I wasn't afraid that it was a person or an animal, I just thought it was the ancestors keeping me company on my late night drive. I was really tired and the tribal members had told me that sometimes the ancestors come with you to protect you and the easiest way to cope with them is to talk to them. It felt a little silly at first, but I started talking aloud. I thought all was well until I'd gotten back to the town where I was living. About a mile away from home, I saw an owl on a lamppost, which to this tribe was considered a bad omen. Although nothing terrible happened immediately after, it was enough to make the tribal elder keep a close eye on my well-being.

I never felt threatened by the ancestors' presence. In fact, I could empathize with them. Who would want their eternal rest ruined by a bulldozer?

Anything Ghost Episode #216
December 19, 2015

The Two-Story House on Lafayette
Christian - (Donna, Texas, US)

Ever since I was a kid, I was very frightened of anything that associated itself with horror and the paranormal. I avoided any and all forms of media associating itself with them, but often would find myself trapped as my cousins and uncles would coerce me into watching horror movies with them. I was a young boy, and like most young boys at that stage, I wanted to be tough, or at least, seem tough.

I wouldn't necessarily call myself sensitive to the supernatural, but I've had several paranormal experiences in my life, and I can say that it's more than enough for me. While one of them did give me a bit of anxiety, the others were all terrifying. One experience in particular cemented the feeling of fear in me to this day; it was an experience that I'll never forget.

Coming from migrant families, my parents moved around a lot and followed certain harvesting seasons all around the Midwest and northeastern part of the United States. Barely starting out from Mexico, my parents worked hard and tried their best until they finally bought their own home in Detroit, Michigan—that's where we all settled down. I was 9 at that time, and my brother and sisters and I all rejoiced at the thought of not sharing a cramped apartment with another family.

When we first visited the home, it was in ruins. The interior and exterior were both charred from a past fire incident, but luckily it wasn't so damaged that my parents had to tear it down. My father and me were hopeful when we decided to take a tour of the inside, but I immediately regretted the decision once I was inside. There was an ominous, heavy atmosphere to the place that had me anxious with every step I took. The living room and kitchen area were the safest places in the home, whilst the second floor and basement were terrifying.

On one particular day, as my father, brother, and I were checking out the house again, and my brother fell through to the basement from the living room. As my father went rushing down towards my brother's location, I was near the hole in the floor trying to talk to him. I heard nothing but crying, along with some strange breathing. I chalked it up to my brother hyperventilating from being so afraid; but after my dad got him out, my brother preferred to not talk about his experience down there for a some time.

While my siblings and I were fully aware of how haunted our home was from the beginning, my parents seemed oblivious to the things happening around us— or at least they feigned ignorance: perhaps trying to keep us in the dark.

I experienced quite a few things by myself and with my siblings, but they each experienced different entities. One such entity I managed to avoid all those years in our home was known to my brother as the "Charred Man." My brother only saw him in the mirrors and considered him even more terrifying than the entity I encountered (I'll address that entity later on in my story). Both my sisters encountered a mother and daughter that were especially active in the kitchen and living room; they got even more active once my mother got sisters a pair of dolls. Every so often, the dolls would move while we were sleeping, or when we would come back from playing outside.

My brother and I also encountered a small boy. He would be either in the basement, which was an area that had one of the heaviest atmospheres; or on the second floor, where I once encountered him while I was running up the stairs. I dreaded thinking of the closet that was located on top of those stairs—it was apparently the source of the fire (according to my parents). All I'll say about the closet is that behind all the clothes and hangers was a dark hole, and that was one terrifying thing on its own.

Anyways, my one big experience with the entity didn't exactly happen right away. After my dad and uncles renovated our home we moved in with ease and comfort, and even if I did avoid the basement as best as I could, my parents renovated the upstairs into one big bedroom for my brother, sisters, and me. We four shared two beds with one another, and spent most of our time upstairs, as we had a lot of room to play in.

It was about a month or two after we moved in that we started noticing little inconsistencies in our home. The sounds of shuffling (the stairs leading to our upstairs bedroom and the entire second floor had carpeting), and light footsteps were heard in intervals during the night; and on other occasions, I would witness my bedroom door open ever so slowly and see that no one was on the other side. With the exception of it being totally dormant for a couple of months, these encounters went on for a whole year. Then there was the night that really cemented my realization of the paranormal. It was an encounter that piqued my interest in the field.

I don't remember how or why, but I was upstairs by myself watching a movie; I do know that everybody else was downstairs enjoying themselves. The sun was setting and my room was illuminated by an orange aura of light. As I was enjoying the movie, I suddenly heard a creaking noise; I turned around and noticed my door was being opened—this time slower than usual. I muted my television and just stared at the open space that befell me. I don't know how long I stared at the space, but it certainly felt considerably long, as I focused my eyes and ears towards the space, trying to catch anything or anyone that caused it. As time passed my body grew more and more relaxed; and just as I was about to return to my movie, I heard one long audible breath envelop my room. I froze and didn't move until my brother and sisters came up for bed.

Small experiences like these kept occurring on and off over a period of months. Then it all accumulated into one terrifying night. I was by myself with the TV on and trying to get some sleep. By this point I certainly knew something was out to "get" me, but I didn't want to worry my parents: my siblings and I kept it secret, hoping it'd be some kind of grand adventure for us. I eventually found the time to sleep, but sprang back up as if waking from a horrible nightmare. Someone had turned the television off and all I could see was complete darkness. As time adjusted my eyesight to the darkness, I could see that my brother was sound asleep next to me while both my sisters were in their respective places on the other bed. I was drenched in sweat, and it was odd since it was a very cold December night.

Minutes passed, and as I tried to go back to sleep, I heard my door slowly creak open. I sprang up and stared at the doorway. Thinking I would see nothing else there like before, I mustered up some courage to face my fears, but what came next shot all chances of me being brave down. A lone, tall, dark shadow of a man stood in the doorway, and it just stood there breathing for a couple of minutes until it apparently opened its eyes or something. I don't entirely know how to explain this, but red eyes just appeared out of nowhere on his face. My body stiffened, my mouth and throat ran dry, and I couldn't take my eyes off of it. I wasn't just afraid, this was another kind of fear altogether that chilled me to my core. I wanted to scream, but couldn't; I wanted to cry, but couldn't; and I wanted to run away, but couldn't.

As a million different thoughts ran through my head, all of them stopped as soon as I saw it walking towards me. Not gliding or floating, but WALKING. Each step it took was audible and rang true as if the floor was made out of glass. It was when it was in front of my bed that I somehow got my nerves to get working and hid under my sheet. Now this is where most people would close their eyes and eventually go to sleep, but I ran into a problem: while shuffling in my bed in an attempt to get under my sheets, I only managed to get the top most sheet on top of me—and it was the thinnest. By the time I realized my mistake, I opened my eyes under the thin sheet and saw the dark figure was next to me—just inches away. I started taking deep, fast breaths out of simple fear, and I knew deep inside that I'd been had. I closed my eyes tightly and held my breath for what felt like an hour. I couldn't sleep, and I certainly couldn't get out of bed; but soon I heard raspy breathing. My body tensed up, and for some idiotic reason I decided to open my eyes. All I could see was a large, black hand over my face. I would have cried, but fear took hold of me. But the scariest thing was that the hand just hovered over my face—as if he was teasing me; knowing full well how terrified

I was...and how terrifying he was. I didn't move a muscle that night until I finally, somehow, fell asleep.

I was awakened early in the morning when my siblings got up to watch cartoons and eat breakfast. It was the weekend, and I decided to sleep in.

I experienced many other things in the house before I moved to where I currently live. It's certainly an experience I'm ironically grateful for as it cemented my belief in the paranormal; but it also dug a crater in me that is filled with nothing but fear, loneliness, and horror.

I'd like to think I would act differently now if I experienced the same thing, but deep down I'm not entirely sure I would.

Anything Ghost Episode #217
January 8, 2016

The Shadow Visitors
Krista (Phoenix, Arizona)

When I was a small child, and was recently old enough to be potty trained, my mother would spend a lot of time standing in the restroom, coaching me (like a good mom). I had a special seat with the head of a horse that squeaked and made googley eyes. As an adult, that seat is one of the few items from childhood that I can recall with total clarity. It lends gravity, serving as a sort of prop, to a story that mom later told me.

One evening, as she stood there with frustrated sighs, I ignored her obvious desire to be elsewhere—making dinner for the two of us and my stepfather (who would be home from work soon). I was entranced by my ridiculous training seat and was taking my sweet time. My mother's back was facing the door to our restroom that was situated in the hallway between the two bedrooms. I was facing the hallway but was blissfully unaware of anything else in the universe.

My mother told me the next part, as I have zero recollection of it: I abruptly stopped playing and fixed my gaze clearly on the open doorway of the restroom. Confused, my mother turned to see what I had been distracted by, and just as she did a thick silhouette walked past the doorway. Before she could form a reaction or explanation for herself, I was up and running after what we had both seen.

Chasing after me, she made a mental note that her husband was home and that I had just run to him. When she arrived where I had halted, staring at the front door, she checked to see if it was locked. Surprised to see that it was, she looked at me and asked me who I was looking for. I didn't answer her, I simply pointed at the door.

Later that evening, my step father got home and my mom asked him if he had been home earlier. He had not.

Over the next several years I had a few more encounters, but many are vague memories.

From the age of three until early puberty, I had many long nights of tucking the covers under every inch of my body. I remember feeling such a heavy weight in the atmosphere of my room. It was as though I was being bared down on by something I couldn't see—like a suffocating evil waiting in the room.

Even in the hottest summer nights, I preferred to sweat unmercifully under the covers, rather than face what I knew I would eventually see: a tall silhouette that would often stand at he entry of my room, or the end of my bed; or his little friend (a smaller version; skittish and much more aggressive), would often crawl onto my bed and press down with the weight of a cat—waking me with it's presence and the dreamy realization that I didn't own a cat.

The women in my family had often seen this man in random places; some in the hallway, some in the rear-view mirror of their cars. He was part of their lives and the lives of their families for a very long time.

Photo by Krista (Phoenix, Arizona)
Krista and her family experienced shadow visitors.

After I moved out on my own, I had no issues with the shadow visitors. I can't tell you what their presence meant, or what they wanted, but I can tell you that they loved fear. I can tell you that fear invited them like the dinner bell. Those that scare the easiest are their bread and butter. I was very easily scared as a child, but eventually grew into an adult that refused to be scared.

I do feel that I'm being watched often, but I make it known that my home is my domain, and that nothing is welcome in it that I did not invite.

Anything Ghost Episode #217
January 8, 2016

Sidewalk Ghost
Roderick (Pas, Manitoba, Canada)

I had this experience back in December 2015; however, I didn't know it at the time.

I'm not sensitive in any way, but I am open-minded. I live in an old two-floor hotel that rents out all of the small rooms. This place moves a lot as it settles, so we know it's just the building. I live next to the kitchen in the upstairs part of the hotel, and it gets locked up at night.

My room shared a wall with the kitchen, and sometimes when I was awake in the wee-hours (I was usually playing video games with the sound turned down, so I wouldn't disturb my neighbors), I would hear the sound of a chair shifting or a drawer opening in the kitchen. I'd hear these sounds around 4 a.m.—just before the kitchen would be reopened at 6 a.m. I wouldn't be surprised if there were similar creepy stories from the other residents. I spoke with a coworker who moved out of my building months before, and he claimed that he'd felt like he was being watched—and even felt someone sit down on his bed.

One night I got called in to work, and my boss said she'd drive over and pick me up shortly.

I hurried to get my winter gear on and went downstairs. No one was around in the lobby, so I decided to wait outside since it was unseasonably warm out. I like listen to music while I wait for someone, so that day I put my backpack on the snow covered bench, and opened my jacket (so I could adjust things accordingly to get my device to play).

About a minute later, I saw my boss approaching in her van and she made a U-turn to get to my side of the street. When I got inside the van, and as we pulled away from the front of the hotel, she asked, "Who was that woman you were standing with outside?"

I paused and replied, "What woman?" I was at a loss for words at that moment.

Photo by Roderick (Pas, Manitoba, Canada)
The hotel where Roderick lived. The bench where he was waiting can be seen covered in snow.

But as we drove towards the workplace, I asked for a description of the person she'd seen. She said the woman was wearing a modern jacket with faux fur around the edges of her hood, and by the way the lady was communicating with it me it appeared we knew each other. My boss added the lady was talking with her hands, and that she was close into my personal space.

But that was impossible. I simply didn't see a woman next to me. In fact, I didn't notice anyone else pass by me, or come and go from the front door of the lobby. I was only outside for about minute and would have heard someone walk behind me while I was putting on music—mostly because of the crunchy snow but also because I am visually alert when I am outside with headphones on.

My boss assured me that she saw the lady—otherwise she wouldn't have brought it up. When she saw this person, her first thought was, "I guess I'm also taking Rod's friend for a ride."

I got a response from one of the residents about my story, and he said that this is an old hotel and a number of people had died in the hotel over the decades. So, he wasn't too surprised.

That's my experience. I felt it was interesting enough to share, as it forced me to sleep with the lights on for a few weeks.

Anything Ghost Episode #218
January 30, 2016

The Knocking Ghost
Lynn (Orlando, Florida)

These two ghost stories come from my time in college in the town of Rock Island, Illinois. I have some great memories and stories from the house I lived in, but these are the only supernatural ones that I can remember.

When I was in college I lived in a house that was almost 100 years old. I found out during my stay there that the house had been home to workers of the paper mill in town. It was hard, dangerous work and it is more than likely that at least one person had previously passed away in the house. My roommates and I had a running joke that there were "nice" ghosts in the house because even though it was just a house for college students it always felt more like a home.

Photo by Lynn (Orlando, Florida)
The view from Lynn's bedroom window.

My room was on the second floor at the back of the house and was rather small—which meant my bed sat in the corner of two outside walls. During the spring of my second year living there, I began to hear what I came to call the "knocking ghost." Every night, just before I fell asleep I would hear a knock on the wall behind my head. It didn't matter what time I went to bed or what the weather was like outside, the knock would always come a few minutes after I had gotten into bed.

One morning, I was lying on the end of the bed that put my head in the corner of the two walls (as opposed to the other end that would have had me lying next to the windows), and I remember I was thinking over some things at the time before getting out of bed to start my day. Soon, my thoughts turned particularly negative and there was a huge bang on the wall in front of my face. Whatever had hit the wall had hit is so hard from the outside that I felt the shock-wave hit my face.

I immediately sprung out of bed and threw open the window, sure that a neighbor had thrown a ball at the house or an animal had made a wrong turn into the wall. When I looked outside there was nothing there—not even a mark on the siding (let alone the dent I had expected to see).

Anything Ghost Episode #218
January 30, 2016

Ghostly Knocks

There have been a lot of experiences shared on Anything Ghost regarding anomalous knocking believed to be a ghost communicating. I've experienced this phenomenon myself. You can read a couple of my experiences in this book:

- **Haunted Guest House in Pasadena, California**
  Lex Wahl - *chapter 1*
- **Clicks at the Freedom Mausoleum in Forest Lawn**
  Lex Wahl - *chapter 5*

Electric People
Lane (Boston, Massachusetts)

When I was about ten or twelve, my mother would buy me little wristwatches. I wore them, but soon grew bored of them because the batteries would die after a few wears. My mom would replace the batteries, but to no avail. The same thing happened with various watches and various batteries. Since there was no point to wearing a watch, I just never did again.

Flash forward to several years later in the early 2000s. I was about fourteen to sixteen. Stereo systems were very popular back in those days. I had my own in my room where I could play CDs, cassette tapes, or the radio. I almost always chose to listen to CDs. I'd turn it off while listening to CDs and then the stereo system would jump back to what I was listening to when I turned it off. I listened exclusively to CDs. In the middle of the night, my stereo began to turn on by itself. Strangely, it would be the radio that turned on. I never listened to the radio. This happened around 3 a.m. many times. I'd always check to see if I'd bumped the alarm button, but it was never turned on. This continued sporadically throughout my teenage years. Sometimes, it would even be the radio on my alarm clock that turned on in the wee hours of the morning. I never used that radio: I used the alarm setting to wake myself up at around 6:30 every morning. At first, it scared me. But this became so normal for me that I'd simply get up, turn the radio off, and then doze back off.

When I was 17 or so, I purchased a small TV for my bedroom where I could play movies on tape to entertain myself. After a while, this electronic device would turn off at random points without being touched. This did not happen during the wee hours of the morning, only randomly while I was watching it. Sometimes it would even turn on by itself. By the time I went to college, I simply started listening to music on my laptop, headphones or an iPod docking system.

The event of electronic devices turning on became much more rare, but on occasion, the radio on the iPod dock—which, again, I never listened to—would turn on. Sometimes, and once when my boyfriend was sleeping over and was able to witness it, my television would even turn on by itself in the middle of the night.

After college, I moved to Philadelphia from Michigan. I was in my new apartment chatting with my boyfriend on the phone in the living room, when I heard my iPod dock's radio turn on in my bedroom. This hadn't happened in at least a couple years at this point, and it scared me. Nonetheless, I turned it off and tried my hardest not to acknowledge feelings of fear. This was the point that I told my mother that this has always happened to me. She didn't believe me. But that soon changed.

The next time I saw my mother was Christmas of that year. We had a tradition of watching all kinds of Christmas movies together. As we were watching Home Alone, the entire sound system and DVD player in our basement turned off by itself.

After that, my mom did some research, and heard about something called "electric people." Apparently, it's people whose emotional state can cause electronics to malfunction.

I still experience rare times when electronics turn on and off around me. I no longer own an alarm clock, television, or stereo of any sort, but I do have an iPad. It's rare nowadays, but on occasion I'll wake up to talking. Without fail, I'll find my iPad (closed in its case), with a movie playing from my Netflix queue. It was never a movie that I had been watching.

Recently, I moved to Boston from Philly. I woke up one night to a light showing from under my bedroom door. Thinking someone was in my apartment, I cautiously went to my living room. There I found that an automatic light in a corner closet had turned on by itself. The door to that closet was closed and everything was in place. There was nobody in the apartment and I don't know how the light could have turned on by itself—as it did not look like anything had fallen from shelving in the closet.

I don't know if what my mother found about electric people is correct or if it has to do with something else, but these things do seem to happen at times when I may be slightly more stressed than usual—but I am not a particularly emotional person. These events happened the most when I was a teenager, and it was almost a weekly thing then.

An alternate theory is this: I've had a number of strange happenings throughout my entire life that usually don't like to acknowledge as paranormal. An Atlantic City boardwalk psychic once told me that a dead relative, whom I've never met, feels a connection to me and stays with me. If that is true, perhaps this could all be some minor mischief from this alleged relative; or maybe it's all just coincidence.

Perhaps I'll never know the truth about why electronics wake me up in the middle of the night and sometimes turn on and off on their own, but I've come to live with it.

Anything Ghost Episode #219
February 24, 2016

New England Ghost Story
Lucas (New England, U.S.)

When you imagine a haunted house, what usually comes to mind is an old dark spooky home, but my parents' home was only five-years-old before we bought it and moved in.

From the first day we moved in, I felt uneasy. I had an overwhelming feeling that we were not welcome in the home. Recurring nightmares of being chased by an unseen entity out of the home, happened for years—until I graduated high school and moved out. Friends who slept over would be awoken by the sound of breathing in their ear, or the feeling that someone was sitting on the bed watching them. Lot's of little events occurred over the years, mostly small, but all unnerving, nonetheless. However, one night, something very different happened.

I was in high school and had come home late from hanging out with some friends. My parents were asleep, and I was in my bedroom chatting online with some friends. Everything seemed normal, until I heard my dog through my closed bedroom door, whining and pacing in the kitchen. My father had an office in the basement, directly below my bedroom. My dog stopped whining, and from below me I heard the sound of drawers being opened and closed. It was a very distinct sound: my father's desk was an old 1950's metal office desk, and I knew the distinct metal-on-metal scraping sound the drawers made when being opened.

My dog began to whine again.

I messaged my friends. "What should I do?! I think someone broke into my parents' basement! I can hear them downstairs"

"Call the police!" My friend offered

"No, it's probably nothing, just wake up your parents and take a look," my other friend suggested.

As we decided what my next move should be, I heard the sound of furniture being dragged across the concrete floor in the office below. It sounded like someone was in the basement rummaging through my father's office and ransacking the place. "Oh my god you guys, I'm terrified! What is happening here? What if they come upstairs!?" I messaged.

Just then, as if in response, I felt what I can only describe as a strong thump directly under my chair, as if someone was standing directly under me in the basement and had punched the floor above them. Thump...THUMP! The thumping was so strong that I actually saw ripples vibrate across the surface of the water in a glass on my desk.

By this time, my dog was pacing and whining in the next room, and I had enough. I had to wake my parents up and call the police. I threw my door open and ran down the hall to my parents' room. In a panic, I woke them up and described what had been happening. We threw the lights on, and my father grabbed a baseball bat from the hall closet. He then instructed me to put a leash on my dog. We got to the basement door and announced ourselves:

"Hello! If someone is down there, you'd better leave! We are coming down and we have weapons!" My father screamed to the door. My mother stood behind us, holding the cordless phone in case someone was there and she needed to call the police. My father opened the door to the basement, turning on the lights to illuminate the pitch-black office.

Nothing. Nothing was moved, nothing was disturbed, and nothing was changed.

We moved through the basement quickly, my dog at my side, my father in front of me. No one was there. No broken windows, no point of entry. There was nothing. My parents by that point were furious with me—thinking I had imagined it all and woke them up for nothing.

"Go back to bed" they said. "Your mind was playing tricks on you. Just go to sleep."

I went back to my room and messaged my friends to tell them what had just happened. "There was no one there." I said.

"It's your house! It's the ghost!" My friend responded.

"I just have to go to bed, there isn't anything else I can do." I said. By then it was two in the morning. I laid down in my bed. Confused, scared and feeling slightly ridiculous to put my parents in such a panic.

As my eyes got heavy and I started to drift off to sleep...I heard it...my dog in the kitchen. She began whining again, and pacing. I could hear her little nails clicking against the linoleum in the kitchen, pacing back and forth, back and forth. Soon I heard the metal-on-metal scraping sound of the drawers being opened in the office below me, along with the sound of heavy furniture being dragged across the concrete floor—the sounds seemed to echo up and through the floor.

I closed my eyes and tried to convince myself that this wasn't happening, I wasn't hearing what I thought I was hearing.

THUMP...THUMP...THUMP!

This time the thumping was directly under my bed, not the chair I had been sitting in earlier. I closed my eyes, and pulled the blankets over my head.

"This is not happening!" I said to myself,

"This cannot be real! It's not possible!" Those were the last words I remember before exhaustion pulled me deep into sleep.

Thankfully, it never happened again. But for the next several years, until I finally moved out, the smaller events continued: shadows in the hallway, a voice that would call out our names when no one else was home, and the bumps and creaks of our haunted little house.

My neighbors all had similar stories and experiences, and after digging into some research, we discovered that the area had been the site of a bloody battle between the colonists and local Native Americans of the area. Perhaps it wasn't our homes that were haunted, but the land itself.

Anything Ghost Episode #219
February 24, 2016

War Ghosts

Many battlegrounds are believed to have paranormal activity. Here are some other stories in this book related to wars and soldiers:

- **The Vietnam Veteran Spirit**
    Lemon (Texas, U.S.) - *Chapter 3*
- **Oriskany Battlefield**
    Alex (Central New York, U.S.) - *Chapter 4*
- **The Forgotten Lodger**
    Chris (Dublin, Ireland) - *Chapter 5*
- **A Small Boy Ghost in Fallujah, Iraq**
    Kevin (U.S.) - *Chapter 5*
- **The World War II Ghost**
    Steve (Kent, England) - *Chapter 6*

The Man Upstairs
Stephanie (Green Bay, Wisconsin)

I met my now husband in 2006. He had already owned a house by the time we decided to live together in 2008. It was built in the 1950s, so it wasn't an incredibly old house. My husband had never experienced anything paranormal in our home; but after I moved in, odd things began happening.

We had three dogs, two of which my husband owned prior to us meeting. Hans was a mini Dachshund, he was our oldest dog. When I first started living here, my husband worked second shift and I worked first shift—so I was often alone with our dogs at night.

The first night I had an experience was when I was sleeping. I awoke to Hans lying over my stomach and staring at the corner of our room. This was very unusual of Hans to lie on me, and when I awoke he was growling. The corner he was staring at had nothing in it: no photos hanging, no items in the corner—it was just an empty space. I kept telling him, "Hans, stop growling. There is nothing is there."

I then proceeded to get up and walk over to that corner to show him it was okay. However, as I waved my hand out, I felt a cool spot in the air. This startled me, as the rest of the room was pretty warm. I jerked my hand back, and Hans began to bark like something was there that shouldn't be. I turned on the lights in the room and sat down next to him. I watched him stare down that spot for probably fifteen minutes.

I mentioned this incident to Matt (my husband) when he got home and asked him if Hans did that very often. He said that Hans had never done that before.

Hans continued to have the same reaction at night about once or twice a week for some time. It wasn't always the same spot, and it happened in different rooms, too. Many times I checked for a cool spot in the air, and it was there.

A few months went by and we were all in bed sleeping and we were startled awake by a loud bang. All of our dogs were in the room with us so we knew it was not them. We turned on the lights and got out of bed to check out the noise. I walked into our kitchen and saw my hand held vacuum in two pieces on our kitchen floor. The odd thing about that was that I had plugged it into its charger and set it on the center of our dining room table before bed. The charger was still plugged in on the table (which was about ten feet away from where I found the vacuum). Matt usually shrugged off these odd occurrences, so in our minds nothing really happened other than we thought it was weird. We went back to bed.

That same week I was on the phone with Matt while he was driving home from work. I was in the kitchen, and it was about midnight. I was picking up papers and empty soda cans while talking to him. I put some stuff into our trash can when I heard a sound from behind me. As a former bartender, the best way I can describe what it sounded like was a can sliding across a table—like someone gave the can a push. I looked up and saw that there was one can of soda sitting on the counter. I walked over to pick it up, and it slid from my hand before I could touch it. It had so much momentum that it slid off the counter and onto the floor. I will admit I gave out a yelp. We were still on the phone, and I told Matt that I would be waiting for him outside until he got home.

Matt tried to explain it by saying the condensation from the can helped it glide; or that I bumped it and didn't realize it. But the can was empty and completely dry—as was the counter top; and I am positive I didn't bump it. So we moved on from that incident as well.

A few months later, I was in bed reading a book when I heard laughter. I was home alone with our dogs. The laughter was loud: like someone was leaning over my shoulder and laughing into my ear. By that point I was beginning to think I might be going crazy. I hoped at the time that it would be an isolated incident, but I still hear random laughs or yelling. Sometimes it happens a few nights in a row, then it stops for a couple weeks.

The next big incident happened after Matt and I were married in 2012. I was taking a nap after work and began to dream about someone trying to get into our house. The dream is vague to me now, but I remember vividly in the dream that I was watching our front door handle jiggle and turn as though someone was trying to get in. My heart was pounding, and I couldn't speak in the dream. I remember thinking in the dream, "Go away! Go away! Go away!"

Then the jiggling stopped. I waited for a few minutes.

I walked to the window, and peeked through the crack in the curtains to see if anyone was still there. Then suddenly in my dream, a voice yelled "Wake up!" And BAM! I was awake. The dream was so vivid and real that I immediately got up and walked to the front door to make sure it was locked. As I reached for the handle, it began to jiggle and turn. I fell backwards onto my butt. The dogs all came running into the living room and began to bark at the front door. I grabbed my phone and dialed 911. As I was on the phone, I peeked out the curtains just like I did in my dream, and saw a young man in a dark hoodie by my front door. I think the dogs spooked him, because he turned and walked away very quickly—as if he had to get away but didn't want to run.

When the cops showed up I described the man as best I could, but I didn't want to say that a dream alerted me to him. I didn't want the cops to think I was crazy.

I know you probably are wondering why this event is paranormal, but the voice that yelled at me to wake up sounded just like the voice I hear laughing and yelling in our house. It's like they were warning me, and from that point on I didn't think the spirit was evil. That doesn't mean that I don't find it to be spooky—because I do.

Some time has passed and we our first child: a little girl we named Isabelle. She is two at the time I am writing this. But when she was about 18 months old, she began to really talk and learn new words. She hit some sort of weird phase where she went from sleeping all night, to waking in the middle of the night and talking randomly. Most of it was babble, but we found it odd because she would sit up and look as if she was holding a conversation with someone. I should mention that we had a video baby monitor, and that's how we could see her having those talks. After a while she would fall back to sleep, only to wake up again crying and asking for us to come to her. No matter if was myself or Matt who went in to her, she always wanted to be picked up and rocked a bit before going back in her crib to sleep again. We both noticed that she would look worried, and her little eyes would be wide open looking behind us at the ceiling.

So finally, one night I asked her what she was looking at, and she said to me "Ghost, momma."

At first I was startled, but tried to rationalize that maybe she was seeing my shadow instead. The only problem with that was that she knew the word "shadow," and would say it if you pointed to one and ask her what it was.

The phase ended, but she would still occasionally wake and want to be held—always with that big-eyed look, and saying there was a ghost in her room. I've asked her if she was scared and wanted it to go away, and she told me no. I'm not sure what to do about it.

Fast forward to just this past December: We had Isabelle's friends Jack, Juno, and their mom Jenni over for a play date. Jenni was my friend so she knew a little about the stuff that had happened in our house. Before I continue, I should mention that Matt and I have an ongoing joke: if one of us leaves a light or TV on in a room, we joke and say, "Oh. Is Gary in there?" (Gary is the name of Matt's uncle who passed away before Matt was even born). I'm not sure how we picked his name for the joke, but it's always been like that.

So we were having this play date, and Isabelle and Jack were having a tea party at the foot of our stairs (the stairs go to the upper floor of our house). We had a baby gate blocking the steps, but the first two steps were accessible before the gate. Jack began to hang on the gate, after which time his little sister Juno also tried to do. We walked over to the kids and explained that they shouldn't hang on the gate. Jack then turned to me and asked what was up there (as we never let them upstairs). I told him that was Ivy's room (I should probably also mention we had our second child in August this past year, and her room was up there).

As we began to usher the kids away from the steps Jack muttered, "What about the man?"

I asked him what he meant.

"What about the man who is up there? Does he have a room too?" Jack replied.

I told him that there wasn't any man up there, and he shook his head in that defiant toddler way and yelled, "Yes! There is a man up there!"

Jenni and I exchanged horrified looks, and got the kids to play in Isabelle's room. I quietly went upstairs while the kids were playing just to make sure we didn't somehow have an intruder. Nobody was up there.

As Jack was leaving, he gave me a hug and whispered to me, "Tell him to leave Izzy and Ivy alone."

I couldn't say anything; I had a lump in my throat, so I just nodded to him.

Photo by Stephanie (Green Bay, Wisconsin)
The stairs where Jack insisted he saw a man.

That night I called Jenni and told her about Matt's and my little "Gary" joke.

She was freaked out about it, and although she insists nothing is wrong, they have canceled all the play dates that occur at my house since that day. We've gone to their place, or to a neutral place for the kids, but they haven't been back here since.

So I have to wonder, if the man upstairs really is Matt's uncle Gary, or something else?

Anything Ghost Episode #218
January 30, 2016

Jealous Ghost
Beth (Salem, Massachusetts)

In the 1980's, I rented my first apartment in Salem, Massachusetts. This was just prior to getting married. It was a four-family home and we lived on the second floor across from another apartment.

Prior to moving furniture into the apartment, I put two glasses in the freezer to celebrate with champagne at later time. When I returned to the apartment a few days later, the glasses were gone, and there were shreds of glass in the corners of each room. We thought our landlord might not have realized we had started to move, and broke them by accident—but it was still strange the way they were spread around.

When we moved in, the fun began.

We heard footsteps pacing back and forth constantly during the night: they came from overhead, and also from our internal hallway; Many nights, the feeling of someone sitting on the bed awakened us; Sometimes, the kitchen water would turn on full blast in the middle of the night; If I went to use to the bathroom in the dark, the doorknob would sometimes turn or shake (even though my husband was sleeping).

Whatever was in that apartment, seemed to have our dog on edge as well: he would crouch in the kitchen doorway, staring into the room with a low growl, and then he would jump in alarm when I'd ask him what was wrong. Very often, we'd hear him whimpering, and when I'd enter the room to check on why he was whimpering, he would run to me with a sense of relief. Once I saw him walking backwards slowly, and growling as if something was coming towards him.

Less than a month after we were married, our wedding gifts to each other disappeared. I had given my husband a pricey watch and I accused him of losing or breaking it. But I soon found that my diamond earrings that were in my jewelry box were also missing.

After awhile, we asked a neighbor across the hall if they ever had anything weird happen to them; they told us that everyone who had lived in our apartment swore it was haunted. He went on to say that the last couple investigated the history of the place, and found that two elderly women had lived there. Eventually, they both died and their wake celebration was held in the apartment (I later found that was common in the those days).

I mentioned all of this to a woman at work who believed in the paranormal and she believed that the two female spirits were jealous of us being married, and had stolen our symbols of commitment. She told me to go into the kitchen when I was alone, put a paper plate on the table, open a pair of scissors and put garlic cloves between the blades; then sprinkle it all with salt and tell the spirits what I wanted.

Photo by Beth (Salem, Massachusetts)
The apartments where Beth, her husband and their dog experienced activity.

I did this one afternoon after work and told the spirits we were sharing the home now. I asked them to please return the items they had moved, and not to scare us (as we had no choice but to live there for now).

That night at dinner, I opened the silverware drawer to set the table, and found my husband's watch lying on the top. I then went into the bedroom, and found my earrings on the bureau in front of my jewelry box.

We continued to feel a strong presence in the apartment up until the time we moved a few years later, but from then on we didn't feel the spirits meant us any harm.

Anything Ghost Episode #222
April 27, 2016

The Ghost in Apartment 9
Celia (Cincinnati, Ohio)

A few years ago I lived with my family in a small two-bedroom apartment. I shared a room with my younger brother, while my mom, dad and baby brother shared the other bedroom.

It was late October when this happened to me. I would have been around nine years old at the time.

I woke up one night and it was pitch black outside. I remember it being very cold, as well. My bed faced the doorway (almost right in front of it) and I was looking out of it into the hallway. It was then that I saw a shadow go past the doorway. The shadow went by very fast, and after a few seconds, another one went past going at the same speed—almost as if it was chasing the first shadow. After seeing that, I rolled over, so that I was no longer looking out of the door. But I couldn't go back to sleep after that.

Not long afterward, one of my brother's toys started to go off. It was a fire truck. The siren on the truck started blaring and I jumped up and ran to my parents' room.

I was crying by this point and woke my mother up. I was so scared that I asked if I could sleep in the bed with them. But my mother wouldn't let me. Regrettably, I returned to my room and hid under the covers until I finally fell asleep.

That was only one of the experiences I had in that apartment. There were also times when I heard footsteps in other rooms—rooms that were unoccupied.

We stayed there for a few more years before moving into a different house.

Anything Ghost Episode #222
April 27, 2016

Ghostly Ship Stories
Minnie (Korea)

Although I live and work in Korea right now, I grew up in Southern California, and I'm still an all-around So Cal girl. These two stories took place in So Cal and both happened when I was in 5th or 6th grade.

The first one happened during an overnight school trip. There was a famous old ship called the Star of India in San Diego. Each year it was a tradition at my elementary school for the 5th graders to visit the ship. I had known in advance about the ship's alleged haunting from the program Haunted History. I'd always loved American history (which is kind of weird for an immigrant girl from Korea, I guess), and have also absolutely loved ghost stories—so this trip was going to be combining the two. I was really excited about the trip because at that age, I had never slept over at another place—but also because I knew that the ship was haunted!

The day itself wasn't anything that special: we just pretended to be part of a ship crew back in the 1800s (which was when the ship was active). I really wanted to see ghosts, but I didn't really experience anything. That is, until that night.

I awoke in the middle of the night (I think it was 1 or 2 a.m.), and went to the bathroom. I made my way back to the spot where I was sleeping and snuggled back into my sleeping bag. I had bad vision, so when I took off my glasses my vision was blurry, but I could still see outlines and shapes well enough. From where I was sleeping, I could see the area where earlier in the evening we had been told stories about history of the ship. It was nothing ghostly, mostly educational stuff. Before I drifted off (with my glasses off), I saw a white figure in that area. I couldn't see the details, since my eye sight was not that great, but the figure was pacing back and forth—and it was pacing in what was a roped off area. The figure was white, but it was also kind of transparent. I was scared, but since it wasn't walking towards me, I just pulled my sleeping bag over my head and eventually fell to sleep.

I woke up in the morning, and remembering what I'd experienced the night before, I quickly put my glasses on to see if anything could have made the pacing figure; but I didn't see anything that could have resembled a person pacing back and forth—and with that kind of transparency. Knowing about the ship's haunted history, I still wonder if it was the ghost from the ship.

The second story happened around the time of the first story as well. I was kind of obsessed about ghost stories and ships, and I found out about the Queen Mary (also in So Cal). I begged my parents to take me to the Queen Mary for several months before they finally gave in and took me there.

I don't exactly remember when my parents took me, but it was either late spring or early summer (I do know it was after the Star of India incident—which had been in late spring). The time frame is kind of important, since So Cal is almost always warm and it was even warmer than usual the time of this incident.

My mom was an early riser (and she still is) and my dad drove us to the Queen Mary early in the morning. When we arrived, we were basically the first guests there. I was super excited and was running around everywhere.

I don't really remember when exactly I started feeling this, but in middle of the ship, in one of the metal-ly areas (I can't describe it well), I felt a hand on my back. But it wasn't a normal hand; it was a super cold hand. Mind you, there were only a few guests there, and they weren't anywhere near me. After feeling the cold touch, I turned around and saw no one.

I was way ahead of my parents and other guests weren't near me. I thought it was weird but I thought it might have been the air conditioning or something. Then I realized…air conditioning doesn't have fingers. I had felt the actual hand with the five digits—and they felt like an adult hand.

Later on in the tour, when we were out in the warmer parts at the top of the ship, I could still feel the hand kind of pushing me. But it wasn't pushing me, it was more of a gentle touch.

I never saw anything that day related to ghosts, but I certainly felt the hand pressing me until I got off the ship.

Anything Ghost Episode #222
April 27, 2016

Children Seeing Ghosts

Here are some other stories found in this book that involve children experiencing the paranormal while playing:

- **Basement Shadow Person**
  Noelle (Michigan, U.S.) - *Chapter 4*
- **Mr. Keen's Halloween Promise**
  Donna (Maine, U.S.) - *Chapter 4*
- **Haunted Birmingham Home**
  Erika (Birmingham, Alabama) - *Chapter 4*
- **Is Emily a Ghost?**
  Alex (Utica, New York - *Chapter 4*
- **Bronx, New York Ghost Stories**
  Errol (New York, U.S.) - *Chapter 5*
- **The Ghost of Llanrumney Hall**
  Gareth (South Wales, U.K.) - *Chapter 6*
- **The Shadow Man at Grandpa's House**
  Barbara (Monterey, California) - *Chapter 6*

Types of Phenomenon Commonly Referred to as a Haunting

Transient Spirits

Similar to a Place Memory (*see Chapter 2*). These entities are experienced once and usually never again. Most likely just remnants of energies without any consciousness.

Courtesy of Al Rauber. All rights reserved. Copyright 2016.

The stories that follow in Chapter 3 are not intended to be examples of the above described phenomenon.

Public Domain.
Dalton. "The spectre of Tappington"

Chapter Three

- My Stay at the Myrtles Plantation
- The Earthquake Ghost
- Devil Dog of New Zealand
- The Doorknob Jiggler
- The Sleep and Snore Ernie Doll
- Philadelphia Haunting
- The Gift of Cows
- "I am the Boogie Man"
- Haunted Colonial Home in the Woods
- The Old Part of the House
- A Walk at Bethany Lake Park
- Emergency Call from the Dead
- The Vietnam Veteran Spirit
- Apparition in My Room
- The Sinclair Library
- Ghost Scars
- A Dark Image in the Hall

My Stay at the Myrtles Plantation
Ryan (New Orleans, Louisiana)

I live about two hours away from St. Francisville, Louisiana. This is where the Myrtles Plantation is located. I have always been fascinated by the stories I've heard surrounding the place, but I never made the time to visit it, until about four years ago.

My girlfriend at the time was very into the paranormal and watched every documentary and reality TV show she could find on ghost stories. After watching a special on the Travel Channel about the most haunted placed in America, we decided that it would be a crime not to go to the Myrtles—since it was basically in our own backyard.

We planned our weekend getaway and booked the Judge Clarke Woodruff suite, because it gave us access to the famed stairwell where a previous owner died after being shot; it also gave us access to the mirror where Chloe is said to make appearances when pictures are taken of the mirror.

Photo by Ryan (New Orleans, Louisiana)
Considered by many to be America's most haunted house.

We were both very excited to stay for the night and also opted to take the guided tour when we arrived. The tour was about $20 a person and totally worth it! You see, when you stay at the Plantation you don't have free rein of the entire house during the night. The house was petitioned off into sections: one room included in the tour was said to have had so much activity that no one was allowed to stay the night in that room any longer. It was very interesting to hear the tour guide tell the history and stories that were connected to the house.

At a certain point of the night, I think about 9 p.m., all of the staff left and we were left to our own devises. They allowed us to roam the grounds, take pictures, videos or just hang out and drink in the courtyard—BYOB.

Photo by Ryan (New Orleans, Louisiana)
After 9 p.m., the visitors were permitted to roam the grounds unescorted by personnel.

My girlfriend and I walked the grounds and took hundreds of pictures with my digital camera. I borrowed a video camera from a friend of mine, but as cliché as it may sound, the battery died about five minutes after I turned it on—despite having a full battery when we arrived—on top of that it wouldn't charge. We also observed many white orbs of all sizes in our pictures—which only added to the eerie feeling brewing in our stomachs.

We started to get sleepy around 1 a.m. and decided to return to our room. The feeling of being watched while in the house was constant. There were no TV's or radios in any of the rooms, so there wasn't much to drown out any noises.

After getting back, we sat up for a while talking and poking fun at each other for being too scared to actually fall asleep.

Photo by Ryan (New Orleans, Louisiana)
The famed stairwell where a previous owner was shot and killed.

Then around 3 a.m. (what the tour guide had referred to as the "witching hour"), we started to hear the faint sound of what sounded like someone sweeping with a broom outside our bedroom door. It started off barely noticeable, but as we listened in disbelief the sound grew louder—to the point that it was unmistakable. I don't remember which one of us broke the silence, but one of us asked, "Do you hear that too?!"

We both nodded in agreement, and stared intently at the door—waiting for it to swing open. The sweeping sound continued for about twenty minutes, and I'm pretty sure we did nothing but stare at the door until it stopped. I even recall slowing my breathing and thinking somehow it would avoid us being noticed—although, all the while my heart was racing due to the adrenaline coursing through my veins.

Neither of us was brave enough at the time to get up and open the door to investigate. Also keep in mind that since the house was petitioned off, we were the only people that had access the area in front of our bedroom door: so I know the sweeping sound could not have been another guest messing with us

Photo by Ryan (New Orleans, Louisiana)
At 3 a.m., Ryan and his girlfriend began to hear what sounded like someone sweeping the floor just outside of their door.

The room seemed unusually colder than it had when we arrived—despite being in bed and covered up to my chest. As we lay in bed in the fully lit bedroom, fighting fear and exhaustion, we began to doze off. But that did last long: as I accidentally touched my girlfriend's head with my hand causing her to almost jump through the ceiling. Her reaction scared me, too; and I decided that sleep was no longer an option. We sat back up in bed, talking some more, and eventually we heard a new sound.

This new sound appeared to be footsteps on the roof of the house! One of the stories that surrounded the house was of two small girls who were accidentally killed by Chloe. They have been seen—and even photographed—playing on the roof. Again, we did not see anything, but the sound of footsteps was obvious, and it went on for several minutes. As for Chloe, she did not decide to make an appearance. And that's probably a good thing, because I think we'd had all the excitement we could handle for one night.

We stayed awake until about 5:30 a.m., and eventually fell asleep. We didn't sleep long: just enough time to get a quick recharge. When we awoke, we packed up our bags, placed the room key in the key drop box and headed home

Although scary, it was a great experience. I always try to rationalize things and I don't dismiss the possibility that our minds got the best of us because our heads were freshly filled with ghost stories from our tour guide.

But I highly recommend staying a night at the Myrtles Plantation to anyone passing through, or within reasonable driving distance. I would do it again in a heartbeat—but only in a larger group.

Anything Ghost Episode #222
April 27, 2016

The Mirror at Myrtles Plantation

The house at Myrtles Plantation has a particular mirror that supposedly contains the souls of one-time residents Sara Woodruff and her two children.

In the century when the Myrtles were alive, many believed mirrors had to be covered when people died—doing so kept the souls of those who passed from being trapped within the mirror.

At that time, Sara Woodruff and her two children were unwittingly poisoned by a vengeful housekeeper. The mother and her two children perished in the house as a result of the poisoning. However, the act of covering a particular mirror had been overlooked. As a result, many believe the souls of the deceased mother and her children reside within the mirror.

There have been reports of marks and scratches appearing in the mirror that some claim to be the hands of Sara and her two children.

This legend was relayed to me by my mother-in-law after she returned from a visit to the Myrtles Plantation.

The Earthquake Ghost
Marco (San Jose, California)

It was the late 1980's. I was in Kindergarten class. It was near the end of the school day and we were all doing our activities with arts and crafts. Half of the class was on one end of the room and the other half was on my side of the room. There were about four kids at my art table.

Suddenly, everything on the table began to shake. The teacher looked at me in a second of confusion, and the entire class looked at each other—very scared.

"Earthquake! Duck and cover!" The teacher screamed while ducking. She was with all the other kids, and they all ducked under her table at the other end of the room. For some reason, the few kids at my table ran across the room to join the teacher's side (probably to feel safer), and that left me as the only kid at my table. As I ducked and covered, while the entire room shook so hard that it sent objects falling loudly left and right, I felt very alone. But during this event, while the ground was shaking, and the toys and color crayons and smiling cartoon posters were falling onto the floor violently, I suddenly felt something warm touch my lower leg. It was a hand. The hand gently grabbed my ankle behind me. I looked back and saw it was a boy grabbing my ankle. He was alerting me with a soft, "Hey." I only looked behind at him for a split second, but seeing him relieved me because I felt I wasn't alone after all. This boy was calmly kneeling behind me and didn't appear to share the same fear I was experiencing: he seemed oddly calm. After seeing the boy, I turned back around to look forward because I heard my teacher scream to me, "Marco, duck and cover your head!"

As I lowered my head, I felt a fast chill run down my body, only adding to the terror of the shaking, because it had only been three seconds since my sight left the kid behind me. With my head upside down in the cover position, I realized the kid behind me was gone. I quickly looked forward to see if he was running to the others, and I only saw a room that was finally coming to a silent stillness: with the aftermath sounds of a few objects rolling off tables onto the floor. There was no sound of running—or any sign of the kid. There was no door near my end of the room, either.

After everything was still and we all came out from under the tables, I realized that the kid who had grabbed my ankle, said something to me, and suddenly wasn't there, was someone I'd never seen before.

I'm am 100% certain that the boy who was consoling me during the earthquake was a ghost.

Anything Ghost Episode #222
April 27, 2016

Devil Dog of New Zealand
Victoria (New Zealand)

I'm from New Zealand, so this story will not be relative to any Native American reservations or anything along those lines. Regardless, I have seen something very similar to this thing called a "devil dog" that has been talked about in the past few Anything Ghost episodes; but I have no idea if it was a devil dog, or something else. Either way, it was creepy.

This happened to me about ten to thirteen years ago when I was still living in my hometown. There was a lookout spot where we used to go to that was kind of rural. It had a really nice view of the city and the ocean so it was a nice spot to stop. One night, a friend and I decided to go up there and spend a bit of time to go watch over the city (we did this quite a bit, so it wasn't unusual). We climbed up to the viewing platform, and were admiring the view and there was no one else there.

A few minutes after we arrived we saw something coming up the road. I don't recall it making any noise, it kind of just appeared. It was a big black animal of some sort, and was way too big to be a dog (although, it kind of looked like a dog). It came up the road and immediately sat under a streetlight—giving us a full view of whatever this thing was. It just sat there and stared at us. I don't remember seeing it's eyes or again any noises, it was just sitting there—this big black beast thing.

In New Zealand, we don't have bears or big fuzzy animals like that: we mainly have birds, lizards, cows and sheep (plus normal sized dogs, cats etc), so I can't think of what on earth this thing was. It continued to sit there for a few minutes, and then it suddenly ran off back the way it came. As soon as it left, once my friend and I got over our shock, we were out of there.

It was awful because we had to go the same way back the way the thing had ran. I was terrified I was going to see it, but we saw nothing. There was absolutely nothing on the way back.

It was really weird, and I've been back since then, but have never seen anything like it again.

Anything Ghost Episode #223
May 21, 2016

The Doorknob Jiggler
Naomi (El Monte, California)

Several years ago, my son and I lived in the back house of our property in El Monte, California. At that time my son was about ten years old.

One night, as we were watching TV in the front room of our small house, we heard and saw the doorknob on the front door begin to jiggle and turn—as if someone was trying to get in. The house had a window that allowed a view of front side of the door. Both my son and myself got up to see if anyone was at the door, but no one was there. After a while we forgot about it, but then it happened a second time. Being that this door was also visible to the neighbor next door, I called my neighbor and asked them to look at my door to see if anyone was out there. While it was happening, they didn't see anyone, and the doorknob then stopped jiggling.

Eventually my son and I moved into the house in the front, and my elderly father moved into the back house. Although my son and I had often shared the story, we had never really stopped to think about what it may have been. We just referred to it as the Jiggler. It was a long time before we would hear from the Jiggler again.

My father was handicapped and can not get out of bed on his own, so we often left his door open (so if he needed us, we were able get to him in a hurry). We did not tell him we left the door unlocked, because he was afraid to sleep in an unlocked house—even though it was behind a locked gate, and we had several dogs to protect the yard.

One morning, I went to help him get dressed and get out of bed. While with him, he asked me, "Did you lose the key to my door?"

I told him, "No. Why?"

He then asked, "Then why were you jiggling the door handle last night?"

I knew the door had been left open. It was then that I told him about the Jiggler.

He said, "I wish you had not told me that. Now I will not be able to sleep."

There was only one other jiggle incident, and it was in broad daylight. I was in the yard between the two houses when suddenly I heard the door handle jiggle right in from of me, and there was no one touching it.

Anything Ghost Episode #223
May 21, 2016

The Sleep and Snore Ernie Doll
Sandi (Stauffer, Alberta, Canada)

One of my first real experiences with the paranormal was about 20 years ago. We moved into a relatively new home. Every so often, I would go down into the basement and would become overwhelmed with the need to get out of there and I would run upstairs.

When I was a teenager, I actually took over the basement bedroom. At that time I had a Sleep and Snore Ernie. I had it placed up high on a shelf. One night, about a year later, I was sleeping and it began talking. I jumped out of bed and turned on the lamp. I then sauntered over to the doll, and stared at it. I was beginning to assume that it was just the batteries dying, but then my dog began to growl and then bark at something behind me. Ever since that night, my dog would randomly begin to stare and growl at things that I could not see.

Years later, I continued to have odd encounters with things being moved, and figures shifting out of the corner of my eye. More recently, I've been smelling strong floral perfumes. One night, I was folding clothes in my living room and I glanced up in time to see what I thought was my husband's shadow walking down the hall to check on our sleeping daughters. I thought nothing of it, until seconds later my husband began speaking to me from behind me in the kitchen.

Anything Ghost Episode #223
May 21, 2016

Sleep and Snore Ernie Stories

There have been three or four stories involving the Sleep and Snore Ernie doll shared with Anything Ghost. Each experience seems to involve when the doll—for no apparent reason—comes to "life" and makes audible noises.

Another of "Ernie experience" is also in this volume of Anything Ghost stories. However, the other story is titled *"Sing and Snore Ernie"* (I'm not sure if it's the same toy). Either way, it leads me to believe the toy may have had a malfunction—rather than it being paranormal activity....but one never knows!

- **"Sing and Snore Ernie"**
  Savannah (Mississippi, U.S.) - *Chapter 5*

Philadelphia Haunting
Maggie (Rochester, New York)

I went and visited my sister in Philadelphia one weekend during my college break. She worked for a nonprofit organization. Half of the weekend vacation was volunteering and in exchange they provided us with housing and food. We were housed in old brick style townhouses, and my one room townhouse was connected to my sister's (she had already been living there for the past year and a half). The interior was out-dated and very simple. That was fine with me because the bedroom had fresh sheets—and that was all I really cared about.

Looking back, I had always felt as though I had a connection to those who have passed; whether it was feeling like someone was staring at me, or just simple things a feeling in my room. But that was nothing like what happened next.

As I was a little bit skeptical of the condition of the townhouse, I asked my sister and her friend if it was haunted. To be honest, I was joking, but as my sister's friend opened her mouth, my sister cut her off and said, "No!" Abruptly. I brushed if off, because I was too excited to explore the city then, and didn't really care.

Later that night, my fiancé and me were exhausted and we went to bed in the small room. That night, I tossed and turned and slept very lightly. At one point, I awoke and found myself looking at the window that was in front of me. There, I saw a woman in a white dress staring out the window. She had long brown hair that was pulled back into a braid of some sort. Shocked, and a little scared, I closed my eyes, and the re-opened them, only to find her still standing there and staring outside the window. She then moved her head slightly, seemingly recognizing that I did see her, and then slowly left through the window. I was so afraid that I woke up my fiancée. He told me it was a dream, and since I was so tired, I agreed.

The next morning, I woke up and went to go tell my sister what I had seen. I ran up the stairs to her connecting room and opened the door.

As I finished my sentence, "You will never guess…"

She immediately cut me off and said, "Did you see her?"

I said, "Her? You knew there was something there and didn't tell me?"

Apparently, many guests who have stayed in that room have seen this woman. Sometimes she was seen in the kitchen, but mainly in the bedroom, right by the window. No one has ever said that she is mean or an evil spirit, but everyone gets the impression that she is just there—maybe curious or protective. No matter what the case was, you can bet that I am never staying in that room again!

Anything Ghost Episode #223
May 21, 2016

The Gift of Cows
Sara (Apex, North Carolina)

Unfortunately, my grandmother ("grammy") passed away about a week ago at 80 years old. I've been picking up the pieces of my heart since then, and trying to come to terms with the fact that I will never again be able to speak to her, or see her through conventional means again.

There was a particular experience that my grammy and I had when I was a freshman in high school. She was staying with me at my house while my parents were away on business. She would drop me off at school in the morning and pick me up afterward. One day, after she had picked me up from school, we were on the way back to my house. It was at least a ten mile drive down the road we lived off. It was a rural county, so there were a lot of fields and farms. While we were on the drive home, we came upon several black cows in the middle of the road. This was particularly funny, as we didn't know of any farms with cows on that particular stretch of road. We laughed at the randomness of it all until eventually they moved and we were able to continue on home.

Sixteen years later, I was extremely sad as I drove my 12-year-old son with me to her graveside service. Grammy lived in another rural area of the state that took me about two hours to drive to. I always knew when I was getting close to her house because I would hit a long stretch of two-lane highway in rural eastern North Carolina. On the day of the funeral, I was traveling on that same road because the graveside service was very close to where she lived. I was thinking to myself that I just wanted the hurt in my heart to stop, because I knew grammy was now without pain and no longer suffering.

A few minutes after these thoughts, my son and I saw some dark figures in the distance. As we drive closer we realized that there on the side of the road were several black cows—much like the cows that were on the road that my grammy and I saw 16 years ago. But what struck me was that in all my travels through rural North Carolina farmland, the only other time I saw cows on the road was when I was with grammy and on my way back from school. And being that it was on the day I said my final good-byes to grammy, I knew it was my grammy—in her true humorous fashion—who put those cows on the road that day. I took it as her sign that all was okay. Grammy was telling me she was where she needed to be, and that she wanted me to continue to be happy and laugh much like we did that day when we first saw the cows.

Anything Ghost Episode #223
May 21, 2016

"I am the Boogie Man"
Liz (Glen Cove, New York)

This happened to me when I was five or six-years-old. I lived with my family in a rambling old apartment in Brooklyn, and I was one of six children.

On this night, I must have fallen asleep watching TV in the living room, and instead of carrying me into bed, my mother must have just covered me with a blanket and left me to sleep overnight in a big armchair. When I woke up, the house was dark & quiet. It was probably about 1 a.m. Standing next to my chair, maybe a foot away from me was a shadowy figure of a very short man wearing a top hat. I couldn't see his face, or any of his features—he was more like just a black, shadowy outline in the darkness. His shape kind of reminded me of the Penguin from the Batman TV show, only much shorter—no more than four feet tall. I was too terrified to summon much of a voice, but I whispered to him, "Who are you?"

He immediately whispered back, "I am the boogie man."

I jumped out of my chair and ran screaming down the hall to my parents' room. They assured me that I had been dreaming, and let me sleep with them for the rest of the night.

Maybe a year ago, around Halloween, I discovered in a Google search that many people (children mostly), have awoken in the night and have seen a "man with a hat." Sometimes he's very short or sometimes he's very tall. I have also read (and heard about on your Anything Ghost Show) of shadow people. I'm not sure whether I find it comforting to know that I'm not alone in this experience, or whether this makes it all the more scary.

Anything Ghost Episode #223
May 21, 2016

Haunted Colonial Home in the Woods
Briana (Virginia, U.S.)

The first haunting took place in a sinister country house my mother, sister and I had moved into after my parents divorced. We lived there almost a year before the activity became too much, and we were forced to leave. The smaller home we moved into later had no noticeable activity—which was a huge relief considering the past events—and that allowed me to finish off my remaining high school years in peace.

Upon graduating I moved back to the city. Unfortunately I had a rocky start, made some poor financial decisions, and quickly realized I needed to get back on track before I irreparably damaged my chances for the future. My father heard about my situation, and contacted me about moving in with him, his new wife, and my little brother while I finished college and paid off my debt—an offer I was quick, and eager, to accept. I got along great with his wife, and it gave my father and I the opportunity to bond again after being apart for so long.

One thing I'd like to point out is that while I am an obvious believer in the paranormal, my father has always openly been a nonbeliever in all things supernatural. If he couldn't see it, it didn't exist. Ghosts, angels, phantoms, shadow people: these were all products of overactive imaginations—and a waste of his time.

My father's house was a large colonial tucked away in the woods on the outskirts of the city, about twenty minutes from the border of North Carolina. Close enough to work and stores, but hidden away from the bustle of the city—a welcome sanctuary after a hectic day of noise and traffic. The family that built the house initially lived in it for less than a year before moving out and selling it to my parents. This detail didn't seem odd at first, but in retrospect should have been a pretty big red flag that something wasn't right.

The bedroom that I moved into was one of four upstairs, and mine was directly above the main living room. My brother's room was across the hall from mine, and my parents' master bedroom was downstairs and on the far end of the home. For the first couple months I was rarely there: only enough to sleep or do homework, and then it was back to work or school. Everything ran smoothly, in the beginning.

The first event happened at night. My brother and parents had gone to bed, and I was settled in at my computer working on an assignment. I was suddenly overcome with a familiar, unsettling feeling that I was not alone in my room. The bedroom door was right beside me, so I could not have missed someone entering the room. I knew that I was not used to the deep silence, and utter blackness that came with being tucked away in the woods, and was initially able to brush it off as I was just letting my new surroundings get to me. Eventually the feeling went away, and I laughed it off.

But as the days passed, other things began to occur. I would be facing the computer (the room dead silent), and I would hear someone sit down on my bed behind me. Because it was an actual sound, and not just a strange, overwhelming feeling, I would instinctively turn and look, only to find the room empty. The sound of someone settling onto my bed grew more frequent—happening on a weekly basis. I quickly trained myself to stop turning around, being afraid that one night I might actually see who, or what, was causing the strange sound.

In the days that followed, I approached my father and his wife about these small occurrences by asking if they ever noticed anything strange. My father, of course, scoffed, saying I was too old for this childishness. His wife, however, turned out to be a believer. She told me that she sometimes felt strange upstairs, but nothing she couldn't shake off, or explain away, just as I had. I decided not to approach the subject with my father again, unless something more solid than mere strange feelings and sounds occurred. As it turned out, I didn't have to wait long.

I came home late from work one evening, surprised to find my dad and his wife had waited up for me. They were sitting in the living room (directly below my bedroom). They both looked troubled, and kept glancing at the ceiling. I finally broke the silence by asking if I had done something wrong. My father shook his head, and then quietly retreated to his room for the evening. I asked his wife what was going on, and she replied, "Well, I think it's safe to say your father is a believer now."

"What happened?" I asked. She went on to explain that they had been watching TV before bed, when they heard my computer chair rolling across the floor upstairs. Assuming it was my little brother, who was supposed to be in bed at that time, my stepmother went up to scold him...only to find that he was, in fact, sleeping in his bed. She opened my bedroom door, just in case, but found nothing amiss. Confused, she returned downstairs and told my father what she had found. Moments later, heavy footsteps stomped around in my room above, followed by the rolling of the computer chair again—this time moving the entire length of the room. My father grew angry and said that it had to be my little brother, and that he was going to be in trouble. He sprinted upstairs and flung open my bedroom door. The room was empty. He then checked my brother's room and found him still tucked into bed. Upon realizing there was no way for my brother to have been able to run to his room, close the bedroom door, get back in bed and calm his breathing that quickly, my father began to accept what was happening.

After about a year of living in the house, I met the man who would eventually become my husband. In the beginning of our dating I had decided to keep my paranormal experiences a secret—afraid that he would think I was insane, and run. I wouldn't have been able to blame him.

Our relationship grew serious, and I began to feel horrible hiding something from him that had such an impact on my happiness. He seemed to know when something happened in the house, based on my changed mood, and he would ask about it, but I just shrugged it off as nothing important. I still couldn't bring myself to open up to him.

But one day something terrifying occurred that made me change my mind. I was having one of those days where nothing seemed to go right. He had made reservations for dinner, and as the hour was closing in, I still hadn't managed to get myself ready. I called him to cancel, saying I just didn't feel up to it. Nothing I wore looked right, and my hair was unmanageable. He said I was being silly and he was sure I looked amazing, and to prove it he wanted me to take a picture of myself with my phone and text it to him, and he would be the judge. In order for him to see the dress I was wearing, and to show how the front and back of my hair looked I used the large, decorative mirror that we had in the upstairs hallway. I had my back to the mirror, and took a picture facing the camera. I will never forget the image that appeared on my phone.

Photo by Briana (Virginia, U.S.)
The mirror where Briana saw an odd reflection of herself.

I was indeed facing the camera in the picture. My reflection, however, was not as it should have been: instead of facing away from me, its head was turned toward the camera. While my hair was twisted up and secured back, my reflection's hair was loose, and wild. My lips were closed, and curved into a forced smile, while the reflection of my mouth was open wide, twisted, and appeared to be screaming. My eyes looked normal but in the reflection they were black holes. Terrified, I ran downstairs and called my dad. Although he had come to be more open about the incidences in the house, this one was a bit far fetched for him. He asked me to text the picture to him. So I did. He emailed it to himself and opened it on his work computer to analyze it, and when he was satisfied that I had not tampered with it, concluded that the activity in the house was more sinister than we had originally assumed.

My husband called me, asking where the picture was, and if I still wanted to cancel the date. At this point I was definitely not in the mood for dinner, and instead decided that it was about time to let him in on this side of my life. If we stayed together, he would eventually find out anyway—so why prolong the inevitable? I showed him the picture as well. He didn't run, as I'd feared he would do. In fact, within a week of showing him the picture, he had an experience of his own in the house.

I had been held up at work and missed our dinner date, so he surprised me by showing up with dinner and a movie. We had just gotten settled on the floor in my room and put the movie in when I very clearly heard the familiar sound of someone sitting down on my bed. I glanced over at my husband. To my dismay, I could tell he had heard the sound as well.

"Did you hear that?" He asked. "I swear it sounded like someone sat on your bed."

He seemed to lose his appetite, and was visibly uncomfortable throughout the movie—constantly glancing around the room as though waiting for something to crazy to happen.

A few months later, only a few weeks before we married, my husband and I stopped by the house to drop something off to my parents. My husband stayed in the car while I went in. When I returned, he looked bothered.

"Is someone in your room?" He asked. I looked up to see my bedroom lights flashing on and off. I grew angry, assuming my little brother was in my room playing—which was absolutely off limits, since I still had not moved my stuff out yet. I ran inside and told my parents, who looked confused, and informed me that my little brother was not even at home. We went upstairs together to check it out, but the lights were off. We all came back downstairs, and I returned to the car. My husband said that right before we got to the room the lights stopped flashing. But as soon as we made it back downstairs again, it started up. Sure enough, when I looked up at the room again, the lights were flashing.

I moved out soon after I married my husband, and my parents claim the activity seems to have stopped since I left. That was six years ago.

Anything Ghost Episode #157
June 16, 2012

The Old Part of the House
Briana (Virginia, U.S.)

My parents divorced when I was 15. I lived with my mother and my little sister, while my brother went to live with my father. I was pretty torn up about the divorce for several reasons—that initially caused quite a bit of tension between my mother and me.

We moved from the big city where I had lots of friends, to a place three states away where I knew nobody. But it was the small town where my mother grew up, so I knew I would have no voice in the matter. And after my mother spoke to a realtor, she ended up rented a house—"sight unseen"—for a very reasonable price.

When we pulled up we were in awe. The house was huge—which didn't really make sense for just three people. It was gorgeous: L-shaped with two stories on one side, and another story on the other side. Inside the home, a thick, heavy wooden door separated the two sides. The one-story side was what they called "new"—meaning it had been built within the past fifty years. On the "new" side there were two bedrooms, a kitchen, a dining room, and a living room; while the "old" side had two stories and had been built in the 1800s.

Upon entering the "old" side there was a large room with built in hammock bed and fireplace. Then there was a set of stairs that led up to two large bedrooms. Next to the staircase was a door that led to a small, dark, wet cellar—every time we went down there we found dead animals. Needless to say, we didn't go down there very often.

The first night we slept in the house, I had been in an argument with my mom. She decided to sleep in the master bedroom with my little sister in the new side of the house, while I chose one of the upstairs bedrooms in the old side—as far away from my mother as possible. A heavy wooden door separated the old part from the new part of the home. Being that it was late spring, the wood in the door had expanded which caused it to stick—making it harder to open. Once the door was open it would close on its own.

That first night, I made my way through the wooden door—slamming it behind me in anger. Then I stomped through the downstairs bedroom (the one with built-in hammock bed), up the staircase and into my bedroom upstairs—where I slammed that door behind me, as well.

It was a sweltering night, so I tried opening the windows in the room, only to find that all four windows were sealed shut. I tried and tried to open them, but they just wouldn't budge. Finally, I gave up and went to bed. I lay there facing the wall trying to sleep in the heat. My damp hair was stuck to my back, and I just couldn't seem to find a cool spot on my pillow. It was miserable, but I just refused to go back to the "new" side of the house where my mom was.

About half an hour after I went to bed, I heard the downstairs heavy door open, and slam shut. This was followed by heavy footsteps pounding up the steps. Then I heard my bedroom door open, and the footsteps walked into the center of my room. I figured it was my mother, and she came up to scold me for giving her attitude (when I slammed the door earlier in the night). But I found it odd that she waited so long to come and scorn me for slamming the door...so I decided to pretend I was asleep.

After a few moments of silence, the footsteps moved to the far window. I heard the window being pried open and then slammed down once. It opened again, then slammed down. Then a third time it opened and slammed once more. I grew more and more angry. Why was my mother being so passive-aggressive? Why didn't she just speak to me if she was so angry? I kept still, facing the wall. Finally, the steps moved back to the center of the room, stayed there for a couple moments, then walked back to the bedroom door, and opened and closed it. I then heard the steps retreat back down the stairs.

I kept listening for the heavy wooden door to open again, but I never heard it.

The next morning I went to the kitchen to have breakfast. My mom was still giving me the silent treatment, so I kept my mouth shut. When she left the room, my little sister said, "Mom's really mad at you for last night."

I said, "For what?—I should be mad at her!"

She replied, "Because we heard you come through the heavy door and to the kitchen, and mom called out to you, but you ignored her."

I said, "I didn't come downstairs last night! Mom came up to my room and slammed my windows!"

My sister replied, "Mom never left her bedroom at all last night!"

There were several other things that happened the first summer we lived in that house. I would be doing my homework in the upstairs bedroom, and suddenly get the feeling that I was not alone. I felt the hairs on my neck stand up, and just knew if I turned around, I would see someone, or something standing there. One day the feeling was so strong and disturbing that I finally yelled out, "Please just leave me alone! I didn't do anything to you!"

One time, when I was walking up the stairs, I distinctly heard a whisper say, "Pick her up and throw her down."

I sprinted the rest of the way up the stairs and slammed my door. After that occurred, any other time I went up or down the stairs, I would always go as quickly as I could—terrified that something would push me down the stairs.

Unable to stand it, I finally moved out of the upstairs room, and to the bedroom directly below it (the one with the built-in hammock bed). But I only slept on the hammock bed for two nights: because both times, I had horrific nightmares and woke up with my entire body hurting.

After the two nights of sleeping in the hammock bed, I moved my bed from the upstairs bedroom to the hammock room. I slept in the downstairs room for a couple weeks, but every night I would awaken to heavy footsteps moving up and down the staircase, and stomping around upstairs in my old bedroom. I very quickly moved out of the old side of the house and into the tiny spare bedroom on the new side.

Some time later, my aunt moved into the old side of the house. She was there for less than a month but quickly moved out. She chose instead, to live in a trailer with her son and his rambunctious family.

We had a dog that refused to go through the heavy door to the old side. The only time she did, we accidentally closed the door and left her over there—not realizing she was there. We began to hear her yelping and barking and scratching at the door. When we opened the door she ran back to the new side and hid. She was a very calm dog, and had never had a problem being left alone.

We lived in the new side of the house for another six months and then finally moved out the next spring.

My mother did research and found out that back in the 1800's to the early 1900's, people in that area rarely went to the hospital (it was several miles away), and generally were treated for illnesses in their homes. It was also standard practice for family members to pass away in their homes, with family, rather than go to a hospital.

Anything Ghost Episode #155
May 5, 2012

The Old Part of the House by Briana, has always been one of my favorite Anything Ghost stories. To me, it has all the elements of a true haunting: an old home that has been renovated; new people just moved in; a child angry with her mother...I just love the story. I especially like the visual of when her back was turned as she listened to someone (she assumed was her mother) pound up the stairs, slam the window several times, then storm back down the stairs. Another great story, that I think is similar to this one, involved a haunted mobile home in Arkansas. I was happy that I was able to include both of these stories in this book.

• **Haunted Arkansas Mobile Home**
   Kia (Arkansas, U.S.) - *Chapter 4*

A Walk at Bethany Lake Park
Robert (Texas, U.S.)

This past April my waist size and age were becoming way too close together for comfort, and my doctor said I needed to go on a diet and exercise. So in April of 2012, I started avoiding fast food and began walking daily. During one of these daily walks was when I believe I caught the glimpse of a ghost.

The park I walked in was Bethany Lakes Park. Certain corners of the path I came across during these early morning strolls were dark, and not illuminated very well by the outdated lights. The park had a concession building, a cancer memorial walking path and, just to the left of the pathway, a tribute to the U.S. Armed Forces. The tribute was a giant American flag surrounded by small bushes. Under the flag were the five branches of America's Armed Forces with engraved names of those who served or gave their life in service.

I would walk early in the morning when the temperatures were cool (because in Texas the temperatures spike quickly to over 100 degrees/40 Celsius during the day). It was dark during these daily walks, so I watched my surroundings carefully so as not to run into other walkers or joggers.

As I was walking around the pathway, I caught a glimpse of a figure near the American flag tribute. This person seemed quite a bit different from those that I usually gave a cheery "hello" to each morning: he was standing very tall and erect like a soldier.

As my walk lead me closer, I noticed the figure was in uniform and appeared to be saluting. I thought to myself, "Well, being that it's close to Memorial Day, this is an understandable thing to do." But there was something strange about this person's manner and I grew suspicious.

As my walk brought me closer...the figure vanished. I quickly refocused my stare again, but it was most certainly gone. This park had very few trees and the land was very flat. I didn't see the figure walk away, and there was no place to hide. My first thought was that I was seeing things because I had not had enough coffee.

For several days after this sighting, I started my walk a little later in the morning so the sun would illuminate the path more. I also drank coffee before my daily walks. But after a while, the heat began to get to me, so I once again began heading out before the dawn. However, during these new pre-dawn walks, I kept a keen eye out for the lone figure.

Anything Ghost Episode #164
October 25, 2012

Emergency Call from the Dead
J. Steven (Texas, U.S.)

Here's a firsthand experience my brother related to me:

A few years ago I was a patrol deputy with a large county near Houston, Texas.

One evening around 20:00 hours dispatch received a call from a residence from an elder female stating that her husband had fallen. Upon our arrival (two other deputies and I) made several attempts to make contact with the home owner. No one would answer the door, and we were unable to see anyone from the outside of the residence. I contacted dispatch and requested they call the residence back and have the wife come to the door. Dispatch stated that they called the number back and it was disconnected. After several minutes and knocking quite loudly, one of the neighbors came out and asked if they could help. We explained that we had received a 911 call from the residence regarding the home owner being injured. The neighbor looked at us puzzled and asked us if we were joking. I explained to him that we were not joking. He then informed us that both husband and wife passed away approximately a week ago.

After a few moments, I asked the neighbor if they might have a key to the residence. He stated that they did, and promptly obtained it for us to gain access. When we entered the house, the neighbor stated that he would not enter. We checked the house unable to locate anyone inside. I further checked the phone and received no dial tone. We thanked the neighbor, and we left the location.

I contacted dispatch and informed them no one was at the residence and requested they check with the phone company regarding the number and phone line. I feared that we went to the wrong address and someone still needed medical attention.

I checked with dispatch to make sure the recording of the original call had not been re-broadcast for some reason, but was told it originated from the home. I contacted the phone company to make sure the phone had in fact been disconnected, and they said it had. I even heard the dispatch recording of the elderly lady. I was later informed that the residents of the home in which the call originated that we responded to passed away the week prior. The husband had fallen due to a heart attack, and his wife passed shortly after (due to shock). Both were very elderly, and had health problems. I was also informed that the call we received was the same call that dispatch received the day they both passed.

We would receive this call for three more weeks, on the same day of the week of the original incident, at the same time. Several of my coworkers would not respond to the call due to the eerie nature of the call. The calls then stopped.

Chapter 3 — Ghostly and Creepy Experiences

Approximately a year later I heard the call go out on the radio, same call, same location. I was no longer in the district, but I responded regardless. When I arrived on location I spoke with the new home owner that stated that all was well.

I have since left the patrol division, and wonder if they still receive the call in late August."

Anything Ghost Episode #142
October 9, 2011

J. Steven (who sent in his brother's Emergency Call from the Dead story), is an excellent photographer. Some of his work can be found at his Flickr account:
https://www.flickr.com/photos/jshorn/
In the early years of Anything Ghost, J. Steven sent me some great photographs of his visit to an abandoned hotel in Texas. Below is one of those photographs.

Photo by J. Steven Horn - **https://www.flickr.com/photos/jshorn/**
The inside of the abandoned Baker Hotel in Mineral Wells, Texas. The hotel has a history of paranormal activity.

The Vietnam Veteran Spirit
Lemon (Texas, U.S.)

I lived in Guymon, Oklahoma in 1985 working at a Travel Agency—actually, it was a satellite office for a much larger office in Amarillo, Texas. It was normal for my boss and I to drive to the main branch in Amarillo for meetings when new travel agendas were introduced (the new launch of a Cruise Ship Line, or a new all-inclusive resort that kind of thing).

Fortunately, these Premiers always occurred on Friday night, so I could sleep in on Saturday morning. It was a long trip; 121 miles each way on a highway that had a 55 MPH speed limit at that time. The programs would usually start at 7 p.m. and would go on until the main office said their good-nights. No one could leave before then, but they were usually a blast: open bar, catered meal, door prizes, and a happy friendly atmosphere.

On this trip there was a midnight drawing for a free trip. We left shortly afterward. Since I was the junior agent, I didn't get to drive and my boss was not one to speed. Our drive was uneventful and terribly boring. My boss couldn't let me fall asleep in fear that she might nod off herself, so she quizzed me on every detail of the new travel opportunity. She dropped me off at my apartment at about 2:45 a.m.

The apartment started out as a garage for the house that was next door. When the oilfield boomed in the Oklahoma Panhandle anyone who had property tried to expand the number of units they could rent out by splitting houses into duplexes and cobbling together small out buildings into one room affairs—like this garage conversion with a shed tacked on. However, my encounter was long after the boom went bust and no one was making nearly the money that they had once been making.

My landlord had wanted me to rent the duplex connected to his. Unfortunately, we could not agree on a price that I could meet. So I rented the one room garage sight unseen. Upon walking through the front door there was a living room and bedroom with its wall to wall closet opposite the door; three steps in and two to the right were the dining/kitchen/bathroom; five steps further to the right was the back door—both the front and the back door opened inward; the bathroom was discreetly hidden behind a bed sheet used as a curtain; the shower was the size of a postage stamp with the scalloped edges cut off.

I felt a presence the moment I brought my first bag through the door. I'd had previous encounters with spirits and haunts without any bad associations, but, this one felt, prickly: it held a sense of deep pain, anger, and confusion. I asked permission to enter, and explained aloud that I had come to live in the apartment for a time and that I would respect it if it would do the same for me. I would talk to the entity like a roommate. I'd say when I was leaving and when I would be back. After a time I gradually felt the atmosphere change from brooding to cool, verging on welcoming. I didn't even think to ask my landlord, Bill, about the presence; and, everything seemed fine until almost four months had passed.

On that night when I opened the front door, and stepped inside, I thought I heard a whispered, "Get Out"! I was very tired though, and I dismissed it as imagination. The presence had never actually spoken to me before. I said hello and talked to the presence about the meeting as I changed into night clothes and lay down. The room was as dark as a pit, save for the line of light that glowed just under the curtain on the front window. As I lay in bed waiting for my mind to slow down, I heard more whispers, but, I couldn't quite make out any words.

The temperature outside was in the lower forties but now it felt colder. Boom! Whoosh! The old wall heater kicked on and a plume of blue flame bloomed out the bottom. I sat straight up in bed and suddenly the whole atmosphere of my apartment had changed! My breath fogged in the light from the heater! I felt sick to my stomach and my left arm felt like it was on fire! The volume of the whispers went way up, it began to sound like a million cockroaches scuttling for cover; and then, it was instantly silent.

I was just beginning to process this when BOOM! My front door slammed open against the doorstop. I felt a chill breath at my ear and a hoarse, gravelly voice full of malice whispered, "Get out!" Screech! Bang! The back door flew open and slammed into the kitchen counter. Somehow I was on my feet then and running out the front door in only my nightgown. I screamed as I ran into the middle of the street.

I looked back at the apartment and the interior lights were flashing on then off then on again. The front screen door was banging open and closed. The lights went on in the house next door, and a moment later my landlord Bill stepped out.

"I can't ever tell who he'll like or for how long." He said as he brought me a quilt.

As I wrapped it around my shoulders he asked me to come into his kitchen to warm up. I agreed. He was a retired military man so I felt safe—and I wasn't going to go back into that apartment anytime soon. He made me a cup of hot tea and asked me to sit down. I asked him what he meant by his comment, and he told me about his younger brother.

They had both been in Vietnam but his brother Jim had come back with some major problems: Post Traumatic Stress Syndrome, a drug addiction and only one arm—his right. He had violent nightmares and was often awake at odd hours. He helped his brother get their parent's rental properties ready when the oilfields began to become prosperous, and did some general construction for others in town, but he was suffering. He would start arguments and get into fights;

and then trouble with the law. He was brought up on assault charges and was supposed to appear in court. The morning of his scheduled court date Bill found him hanging from a roof beam in the garage apartment. He suspected foul play but the police ruled it a suicide and closed the case.

He told me that he hadn't rented the garage for two years; but, then he had a young man who really wanted to rent it and everything went real well for five years. No complaints came from the young man and then he married and moved on. The next renter bailed out in the middle of the night and never came back.

He said that sometimes the renters would stay a few years and others would make it a few weeks or months before leaving—usually without notice. He apologized for not telling me about Jim before.

Then he went back into the apartment with me while I gathered a few things. Then I drove to a motel. I moved out on Monday morning leaving him a forwarding address. A month later, I received a check for my last month's rent and $40 dollars extra—I guess he knew I had to stay in a motel over the weekend. Since then I've always given rentals a thorough walk through and let my senses tell me everything they can before I've laid down a penny.

Anything Ghost Episode #170
March 2, 2013

War Ghosts

Many battlegrounds are believed to have paranormal activity. Here are some other stories in this book related to wars and soldiers:

- **New England Ghost Story**
  Lucas (New England, U.S.) - *Chapter 2*
- **Oriskany Battlefield**
  Alex (Central New York, U.S.) - *Chapter 4*
- **The Forgotten Lodger**
  Chris (Dublin, Ireland) - *Chapter 5*
- **A Small Boy Ghost in Fallujah, Iraq**
  Kevin (U.S.) - *Chapter 5*
- **The World War II Ghost**
  Steve (Kent, England) - *Chapter 6*

Apparition in My Room

Kong (Eau Claire, Wisconsin)

My name is Kong and I'm a 31-year-old man. My "encounter" happened when I was young, around ten years of age, at an old house my family used to live in. I still remember that night very vividly, and when I think about what I saw it still gives me chills.

At the time we lived in a very old house in a city called Eau Claire, Wisconsin. In the basement of that house was a bricked up room. As the years went on, the bricks that concealed the room crumbled bit by bit, and soon we were able to squeeze through into the room. It was a small 8' square room that it was filled with nothing but rubble, insulation and toy parts. Needless to say it was quite a scary room, but as children we didn't even think of it that way—my siblings and I would sometimes play in that room. I have no idea if the room was in any way connected to what I saw one night, but I have no other reason to believe it wasn't.

The house we lived in was old and creepy, at night there wasn't enough light in most of the house and it would get pitch black. Most nights I couldn't even see the hand in front of my face if I wasn't by a window with the shades opened.

I shared a room with my older brother who was about ten years older. The room was rectangular. We each had twin beds that were set adjacent to each of the two windows. The door was on the opposite side of the room, and right next to the door was an old dresser that my brother and I shared.

As far as I can remember, I have always had problems falling asleep. I'd stay up and fantasize about things when trying to fall asleep—things that usually involved me being a hero of some sort. Also, when I can't fall asleep I like to put my head under my blanket for the extra sense of security.

One night I saw something curious, after I pulled the blanket down to get some fresh air. Next to the dresser and in front of the door to our room, I saw a faint light. As I stared at the light it became brighter and brighter. The light shone like a distant flashlight, and it was translucent. As I stared at this light it started to move. The light slowly flowed downward like a waterfall, and as it did a figure started to appear. At first the light appeared at the top of the figure's head, then it slowly descended down the figure's body revealing the figure. The figure was that of an attractive African American woman wearing a summer dress. I could tell she was young—in her mid to late 20's or early 30's. She didn't appear threatening but I felt uneasy and scared because she was looking directly at me. I immediately put my head under the covers and shut my eyes tightly.

When I worked up some courage, I pulled the covers down and looked in her direction again. I saw her exactly how I'd seen her the first time: first the faint light got brighter, then the light flowed down like a waterfall revealing her full apparition.

By this time I was so scared I was shaking under my covers—knowing she was staring directly at me. I yelled for my brother. I asked him if I could sleep with him in his bed and he mumbled, "Yes," with his eyes still shut.

I don't know why I didn't tell him: I think I was too scared to say it out loud for fear of what the ghost might do if it knew I could see it.

I moved swiftly to my brother's bed, without looking in the ghost's direction, and slept on the far side behind him—away from the ghost. I was sure I was seeing things. I looked out the other window adjacent to his bed, and saw a street lamp illuminating a small area below it...nothing was out of the ordinary.

After a few minutes of shutting my eyes tightly, I looked back in the direction of the ghost over my brother's shoulder. Again, I saw it exactly as I had before with the faint light, etc...and now the apparition had turned to look directly at me.

I had the feeling that it meant me no harm, but I still couldn't help but be scared—because in my culture, the paranormal and non-human entities almost always mean the living harm. I shut my eyes tight, and surely enough I fell asleep. That was the first and only time I saw her, but I still remember her to this day—over 20 years later.

Other things happened in that house too. When one of my younger brothers was diagnosed with epilepsy he used to run high fevers and tell us he'd see ghosts lurking in every corner of the house. This would scare the rest of us, as often times he'd point directly at the spot the ghost was.

There are times when I think about her, and I wonder why I saw her—and what she may have wanted. I have always wanted to investigate the history of that house, but I wouldn't even know where to start. When I do think about what I saw that night, the hair on my body stands on end and I get goose bumps—and still, I can't help but wonder why I saw her.

Anything Ghost Episode #127
January 22, 2011

The Sinclair Library
Mike (Manoa, Honolulu, Hawaii)

This happened to me in my third year in college, during the spring semester at the University of Hawaii at Manoa.

This university is known for mysterious occurrences, but I never thought that I would actually be witnessing or experiencing one. This particular occurrence happened during daylight hours—a seemingly unlikely hour to expect any type of haunting.

I was studying for an upcoming midterm. During that time of the semester it was quite busy at both libraries on campus. I found a quiet spot in the less crowded of the two libraries, Sinclair. I went to the second floor and sat at a desk at the end of one of the bookshelves. This library was configured strangely, so I had no problem finding an area with the least amount of student traffic. It was against one of the less used bookshelves.

About thirty minutes into my studying, I began to feel a slight tapping on my left shoulder. Thinking it was muscle spasms or a bug, I brushed it off. Within a few minutes the tapping continued even harder this time. I looked down both sides of the bookcase and saw nothing. This began to make me feel a bit unsettled. I was thinking it was either a friend playing a trick, or perhaps I was just starting to feel the effects of studying too long. Just as I thought the tapping had ceased, it started all over again. However, this time I could see the indentation of my shirt where the tapping was occurring. I finally asked, "Who is that?"

I bolted up and stormed around the nearby bookcases. I was looking frantically down the aisles to see if anyone was hiding or laughing at me from behind stacks and carts of books. I found no one I knew. The only people present were a few international students staring at me from their books and laptops, probably wondering if I'd cracked up. Frustrated, I moved to another part of the library and the tapping stopped.

To this day I cannot explain what happened or why it happened. For all I know, I may have been in the way of a wandering spirit whose ghostly path I had accidentally blocked.

Anything Ghost Episode #115
June 6, 2010

Ghost Scars
Ben (Fort Smith, Arkansas)

In 2003, I was living in my hometown, Fort Smith. Two coworkers and I agreed to rent a large, 6,000 square foot Victorian home for about $650 a month. It was a great bargain extended to us by a friend who had bought it to rent out. Each of us had our own bedroom, extra room and bathroom. They were more like bedroom suites than bedrooms.

I moved in on March 30 with help from some movers. I got my bed set up in the one downstairs bedroom suite, and that night went to sleep at the new address. My house mates were moving in a day or two later, so I was all alone.

Photo by Ben (Fort Smith, Arkansas)
The large 6,000 square foot Victorian home in Fort Smith, Arkansas where Ben resided.

Being early spring, it got quite cold in the night. At one point during that first night, I awoke to light a gas space heater in my adjoining room. I left the door open between the two rooms, and then went back to sleep.

When I awoke in the morning, and before I had even had gotten out of bed, I noticed about a dozen long scratches down the back of my right hand. One was an inch or two down from my index finger and was quite wide. I remember thinking, "Well, those aren't too bad. They'll heal up and won't scar, but how the hell did I get them?"

At first, I thought I had scraped my hand on the grill in front of the heater's burner. But the pattern was all wrong for that. My second thought was that maybe rats or mice had made the scratches. But I saw no evidence of vermin in the home. Besides, these scratches were long and swept down from my own fingers as though they had been made by a hand or tonged trowel. Eventually, the scratches did heal up without a trace—almost. The widest mark, mentioned earlier above, mostly disappeared it but left behind a quarter-inch long scar that I still have to this day. It's maybe a millimeter wide at most.

Photo by Ben (Fort Smith, Arkansas)
The scar left on Ben's hand remains to this day.

I have a master's degree in history, and was a journalist at that time. As you can imagine, I was interested in the history of the house—even apart from the weird incident—so I did some research.

A Memphis cotton broker had built the place in the 1890s. He had moved to Fort Smith in the late 1800s with his family. He was struck by a car in the 1920s and died. His funeral had been in the home—which was not an unusual practice at that time. His family and some descendants whom continued to live there into the middle of the 20th century. Our landlord and friend told me she had heard that for a while in the 1950s, the property was used as a small rest home. I couldn't find evidence to refute or confirm that.

While living there, several times we had strange but explainable things happen. We'd hear weird noises on the second floor while we were downstairs in the common rooms. One time a house mate and I watched as a balloon at the top of the ceiling in one common room, floated down into the hallway, floated up, crossed, floated down, drifted slowly and then floated up again into my bedroom suite through an open doorway. Even my house mate, a strong skeptic, said that was a little weird. We easily could imagine how a deflating party balloon might migrate from one room to the next over hours but not in 90 seconds.

A year or two went by, a house mate moved away, our landlord decided to sell the house and I was about to get married, so we all moved out.

Fast forward to January. I was expecting a Christmas present that never arrived. Finally, it occurred to me it might have gone to my previous address. I called the new owners (after getting their number from my old landlord). Sure enough, the gift was sent to my old address. They'd been trying to find me. With their permission, I dashed over to pick it up.

While talking to one of them on the front porch, the new tenant asked me if I'd noticed or experienced anything weird while living there. I told him my story.

"That's very strange. What room were you in again?" He asked.

I told him.

He proceeded to recount to me how he had slept alone in the house on his first night in the same room. In the middle of the night, he had awakened to a sharp pain in his index finger at the point of his topmost knuckle. He said it felt like someone was driving a fingernail into his hand with all the force possible. Next, he showed me a scar that was hidden in the folds of the skin around his knuckle, and how he no longer had full mobility in that joint.

Furthermore, they had seen a white apparition move from room to room—usually in their peripheral vision. They had also heard noises and had witnessed a few other phenomena of lesser note.

The fact that consecutive occupants of the house had been scarred (and scared) during their occupation was a little unnerving. I almost feel like some spectral spook was tagging or marking us. Maybe it was even a necessary evil—a good ghost marking us for protection against a bad one—or maybe it was a warning or a failed attack. I don't know.

Last fall, not long before Halloween, the house was gutted by fire. It was a great loss, ghosts or not, because it was a beautiful old home with many fine Victorian features. The owners had moved out a few months before, and it had been vacant. I was sad to see it go.

However, I still have the 'ghost scar' to remember it by.

Anything Ghost Episode #164
October 25, 2012

A Dark Image in the Hall
Natarsha (Massachusetts, U.S.)

I had just moved to Georgia and was living with my mom, sister and my three-year-old daughter. The house was setup so that after walking up the stairs my mom's room was on the left, and my sister's room to the right. At the end of each room was a bathroom. My bedroom was the only one downstairs. At that time, my daughter usually slept with my mom.

I was always the first to get up in the morning. Being that it was fall, it was still dark outside. So my light would be the only one on when I was ironing my clothes at that hour. As I was ironing in my downstairs bedroom one morning, I thought saw something white out of the corner of my eye that went into the bathroom (which was kitty-corner to my room). At first I thought it was my daughter coming downstairs—as she often wore a white t-shirt to bed. Obviously it wasn't her because she didn't come in the room and it was dark in the rest of the house. I kept ironing trying to ignore what I thought I saw. I couldn't. So I went into the bathroom, but found nothing was there. I chalked it up to my eyes playing tricks on me, got dressed and went to work.

When I arrived home from work that evening, my sister immediately summoned me upstairs. Having been sitting in Atlanta traffic for well over an hour, I was a little agitated. So I yelled, "What?!"

She insisted that I go upstairs. So I trudged upstairs. As soon as I got up stairs she began talking to me about something that I couldn't understand—her eyes were watering as she was talking. So I asked her what the heck was wrong, because it was unlike her to start crying like that.

She said she had fallen asleep on the couch (which was downstairs next to my room) and heard our mom calling her name. It was early in the morning, so she figured our mom was telling her to shut the TV off and go upstairs. She kept asking "what" in response to her name being called, but each time my mom never responded. So she lifted her head up, and to her surprise there was a black mass standing about twelve feet away from her. She said she counted to three a few times to psyche herself up in order to run up the stairs—because in order to run up the stairs, she would have to pass the black mass. She finally got up the courage and darted up the stairs, past my room, into her bedroom and turned the lights on.

Later, she asked our mom if she had been calling her and our mom told her that she too had been sleeping.

When she started telling me the story the hair on my arms started to stand up. I basically stated in manner when one doesn't want to believe what someone is saying but knows is true. I kept saying, "Stop lying! Stop lying! Oh my goodness! I saw something this morning!"

I was super excited at that point. I went on to tell her what I thought I saw going into the bathroom that morning. She told me that when she saw the black mass, it had happened a couple of hours before I left for work. I sarcastically thanked her for being a jerk and leaving me downstairs with the thing.

I thought it weird how we had separate encounters only a couple of hours apart. I wouldn't have known about any of this if she didn't tell me her story. I would have gone on with my initial thought that my eyes had been playing tricks on me, and wouldn't have thought twice about it.

As I said earlier, my daughter would mostly sleep upstairs with my mom. But from time to time she would sleep with me. I wake up randomly at night to re-position myself; but one night I woke up and thought my daughter was moving around on the bed. The room was pitch black until my eyes adjusted to the darkness. My daughter had apparently been awake, and I heard her whisper to me that someone was standing by the closet. I could feel my heart pounding, and my stomach went into my throat. I didn't want to scare her, so I told her nobody was there—even though I was scared out of my wits.

On another night, my daughter had a similar experience, but this time she saw someone standing by the window. I once again told her again that nobody was there, and somehow we managed to fall asleep—even though my adrenaline was through the roof.

We told our mom about the stories, and she shrugged it off by telling us to stop watching all that ghost stuff on TV. But a few days later, she called the pastor of our church and asked him to pray in the house.

It wasn't until my mom and sister moved back to Massachusetts and I was visiting, that we talked about it again. To me and my sister's surprise, my mom told us that a neighbor told her we had lived there the longest out of all the tenants. Hmmm. So she knew all along we were telling the truth.

Anything Ghost Episode #162
September 18, 2012

Types of Phenomenon Commonly Referred to as a Haunting

Poltergeist Activity

Sometimes referred to as a Poltergeist Infestation. Phenomena includes rapping's and knockings, opening and closing of doors, or drawers. Objects will be hurled or thrown, fires started, furniture moving or overturning, beds shaking, showers of water or rocks, etc. Objects may fall through ceilings or come through walls. These objects, known as "apports" are often warm to the touch suggesting a physical change in the structure of the part. Poltergeist activity is not caused by a spirit but by a living person under stress through Psychokinesis or PK. When this activity occurs over and over again we refer to it as Recurrent Spontaneous Psychokinesis or RSPK. This is a Poltergeist Infestation.

- Always occurs in the presence of a readily identifiable person who is called a Poltergeist Agent
- This agent is often an adolescent who is dealing with repressed sexual energies but this is not always the case. The activity is caused by an unconscious release of energy. Very often this agent is found to have psychic abilities
- The intensity of the activity is directly proportionate to the amount of stress placed on the agent. Remove the stress, and the activity subsides

Courtesy of Al Rauber. All rights reserved. Copyright 2016.

The stories that follow in Chapter 4 are not intended to be examples of the above described phenomenon.

Public Domain.
Newell, Peter. 1862-1924.

4 | Chapter Four

- Louisiana Library Ghost
- Las Luces Fantasmas
- Haunted Office Space
- The Museum Stories
- The Children's Tea Set
- Oriskany Battlefield
- Basement Shadow Person
- Home for Troubled Teens
- Mr. Keen's Halloween Promise
- Haunted Stockton Apartment
- Haunted Birmingham Home
- Ghostly Rail Sounds
- Haunted Arkansas Mobile Home
- The Haunted Victorian Home
- Room 212 in the Stanley Hotel
- Peek-a-Boo, I See You!
- Is Emily a Ghost?

Louisiana Library Ghost
Lora (Louisiana, U.S.)

My workplace is haunted. I work in a medium sized library in the downtown area of my city. I mainly work in genealogy and my boss, Wayne, works upstairs in our Special Collections room—where old, rare and local historic items are housed. The Special Collections area seems to be the center of most of the activity. Our ghost is female, and seems to be more of a poltergeist than an apparition.

The earliest known instance of our ghost was back in the 1980's. Ellen was the head of this particular branch library. No one had been hired yet to oversee the department, so it stayed locked until a patron needed to see an item from it. Ellen had the only key to the door. When things were slow, she would go upstairs and familiarize herself with the items inside. All walls in the department were covered with locking cabinets that almost reached the ceiling. As finished looking at a section of books, she would shut the cabinet and lock it. After she left the room, all the cabinet doors were locked and the main door was locked behind her, as well. It would often be weeks before she entered the department again; but when she did, several of the cabinet doors were standing wide open.

Wayne had a slight sensitivity to the paranormal. I have seen him enter an old building, look at me and say, "Can you feel that! This place is almost vibrating!"

I guess, due to that openness, our ghost had taken a liking to him! He has heard knocks and thumps, seen things fall and be thrown—as well as witnessed the cabinet doors standing open—when he knew he had locked them.

One thing Wayne has learned is that our guest does not like technology. Many, many times, to the bafflement of our IT department, Wayne's computer has crashed and the hard drive has to either be reloaded or replaced. Our ghost is always blamed. Wayne and Ellen believe the ghost is a former department head by the name of Hazel. She was known to despise technology. She retired just so she would not have to learn to use a computer. Not long after her retirement, she passed away in her shower at home.

A colleague of mine, whose office is across the hall from Special Collections has seen our ghost several times—and felt her. Sometimes my colleague would walk into our room and say, "She doesn't want me in here right now." Then she'd turn and walk back out again. When she saw her the clearest, she described a woman in a long dark flowing skirt, white blouse, and her hair in a bun. It was the stereotypical description of the old maid librarian type. Kami caught a glimpse of her through a window as she walked around the corner, but only saw her back. Wayne has seen her once and had the same description. But this description of our ghost is puzzling. The building was built in the late 1950's; long after this style of librarian had faded into history.

My experiences with our ghost have been limited. Whenever she acts up the most, Wayne will call me upstairs and tell me to sit and listen. I have yet to hear a thing. She did act up once when I was in the room and unfortunately, my back was turned to the action.

Several years ago, Ellen was made the head of our IT department. We were getting new carpet installed throughout the building, and things had to be removed from the floor to be put in storage. Wayne used one of the locking closets to place our more rare items for safekeeping. Unfortunately, Ellen had plans on storing some of her computers in it. This resulted in a civil but heated argument between the two. I happened to be sitting in a chair with my back to them trying not to listen, when I heard a very loud hollow thump followed by complete silence. I then heard Ellen say, "Boy, she's pissed!"

Upon turning around, I found the two staring at an empty box lying on the ground between them. Due to lack of space, Wayne uses the top of the cabinets to keep the empty acid free boxes used to store fragile books and materials. The walls of the cabinets extend about two inches above the top creating a hollow space. If the box had just shifted, it would have fallen into the hollow space and not to the floor. The box is about three inches thick and large enough to store a newspaper in so it was not top heavy. It had been solidly placed on top of the cabinet, with no possible way it could fall. Both Ellen and Wayne described the box sliding straight out as if it had been pulled out and slammed to the floor between them. Ellen let Wayne store his items where they were.

As I said, our ghost is mainly seen in the Special Collections department, but there have been instances of her elsewhere in the building. Several years ago, early one morning, two circulation employees were taking the elevator to the second floor so they could turn on the lights before we opened. As the elevator doors opened, they heard a female screaming from the bookshelves where our fiction books are found. When they walked towards the sound, the screaming grew louder. Both women ran back to the elevator, flew downstairs and refused to go back upstairs alone from then on.

One morning, a colleague from our Cataloging department stopped me in the hall. She informed me, "Your ghost has moved downstairs into Genealogy." Shelly was the first to arrive each morning to work. As she passed by our locked and dark department, she heard low murmuring voices coming from inside. She could see no person inside and quickly went to her own department. An hour later when I arrived and opened the room, there was no one inside.

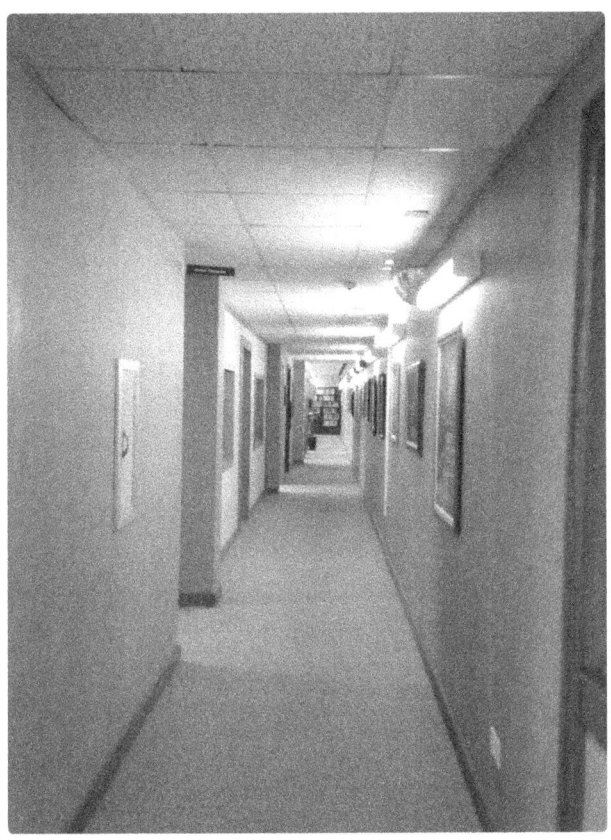

Photo by Lora (Louisiana, U.S.)
The ghost has been seen in other parts of the building, such Genealogy. Shown is a hallway in the building that runs between departments.

Just who is our friend? Could she be attached to an item in Special Collections or is she connected in some way to the building? As far as we know, there have been no deaths on the property. Being a researcher, it is frustrating to not have any clues to help solve this mystery. As long as she doesn't behave too badly, she is welcome to stay for as long as she likes.

Anything Ghost Episode #158
June 30, 2012

Las Luces Fantasmas
Rob (California, U.S.)

My mother, Magdalena, was born and raised in rural southeastern Arizona. Globe, Miami, and Thatcher-Safford are small hamlets that developed around the vibrant mining industries that once pulsed expansively throughout the region. As children, my brothers and I would gather around the kitchen table and listen to my mother's stories about the Arizona desert. One story, in particular, remains with me to this day.

It is the story about Las Luces Fantasmas (i.e., ghost lights) that scared my mother when she was a little girl. These ghost lights would appear only at night, in the distance, and hover just above the desert floor. The lights seemed to move under their own power and change color as they flickered incandescently.

My grandmother, Petra, warned her children not to venture out at night because the evil spirits, Las Luces Fantasmas, were waiting to abduct them. Generations of Arizona residents have claimed to have seen these spirit lights. In fact, I once thought I saw these lights as a small child on one of the many summer trips that our family took to Safford, Arizona…greenish foggy orbs that drifted just off the desert floor…was it the devil that I saw dancing? Or were these lights just the basis for a story told by my grandmother who simply wanted to keep all her children indoors at night?

Anything Ghost Episode #164
October 25, 2012

Haunted Office Space
Randy (New York, U.S.)

I have been having paranormal experiences since I was a kid. The most recent happened last month. I was at work and had experienced a few things at my job. Since having a baby, my bosses let me come in early (as that is the time my baby wakes me up), so most times I am alone in the morning. I work in mid-town Manhattan in a building that is over 200 years old. I was walking around in the large classroom (the only sounds were those of my footsteps). As I continued to walk I began to notice the sound of my footsteps get out of sync with my footfalls. Confused, I stopped walking. The sound of footsteps continued. This freaked me out so I headed back to my office. It was then that I realized that my footsteps weren't making any sound, because the classroom was heavily carpeted.

As I said, that was just the latest of incidents.

Years ago (when I shared the main office), I would hear someone at my boss's desk. This was after hours, at a time I thought everyone had gone for the day. The office was set up so that there was a partition dividing the room. My boss's desk was directly on the other side of the partition, and I was in a position so I could see anyone entering the office. I was working late one night and I started to hear noises: it sounded like someone was swiveling in a chair. Then I started to hear the sound of someone typing on a keyboard. Thinking maybe someone came in while my attention was distracted, I called over, "Is that you?"

No answer.

So I got up walked over but saw no one. I tried to figure out how this was possible—maybe the window was open? Were there mice? I could find no reasonable explanation. After a while I went back to work.

Soon, I started hearing the noises again, only this time louder. And although I was scared, I jumped on my desk to look over the partition. No one was there and the chair was in the same position as I left it. I went back to work, but after a while the noises started again. From then on I started wearing headphones and listening to music while working. I decided not to tell people at first, as I thought they wouldn't believe me.

One day one of my co-workers stayed working late with me. After a while she began to hear the sounds of the chair swiveling and someone typing on the keyboard. My co-worker asked me if someone was there. Knowing that she was a firm non-believer in all things paranormal, I just shrugged my shoulders instead of telling her what I suspected it was. I told her, "Why don't you check it out?"

She did and all she could say was, "No way! No way!"

She asked me how I was doing that. I told her there is no way I could make those sounds. She had no explanation.

But she wasn't the last person to hear the sounds: there were several occasions of people visiting my desk and being spooked. I guess I kind of got used to it.

One night the sounds were really loud, and I of course was alone. As I sat working on my computer, I suddenly got the feeling that someone was right behind me. It felt as if someone was reaching over to touch my shoulder. So much so, that I turned around and punched at the air where I thought someone was. I left early that night, and on the way out I asked the maintenance men and doormen if they had seen anything. They told me they had indeed seen things, and that they also got a spooky feeling from building. Well, I was able to get some history from them, but nothing related to my floor.

On another night, I had to work very late into the evening. The building manager gave me special permission to stay in the building, and the only other person in there was the doorman (who was responsible for locking up after I left). The doorman was a friend of mine, so he decided to hang out in my office while I worked. I told him my stories of hearing weird sounds and he would try to explain them away—I always felt that he didn't really believe me.

Around 2 a.m., I was making copies. He was surfing the internet. We began hearing footsteps coming from the main hallway. Mind you the door was closed and usually you can't hear anything on the other side of the door. So, whoever was making the footsteps must have been stomping their feet hard. I started to laugh and told him, "Why don't you check out who is making those footsteps?"

The expression on his face was hilarious. He shook his head.

The footsteps went on for ten more minutes. We knew that no one was in the building—as my friend had checked the building before coming to my office, and locked the building tight.

The next time I saw something was during working hours with the office full of people. I was looking for my assistant, and passed by a storage closet. I looked in the room and saw a slim person moving books around. My assistant at the time was quite rotund, so knowing it wasn't who I was looking for I kept walking. I then felt the hair on my arms and neck rise, and I asked myself who that was? I went back to the doorway, looked in the room and saw no one there. This was all in the matter of seconds. I would have seen anyone exiting that room. Standing there, I must have had a perplexed look on my face, because my co-worker walked up to me and asked me if I had seen her, too. I asked my co-worker what she had seen. She told me she has seen a slim lady with dark clothes and dark hair, moving books around—the same thing I saw.

I saw this woman again last summer. I was in my office on a Saturday (which meant no one else was in the office). I was sitting in a smaller office when I looked up and saw someone walking through the classroom. I thought perhaps it was my cousin, who I was meeting at my office. I got up and looked around—but no one was there. The impression I got when this woman passed by was a face that looked serious: she had dark hair and dark clothes, and was walking very quickly—almost gliding. I looked all around the office to make sure no one was there. Nobody.

Since stuff like this happens to me on and off. I try and explain the experiences away. Even though my gut reaction is to say, "Feets don't fail me now!"... while running out of the office, and I making myself check everything to see if there is a rational explanation.

I asked around to see if I could find any history on this woman. No one knows of any women who had died in the building. There are a few men who died in the building, and there have been sightings of them.

Anything Ghost Episode #127
January 22, 2011

Haunted Office Spaces

One of the most popular haunted office space stories on Anything Ghost was about an office that was located inside a hospital in Utah (it was an emergency paging company for doctors and staff). The story was titled, "Confessions of a Fixer." It was a self-narrated story told by Eric.

In the story, an employee, with a reputation for always leaving early, asked Eric (his supervisor) if he could leave because he wasn't feeling well. Eric, thinking it was another excuse for the employee to leave early, told him to finish his shift.

Eric went home when the day was done, and while he was sleeping he received a phone call. Annoyed for being bothered at home sleeping, he looked at the call: it was from the employee who had asked to leave early...but nobody was on the other end. Not too long after that phone call, Eric received another call from his work: they told him that the employee had passed away because something had ruptured in his stomach.

After that incident, strange things began to happen at the office—things that were disrupting to the business—and could ultimately be life-threatening (because of the nature of the business).

A co-worker told Eric about Anything Ghost, and Eric decided to share this story. He thought that by sharing it may reach out to the employee who died—telling him that he was sorry; and asking him to please accept his apology and move on...so the company could function normally again.

The sincerity and emotion in Eric's recanting of the story is a big part of the experience. Eric's recording of the story can be found on the Anything Ghost YouTube channel.

The Museum Stories
Claire (U.S.)

A museum is the perfect place for a haunting: from its architecture mimicking ancient temples, to the exhibit cases filled with timeless objects, there are many opportunities for ghosts and other entities to make it their home.

I used to volunteer in a small, local museum that was a former Carnegie Library. Thanks to a large endowment from a wealthy donor, it was converted into a museum that documented local history. The summer I was there, it was a hot one—over 30 consecutive days with temperatures breaking 100 degrees.

Photo by Claire (U.S.)
A glass case in the museum where Claire volunteered.

The museum, of course, being quite old, didn't have air conditioning, and I was miserable as I sorted through prints and moved boxes full of artifacts. Imagine my surprise when I happed upon a pocket of cool air! I hesitated a moment, and moved away (back into the sticky heat). Then, I returned to that same cool area, and looked around for a vent or possibly a fan that was tucked out of sight. There was nothing that could have created that sensation. I wasn't panicked, or scared, but I knew that it had to be a ghost. I stood there for a while, contemplating the possibility of a haunting, then it came to me: a librarian. A woman? Yes.

I decided she must have been a librarian here in times past. I had been moving artifacts and objects that hadn't been disturbed in decades—perhaps I had stirred up more than dust.

As the summer progressed, I came to greet my ghost whenever I came into the basement—she seemed to follow me, and linger nearby as I went about my work. I never saw her, I could only sense her presence. I had a feeling that we were close in age—or near enough. I think she felt some camaraderie with me, and felt the urge to watch over me.

The museum was poorly run, and I ended up leaving at the end of the summer on bad terms with the management. The night I left, I said goodbye to my ghost and explained to her that I wouldn't be coming back, but that it wasn't her fault, and that I was leaving because the curators were treating me poorly.

The next day, I woke to a voice mail from the head curator. She informed me that the security cameras had captured something strange after I left. Not five minutes after I exited the museum, the glass shelving in the gift shop adjacent to the basement stairs had spontaneously shattered, sending the merchandise hurtling to the floor.

Anything Ghost Episode #210
August 16, 2015

Photo by Claire (U.S.)
The creek that runs near the museum.

The Children's Tea Set
Isidro (Salt Lake City, Utah)

By April of 2012, I had been renting a house for four years. I was installing a new water faucet in the basement. There was a crawlspace alongside the water heater and furnace that was barely wide enough for me, but that's where I needed to go to get to the water shut-off, and there was no light back there. So I got my flashlight, wrench and some pliers and made my way back there. I was surprised that it wasn't as dusty as I expected it to be and there were hardly any spider webs the further back I went.

I followed the water pipe, which was about shoulder high, to the far corner of that little room, and I saw the shut-off. But then I noticed on the floor, almost right under that valve, was a box; it stood about a foot high and when I shined the light on it I saw that it looked like a children's tea service. There were brightly colored cups and plates, a little teapot and some other containers. It looked new and clean. I picked up a couple of pieces, looked at them and then put them back. I didn't feel I should disturb them or move that box any more than I already had. Then I got to work turning off the water, installing my faucet, then going back and turning the water back on.

I don't know why that box was there. I avoided looking at it too much. My room is on the other side of the wall where that box is, and sometimes at night I'd hear something like a pencil drop or a book being shifted—and the noise came from that end of the room. But even when I'd get up, turn on the light, and take a look around, I really wouldn't know what had made the noise. I would not find a dropped pencil, nor a book moved out of place.

On the other side of the other wall where the box was, there was a small room that I used as an office. It didn't have any windows and the feeling from that office used to be a scary one—especially if the door was opened just a crack, and all I could see as I walked by was the black inside of the room. I used to get the feeling that there was something bad inside there, but that's changed and I don't get a menacing feeling anymore.

As for the little box, I didn't ever have a feeling that it was threatening in any way. I just wanted to leave it alone and not provoke whatever might be there. The noises in my room also didn't seem like scary events. They would happen about every two or three weeks, but I still couldn't explain them.

At the end of summer, I think it was in August, about four months after we found the little box, something happened in my friend's room. He came home from work one day, went into his room and found that the glass cover for the ceiling light was on the floor underneath a small wooden table. He didn't know how it got there without breaking if it had fallen, or how it had gotten under the table since the table was directly under the light. As far as we know, no one had been in the house. It was empty while we were at work.

Photo by Alice (Bendigo, Victoria, Australia)
A small cabinet found in a crawlspace of Isidro's home, contained a children's tea set.

Another thing about my room at night is that when I close my eyes and I'm trying to go to sleep, I'll often see a pair of eyes looking at me. This has happened hundreds of times and it goes back to about a year before I discovered that little box. It has never been the same pair of eyes, and until recently, none of the eyes looked like they were from a human. And though some of the eyes have looked really frightening, none of them looked like they were trying to scare me. They just looked like they were surprised that I could see them and that I was looking back at them. I was surprised, too, and even though my eyes were already closed, I would blink and the strange vision would be gone in an instant.

Anything Ghost Episode #170
March 2, 2013

Oriskany Battlefield
Alex (Central New York, U.S.)

My story begins at the Oriskany Battlefield. One summer, about 5 or 6 years ago, I was introduced to the field and its haunting history. For those who don't know, the Battle of Oriskany was considered one of the bloodiest battles of the Revolutionary war. In the battle, native Americans sneaked out of the woods and ambushed American soldiers who had set down their arms while drinking and washing from the creek. The creek that divided the two fields was appropriately dubbed "Blood Creek"—because as the stories have stated, within five minutes of the battle, the creek was red with blood.

Over a two year time frame, I have visited the area 20-30 times, and have experienced a variety of unexplainable events.

The battlefield is split into to open fields with a wooded ravine dividing them; this ravine is where Blood Creek resides. When facing the battlefield from the road, the larger well lit portion of the field is on the left (donning what looks like a miniature version of the Washington Monument). The right side, where we would usually enter (due to its lack of light) contained a square monument stone. The two fields are connected by a winding trail through the woods, and over a small, eight foot bridge above Blood Creek.

The first night I visited the field I was with two of my friends, Bob and Matt. Bob was already familiar with the field while Matt and myself were first timers there. We entered on the dark, right field and began walking towards the trail in the woods. As stated earlier Bob was familiar with the area and the most comfortable with entering the woods. After some hesitation, Matt and I began walking in. About five feet from the tree line we heard a loud THUD (as if someone, using all their weight, had stomped their foot in front of us). We froze, listening. Soon after this incident we began to hear footsteps, walking through the woods. It sounded like a large group of people walking through the dead leaves—sticks breaking and such. It is important to note that the well lit portion of the field provided us with some light and we could see that no one was in the woods—especially where the sounds were originating from.

Despite these events, we continued down the steep, winding path to Blood Creek. When we arrived, we stood leaning on the bridge and listened: the only sound we heard was running water. But after about 2 or 3 minutes we started to hear talking behind us. It was muffled (as if the two individuals were speaking behind a closed door), so we couldn't distinguish any words—but it was absolutely present. There was no possible way someone could have been standing in that location—especially at that hour. Since that night, I was hooked, to say the least.

Photo by Alex (Central New York, U.S.)
Mist in a photo taken at the Oriskany Battlefield.

The second night I returned with another friend. We entered in our usual spot and sat down on a picnic table, just listening. First we heard what sounded like a giant walking through the woods on the far end of the field. It sounded like trees were being uprooted and torn down—crashing to the ground. The only animal we could think that would replicate this sound would be a moose—which Central New York has none of—this freaked us out, but our curiosity kept us there.

Other times we sat on the picnic table, we would often hear cars coming from a distance and pass by. Then there were other times when we would hear this sound, and realize that, though the sound continued, no cars would pass. This caused us to listen a little more closely, until we realized that the sound was actually a sickly breathing noise—right behind our shoulders.

Another night, we were sitting on the table listening and watching for quite a while (I was sitting closest to the woods). As usual, the lights from the far side of the field showed the silhouettes of the trees; this allowed me to see quite clearly into the woods. As we sat, talking and listening, I saw something that caused me to jump from the table—and I demanded that we leave. Though my friends kept asking what happened, I would not tell them what I saw until we got in the car and drove off. And here's what I saw: as I sat on the picnic table,

I watched a shadow figure walk from one tree to another—almost as if it was stalking something. It was crouched and appeared to be looking down the hill towards the creek. It did not continue through the woods, just between the two trees down in the woods. This was enough to cause me to jump up and run out of there.

Anything Ghost Episode #157
June 16, 2012

Basement Shadow Person
Noelle (Michigan, U.S.)

I was in second grade, and after school one day I went with another girl to play at our friend Melanie's house. I just got a new pair of Barbie roller skates and we were planning on skating in her unfinished basement. Melanie was always talking about how her house was haunted, but she'd never mentioned being actually afraid of the ghosts—plus, she was the kind of girl that made up stories a lot, so I didn't think anything of it before going over.

The basement wasn't too big: there were a couple of small glass block windows in the front, a washer and dryer in the back, a big pile of boxes, and the stairs lead back up to the left. While we were roller skating, one of us, I don't remember which one, said, "Hey! Look!"

We all stopped right where we were and looked. There was a shadow of what looked to me like a man on the back wall by the washer and dryer (the light was coming through the windows at the front, so it was a plausible place for a shadow to be) and it was getting larger as if there were a person walking away from the wall and towards us. The strange part, though, was that the actual source of the shadow was nowhere to be seen. All three of us were standing frozen in fear and we were not close enough to the wall to be making shadows onto it. One of us screamed and broke the trance and we all ran up the stairs with our skates on.

Later, when we were in high school, Melanie's family moved away and my friend Christine's family bought the house with the intentions of fixing it up and renting it out. Christine had been pretty good friends with the Melanie's younger sister and had stayed the night a few times. She said that it seemed like there were at least two ghosts there: an old man and a younger man. Every single time she slept over she would hear footsteps going down the stairs and the back door would slam. It turned out that the Melanie had a much older brother who had been killed in a car accident as a teenager and they always thought that this was his last action before leaving the house the night he was killed.

Christine also said that one night she took a necklace off before going to sleep and put it on a dresser. In the morning it was gone. When she told Melanie's sister, she immediately went into the attic and came back with the necklace. She said things disappeared frequently in the house and they always found them in the same place in the attic a couple hours later.

*Illustration by Noelle (Michigan, U.S.) - **www.noellewezner.com***
Noelle and her friends witnessed a dark shadow against the basement wall.

After Christine's family bought the house, they had to completely gut it to make it suitable to rent. (Melanie's mom hadn't been well for a few years and was unable to keep up on housework, so it was very messy inside and cluttered with junk and dirt) They were repainting the whole house and it soon became apparent that no one wanted to be alone while painting in Melanie's mom's room—particularly in her closet. They kept trying to pass painting the closet on to someone else. Christine said when you were inside the closet, you got intense overwhelming feelings of helplessness and negativity. In the end, the closet never ended up getting repainted and they ended up selling the house instead of renting it out. It looks very nice now—all fixed up and clean. The current owners seem to be taking very good care of it. I can't help but wonder if they ever see anything strange or get any weird feelings, though.

Anything Ghost Episode #159
July 15, 2012

Home for Troubled Teens
Shannon (Layton, Utah)

For about three years I worked at a locked-down residential treatment facility for teenagers with mental health and behavioral issues. The kids were all in state custody, and all of them had come from pretty horrible backgrounds. Most of them were very troubled due to years of abuse from their parents and the traumatic experience of being in foster care.

The facility occupied the entire top floor of a two-story building, and like I mentioned before, it was completely under lock-down—with every door requiring a key-card. At any given time there were eight boys and eight girls, and the genders were separated between two hallways.

My shift was typically from 4 p.m. to midnight, and after two of the staff went home at 8 p.m., there were only three of us left working there. The kids were all sent to bed around 9 p.m. (most were asleep by 10 p.m.), and were woken up at 6 a.m. every morning. Every bedroom had a camera in it so the staff could monitor the kids, due to the fact that many of them were "self-harmers" or suicidal.

With only three awake staff on the whole floor of the building, and with all the main lights off (leaving only a single light on at the end of each hallway), and the dim glow from the monitor in the office, the place became very creepy after bedtime. What made it even creepier was watching the kids sleep through the monitors: it reminded me very much of the movie Paranormal Activity.

Many of my coworkers were quite the characters, but one of them, a woman named Jen, was a married mother of two in her mid-forties who worked there part-time while she was finishing up her master's degree. The point I'm trying to make is that if any of my other coworkers had told me the story I'm about to relate to you, I would have chalked it up to them trying to scare me—or just being downright crazy. But Jen was completely sane, completely normal, and I was completely shocked when she told me this story.

We were required to check on the kids every 15 minutes after they went to bed, and we did this by assigning one person each night to go into the office and glance at the monitor to make sure each kid was asleep in bed.

I had worked with Jen for a couple of years, and we were sitting in the hallway at work talking one night. She mentioned, very nonchalantly, that she used to regularly see a ghost in the monitor while doing checks. There were eight kids in eight rooms, and the monitor could only display four rooms at a time. So the monitor would constantly switch from room to room, displaying the first four rooms, then the second four rooms. It would switch rooms about every three seconds.

Jen told me that sometimes she would see a person. She described it as a black figure of a man standing at the foot of a bed, and staring down at a sleeping kid. She would see it in a room as the monitor switched back and forth, but after a few times of the monitor switching, the figure would eventually be gone.

The first time she saw it, she said she almost freaked out—thinking that one of the other kids had sneaked into another's bedroom. But it disappeared so quickly, and after quietly going into the boy's room to make sure no one was there, she chalked it up to just being her imagination. One other thing is that two other staff were always sitting at the end of the hallway in full view of all eight rooms. They would have been able to see if someone had sneaked in or out of a bedroom.

After having seen the figure a few times, she decided it was a ghost. At first she figured a specific room was haunted. But then she noticed that the figure appeared on a regular basis, but was sometimes in a different room.

The kids at the facility would rotate bedrooms once a week, and after a while Jen noticed that the figure would always be standing at the foot of the bed of one specific boy. It would follow him, no matter what room he was sleeping in.

The boy had left the facility nearly three months prior to her telling me this story, and Jen had not seen the ghost since. I asked her how this had not frightened her, and she told me that the figure never appeared to be doing any harm, and she simply found it fascinating.

I have heard things about hauntings being tied to trauma, like if someone dies traumatically their death is more likely to result in a haunting. This story made me wonder that if a certain person has experienced enough trauma in their life, it could open them up to paranormal happenings. This particular boy had been through more abuse in his short life than one person should ever have to face—let alone as a child. I have thought that perhaps it was a deceased loved one watching out for him.

In talking with a few of my friends who also worked at this facility, we agreed that any hauntings there were probably a result of all the abuse and trauma these kids experienced—it seems to bring about a negative energy.

The graveyard-shift workers had many-a-story to tell about things they heard or saw in the middle of the night. There was one hallway that was used as a day treatment, so it was completely empty at night, but it had the nicest bathroom and provided a bit of privacy. However, all but a few of the graveyard workers refused to go into that hallway at night—even to use the nicer bathroom. One of my close friends who worked a graveyard shift, who is very religious and does not believe in the supernatural at all, admitted that she was alone in that hallway washing some dishes, when someone shouted her name right in her ear. She immediately found another staff and would not leave that staff's side for the rest of the night. She didn't even go back in the morning to finish washing the dishes.

Anything Ghost Episode #163
October 2, 2012

Mr. Keen's Halloween Promise
Donna (Maine, U.S.)

This story comes to my mind every Halloween because the experience took place the day after Halloween. I was seven years old at the time, and it was the mid-seventies when kids would play outside all day long—climbing trees and riding bikes. I grew up on a beautiful dead end road in Maine where several children of my age lived and played.

At the end of our street, and just before it intersected with the main road, there was a little brown house. A sweet elderly couple, Mr. & Mrs. Keen, lived there. They would often ask us neighborhood kids to do odd jobs and errands for them, and would always pay us in caramels—which I loved!

On the Halloween of my seventh year, my mom made me an amazing mummy costume. I was sure I wouldn't be recognized by anyone! I joined my friends outside, and we excitedly and loudly scuffled along in our costumes, knocking on doors and screaming, "Trick or Treat!" Smiling families greeted us and gave us goodies, after which time we would continue on our march to the next house.

We finally reached the end of the street: the Keen's house. Here my hope was that I would see handfuls of caramels. Mr. Keen answered the door, and though his hand was shaking wildly, he didn't disappoint any of us: he dropped caramels galore into our eagerly awaiting opened bags.

When he was finished filling our bags, I stood there, frightened by his shaking white hand. Being nosy, I asked him what was wrong. He gazed at me kindly and said, "Is that my little redhead under there?"

I smiled.

He told me he was cold, that's all, told me not to worry, and that he'd see my little face tomorrow.

The next day was cold and sunny. Fallen leaves scattered the road. Me and my friends, five in all, were having a blast riding our bikes and big wheels up and down the dead end road. At one point, I looked over towards the Keen's house and noticed Mr. Keen standing on his porch. I waved and yelled, "Hi Mr. Keen!"

The other kids joined me in this greeting. But Mr. Keen didn't respond. He just stood there. A chill went through me. I felt something that I couldn't explain. A fear. A knowing that something was so wrong.

We all stopped on our bikes, and became silent...just staring at Mr. Keen on his porch. He was staring back at us from maybe 20 feet away. He looked so very still with his plaid red shirt and suspenders. He had a grayish pallor—a strange appearance. Fear began to take hold, and we all began jumping back on our bikes, and made a dash to our homes.

In my house, my mom had several of my friends' moms over for a visit. I ran in with tears in my eyes, crying out that something was really wrong with Mr Keen!

"What do you mean?" Asked my Mom.

"He's on the porch! He didn't say hi! He's not moving!" I cried back.

My Moms face turned white. She asked me if I was sure. I shook my head frantically telling her yes.

"But...that can't be, Mr. Keen is gone. He passed on early last night," she said.

Anything Ghost Episode #163
October 2, 2012

Children Seeing Ghosts

Here are some other stories found in this book that involve children experiencing the paranormal while playing:

- **Basement Shadow Person**
    Noelle (Michigan, U.S.) - *Chapter 4*
- **Haunted Birmingham Home**
    Erika (Birmingham, Alabama) - *Chapter 4*
- **Is Emily a Ghost?**
    Alex (Utica, New York) - *Chapter 4*
- **Bronx, New York Ghost Stories**
    Errol (New York, U.S.) - *Chapter 5*
- **The Ghost of Llanrumney Hall**
    Gareth (South Wales, U.K.) - *Chapter 6*
- **The Shadow Man at Grandpa's House**
    Barbara (Monterey, California) - *Chapter 6*

Haunted Stockton Apartment
Priscilla (California, U.S.)

These two stories take place when I lived in my first apartment back in 2004. A little background on myself: I am Mexican-American with religious parents. I was raised with the cultural and religious up-bringing that you do not leave your home until you marry. At one point in my life, I knew it was now or never, and I figured it was time to be out on my own. So, I moved to Stockton, California into a two bedroom apartment.

Within a week I acquired a roommate, her name was Amy. She was a co-worker of mine and she worked the swing shift. Since I worked days we never really saw each other, except on the weekends.

About a month after I moved into the apartment, something peculiar began to happen. Being that it was my first apartment, I didn't have all the furniture needed; so my bedroom only had a bed, a small clothes dresser, and that was about it. I did have the larger bedroom of the two, so needless to say the room seemed quite large. In fact, my closet was very large. It had wall-to-wall sliding doors, and the way my bed was set up in the room was that if I were lying on the bed, I would be facing the wall-to-wall closet.

One night I closed my closet doors completely—as I had always done before—but when I woke in the morning my closet doors where completely open from one end to the other. Not paying much attention to the incident I went on with my day.

That night I again closed my closet doors as normal. As I was doing this I remembered that I woke up earlier to find them open. I ignored it and smirked it off. I fell asleep fast as I was very tired.

The next morning, to my horrific surprise, the doors were again completely open. As my eyes adjusted to the early morning darkness and the small amount of light that was coming through the window, I realized that my eyes were not playing tricks on me: the doors were actually opened. I froze. I quickly started to mentally process all possibilities, but quickly dismissed them. Could it have been Amy playing a trick on me? No, I thought, she doesn't have the key to my room. I would always sleep with my keys in my purse. It wasn't her...could it be me? Did I suddenly start to sleep walk? No, I can honestly say I've never had a "sleep walking" incident. I simply couldn't explain it. My mind would fall back on my religious upbringing beliefs. I was always taught that when things like this happened...the strange and unusual kind of things that most of society calls ghosts, they were demons—so this most definitely rattled my fears!

I told my roommate about this incident and she quickly said it must be a ghost, because from time to time she had the feeling of being watched. But being that she had no significant incidents herself, I ignored her comments.

Waking up to open closets doors must have happened at least six times—at least that I can remember. This of course was nothing compared to the final incident that left me in tears, and was the final push that lead me to move out of that apartment.

It was evening and I was waiting for my boyfriend to come home and spend the weekend with me. I was watching TV and clicking through some channels trying to find something with no luck. Out of the corner of my eye (which was practically directly in front of me), I saw what looked like a bluish human figure walk from the hallway into the kitchen. This bluish apparition walked like a human, with swaying arms. In those few seconds I could honestly make out the head, shoulders, body and legs. As soon as it caught my attention, I directed my focus and watched as it walked in front of where I was sitting. I was completely shocked, and wasn't sure if I had imagined it. I could only do one thing: I held my breath. My eyes stayed focus in the direction of which I saw the apparition. It walked into the kitchen. It then proceeded to peek around the corner from where it had just walked into. It peeked out in a manner consistent with someone making sure somebody was watching. When I saw this happen, I couldn't resist the fear that overwhelmed me, and tears began to run down my face. I gathered whatever nerve I had left in me as I sat scared and frozen. I picked up my cell phone and quickly called my boyfriend to see how close he was—I knew he had a 2-hour drive. When he answered, I couldn't even speak.

He said, "Priscilla? Priscilla? Hello! Hello! Are you okay?"

I busted into a crying spell that was uncontrollable.

He said, "I'm close to the parking garage, I'll be up in a few minutes."

He stayed on the phone with me for what seemed like two long minutes, until he walked through the door. He arrived to find me completely shaking and unable to tell him what I had just seen. After a few minutes I began to describe my experience. He looked shocked, but believed me.

That night we slept with the lights on throughout the apartment.

I moved out a few months later.

Anything Ghost Episode #165
November 12, 2012

Haunted Birmingham Home
Erika (Birmingham, Alabama)

I have three stories to tell you tonight. The first story is about the house I stayed in with a roommate during 2011. I am a mother to a beautiful little girl who is two years old. After ending the relationship with her father when she was just a couple months old, my daughter and I moved back into my parents' home. There really wasn't much room for us, and at night my daughter slept in her pack-n-play and I slept in a recliner. The arrangement was appreciated, but after several months it grew very physically painful for me. A friend of mine brought up that her mother had been wanting to move back into a home she used to live in, and she asked if I would want to be her roommate. I jumped at the chance to sleep in a bed again.

There had always been awkward little feelings I'd feel in that house. But living there at the time, felt right. I didn't really mind being there alone with my daughter or by myself as long as I didn't think too much about the silence around me. My roommate never felt comfortable there alone, and did not feel comfortable in the master bedroom (as it had been the room she shared with her ex-husband), so it became my room. The house had been sitting empty since their split. There were a few times she attempted to live there alone, but subsequently she would move back out because the silence and shadows of the house would eventually get to her every time.

I enjoyed taking little videos with my phone of my daughter doing cute things so I could share them with my family and friends. All of the "feelings" came to a head during one of those recordings. My daughter and I were in the dining room. I was seated at the table while my daughter was in her high chair. In the first recording, she was playing around, then suddenly acted strangely, leaning to the side as if something was there. She kept looking to the wall that was closest to us, pointing and saying, "Uh oh."

I just chalked it up to her being a toddler.

I recorded again and she said, "Uh oh" again, before dancing to the sound of the Taco Bell TV commercial (on in the background) right before the loud gonging bell was rung. Then my daughter said, "Yeah!"

I repeated her "Yeah."

When I went back to watch the cute video of my daughter, I was very surprised as to what I heard. Following the bell sound on the commercial, very distinctly a voice can be heard whispering loudly, "Yessss!" Which had apparently been what my daughter said "Yeah" to. I shared the video and story of what had happened with my family and friends and they were all pleasantly horrified.

While there was never a sense of danger in the house, the spirits that lived with us made their presence known frequently. One morning as I got ready, and my daughter sat in her high chair eating breakfast, I noticed her laughing and giggling again toward the wall. This time it was the opposite side. When I asked her who she was talking to, she responded calmly, clearly, and happily, "Uncle!"

This was a word she did not know yet. My roommate's uncle had passed away many years before, and had become a friendly ghost to the children that came around his family. My roommate's younger daughter was a baby when her ex-husband and my friend noticed the distinct playfulness and babbling of the baby directed to something unseen behind them.

Also in the house was a frail and fragile apparition that I would see out of the corner of my eye, when I was standing in my bathroom facing the mirror. To the right, I would see a mist in the form of an older woman: hunched with arthritis, walking to the bathroom from the bedroom, and then the image disappeared as the doorway was reached. This same old woman had died in the house many years prior.

There were unpleasant times in the house as well... unexplainable pounding on my closet doors; a giant clipboard positioned sturdily on my dresser would suddenly slam to the ground as I walked in the room; I heard the screened porch door opening and swinging shut; I heard the front door being unlocked and opened, and closed again—but found the door's inside sliding latch was still locked.

In January 2012, our friendship dissolved, and we moved out of the house. She moved in with her older daughter, and I moved back in with my parents where I have continued to live since.

Anything Ghost Episode #167
December 23, 2012

Ghostly Rail Sounds
Nick (Connecticut, U.S.)

My wife and I bought our first home in July of 2011. It was a modest Cape Cod in a quiet suburban neighborhood. The previous owners did many updates to the house, built in 1949, making it move-in ready and modern looking. We fell in love with the place.

There was nothing outwardly spooky about the house. The landscaping was beautiful, and the rooms got plenty of natural light through new windows. Even the basement, a standard concrete one with a laundry room, a work shop and a pantry, was tidy and welcoming. That's why the occurrences I'm going to share, caught us off guard.

The first strange incident happened soon after we moved in. One evening, I found our cat, Max, who is the furthest thing from a "scaredy cat," frozen in a defensive pose in the dining room—the fur on his back spiked. He was focused intently on, apparently, nothing. But he was clearly frightened.

Granted, for many cats this behavior would not be perceived as odd. But Max is unique. This is a cat who runs towards the door like a dog when someone knocks. Nothing fazes him: not loud music, nor children playing—nothing. So his demeanor in this particular case was very out of the ordinary. We'd never seen Max act in such a way before, and we haven't since.

The next odd thing to happen in the house was experienced by both my wife and I. We were unpacking boxes in the kitchen one afternoon, and I was whistling a little tune. When I stopped, I heard another whistle. It was a whimsical, old-guy-strolling-along-type whistle. In unison, my wife and stunned I said, "Did you hear that?"

There was no music or TV on in the house, so I immediately looked out the front door to the street. No one was around and I could see quite a distance in both directions. This happened in the heat of summer. Our windows and doors were closed and the central air was on. So even if someone had walked by the house whistling, it's highly doubtful we would have heard him or her so clearly. But the whistling story was soon pushed to the back of our mind (as was the one about Max), and we carried on with making the house our own. What else were we to do?

In October of 2011, I had another bizarre experience in the house. One night I lay awake in bed thinking about some major changes that had recently taken place at work. Around 2 a.m., I heard a strange sound coming from downstairs. I focused. What I heard was a slow, metallic scratching. The sound would then stop for a few moments before continuing. This went on for several minutes, and then stopped for good. We'd been in the house for three months at that point, and I knew all the normal sounds of the place: The boiler turning on, water rushing through pipes, the freezer producing ice cubes, etc. But I had never heard a metallic scratching.

Unable to identify the noise, I made my way downstairs. I found nothing unusual. My cat was asleep on the couch, and a quick peek out the window showed a quiet neighborhood on the chilly fall night. I headed back to bed, perplexed yet again.

Because she was pregnant, and could do without the stress, I decided not to tell my wife about the metallic scratching. Instead, I asked if she could get some history on the house from the previous owner, Jessica (a girl she had become friendly with).

The next day, my wife called me at work excited to tell what she had learned. The good news was Jessica and her husband experienced nothing strange in the house during their five years there. The only semi-eerie thing Jessica could come up with was that her grandfather (the original owner of the property) had died in the home. She went on to share that, in a weakened state at the end of his life, a system of tracks had been affixed to the first floor ceiling that allowed her grandfather to get around more easily. The old man would be hooked up to the tracks via a sling.

"Not too scary, right," said my wife, her mind at ease.

"Yeah," I said, but not really meaning it.

"You're freaked out that someone died in the house?" She prodded.

"Of course not," I responded. "It is what it is."

The rest of the day I thought again and again about my terrified cat and the mysterious whistling. But mostly, I recalled the late night metallic scratching—scratching that I now imagined came from the old man's ghost maneuvering around the long ago-removed ceiling tracks.

More than a year passed, and we had our baby. I'm glad to report that nothing else unnerving happened in the house. Perhaps the old man just wanted to see who the new tenants were.

Anything Ghost Episode #167
December 23, 2012

Haunted Arkansas Mobile Home
Kia (Arkansas, U.S.)

From time to time, when I was very young, my father and I shared an intense love of scary things. We were both horror movie aficionados who decorated for Halloween the way most people decorate for Christmas, and we always loved telling ghost stories. In fact, one of my favorite memories of my father has to do with him dusting off an old urban legend and working his magic as a master storyteller, to frighten the wits out of my childhood friends during a slumber party at our house. My father had a flair for the fantastic, but he was also a hyper-sensible (I take after him in both regards), so despite our passion for the paranormal, we never laid claim to any ghostly encounters of our own.

However, a little more than a decade ago, when I was seventeen, my dad took a job as a second shift maintenance worker at a factory in my hometown. After he and my mother divorced a few years earlier, he moved to an apartment in the next town over. But with the long shifts and irregular hours, the extra commute was impractical. He had only been working at the factory for a few days when he started looking for some kind of accommodations in my hometown—which was no easy feat, given that my town had less than two thousand people and rental property was scarce. It wasn't long before he heard of a mobile home for rent and contacted the landlord. Because his shift at the factory was at such an irregular time, he asked me to go survey the place. He gave me his checkbook and said, "If it's even remotely habitable and you think it's okay, go ahead and pay the deposit and first month's rent."

The landlord took me to the mobile home. It was located only a mile-and-a-half from the factory, and a little over two miles from where I lived with my mother. As I looked around the rooms, and something just felt off. The place was nothing special: a small bathroom and bedroom on one end, a spacious living room, a nice sized kitchen, then a large master bedroom with a walk-in closet and bathroom of its own. But the air felt thick enough to smother me. Maybe this was only because I had lived in northeast Arkansas where we had our fair share of tornadoes each year. So I really didn't relish the thought of spending every other weekend in a mobile home—after I'd seen first-hand how they fared in such turbulent weather. Assuming those thoughts were the reason for my uneasy feeling (and because my dad needed a place to live), I set aside my feelings of discomfort and signed a check for the landlord. That weekend, my father moved into his new home.

It wasn't long after my dad settled in that I had to go back to school. It was my senior year and I was involved in an overwhelming amount of extracurricular activities. Taking my hectic social and academic schedule into account with my dad's inconvenient work hours, it was well into October before I had a chance to stay the night with him.

One Friday night, after I'd finished cheerleading at a basketball game, my dad and I went out to dinner and then rented a stack of movies that I intended to watch while I stayed there. By the time we got back to the mobile home, we were both incredibly exhausted. As it always happened when I stayed over, he slept on the couch and I took the bed. When he and my mom divorced, he developed a habit of sleeping on the sofa with the television running all night, so the bed was rarely ever used.

It only took a few minutes for my dad to pass out on the sofa and I carried my things into the master bedroom to get ready for sleep. As I changed out of my cheerleading uniform and into my pajamas, I couldn't shake the feeling that I was being watched. But as tired as I was, I ignored the feeling and quickly turned out the light and climbed under the covers. Since I wasn't used to the new mattress, I tossed and turned for quite awhile.

I had just wriggled into a comfortable position and closed my eyes. Then I heard the door open; that was followed by the opening of the closet door, and the click of the pull-chain (which illuminated the walk-in closet). Assuming it was my dad coming in to hang up his clothes, I didn't react...but I never heard any other sounds. Curious, I opened my eyes. Sure enough, I saw the bedroom and closet doors were open, and the bright yellow bulb blazing in the walk-in, with the pull chain swinging slightly—however, my father was not in the room.

"Dad?" I said, thinking he might have ducked into the master bath.

There was no reply. After a moment, I climbed out of bed and walked into the kitchen. From there, I could see my father fast asleep on the sofa. I felt my insides begin to tremble as I turned and walked back to the bedroom. I gave a quick, hard tug on the still swinging pull chain in the walk-in and extinguished the light, used my bag as a doorstop to prevent the door from coming open again, and locked the bedroom door.

When I got back in bed, I stayed awake for a time, coming up with a dozen logical reasons for what had occurred. It was then that I started noticing how the shadows played on the walls, and how one shadow in the corner seemed much darker than the rest. It undulated and seemed almost palpable. Immediately, I clamped my eyes shut, turned toward the other wall, and eventually fell into a restless sleep.

It was around eight the next morning when I awoke and was automatically grumbling over the poor quality of my rest I'd had. Remembering the plans my dad and I had made, I gathered my clothes and went into the master bath to take a quick shower. I had almost finished when I heard drawers and cabinet doors opening and closing. "Whatcha need, Dad?" I asked, thinking he'd come in to retrieve something. When he didn't answer, I didn't think much of it, figuring he didn't hear me over the running water. Once I'd dried off, I wrapped a towel around me and pulled back the curtain. Through the curling wisps of steam, I saw the drawers at the sink were open, as were the three doors of the towel cupboard. My brow furrowed in confusion. My dad was known for being a practical joker, but that seemed an odd choice for a gag. Once I closed all the drawers and cabinets, I went back into the bedroom to finish getting ready. It wasn't until I was done and on my way to the living room that I noticed the bedroom door was closed and still firmly locked.

When my dad and I were ready to leave, I asked, "Did you come in to the master bath while I was getting ready?"

He shook his head. "No, why would I?"

I shrugged and said, "I don't know. Maybe to get your toothbrush or something."

He told me, "Nope, I keep all of that stuff in the other bathroom. It's easier to get to when I roll off the couch and get ready for work."

Before I could explain what I had experienced, he changed the subject and we were out the door.

Months passed and little inexplicable things occurred occasionally. Items were never found in the places they'd been left, rooms would begin to feel noticeably colder, and sometimes I heard what sounded like growling noises coming from that strange, substantial looking shadow in the master bedroom. Of course, I found logical reasons of explaining it all away: bad memory, a powerful air conditioning unit, and what was likely an animal that had found its way under the mobile home. More than anything, it was the pervasive feeling of continually being watched that was the most disconcerting.

Then in April of the following year, my dad was at work when he stabbed his left index finger with a drill bit. The wound became infected and my dad was seriously ill for a week or two. One afternoon when he was home sick, my mom dropped me off at the mobile home so I could look after my dad for a few hours. He asked me to take his truck and get his prescription, and some sodas and snacks. I did as he requested and eventually finished my errands. While I was gone, it started raining pretty heavily and I ended up standing on the front steps of the trailer, loaded down with bags and getting thoroughly soaked—unable to open the front door. I knocked, but it was difficult with my hands full, so I kicked the door a couple of times.

Looking up, I saw a heavy shadow behind the thin curtain of the kitchen window. It seemed to be peering out to see who had come calling. Then it moved in the direction of the door and I sighed gratefully, expecting my dad to open the door any second. I waited for at least another minute before heaving a frustrated sigh, dropping a bag of two liter sodas onto the rain soaked steps, and fishing my keys out of my dripping wet purse. Grumbling, I opened the door and set the bags inside. There I saw my dad asleep on the couch. Somewhat warily, I went to the kitchen, stored the groceries and then changed into some of my dad's extra sweats and a t-shirt while I put my own soggy clothes in the dryer.

    The sofa was one of those large L-shaped sectionals and while my father slept feverishly on one end, I had a whole love seat sized area for myself where I stretched out with a blanket and a book. The only other furniture in the room consisted of a coffee table, that I was using as an ottoman, and an armchair that was on the side of the room. The armchair wasn't exactly a regular, stationary armchair: it could swivel and rock a bit as well. But I never really sat in it much , as I just never found it very comfortable. What happened next made certain I never wanted to sit in it again. I saw some movement out of the corner of my eye, so I lowered my book and sort of scanned the room—looking for whatever might have caught my attention. Then, I noticed the armchair was rocking back and forth, ever so slightly. Horrified, I watched as it did one slow, perfect revolution of three hundred and sixty degrees before stopping completely as if it had never been touched. Immediately, I reached out and shook my dad awake. He'd been tossing fitfully for a while and a light touch was all it took to rouse him. Without me saying a word, he instantly looked over at the armchair when he came to full consciousness. I didn't tell him what I'd seen. I just never could form the words.

    It wasn't long after he recovered from the infection that my dad moved out of the mobile home. He didn't tell me what prompted the decision to move and I never asked.

    That Christmas he and I were having a quiet, late night conversation with my aunt at her house. During a lull in conversation, my dad suddenly mentioned the mobile home. He told us that the whole time he lived there, he'd been tormented by grotesque, hellish nightmares and that he'd never gotten a good night's sleep. He spoke of seeing shadows at the edge of his vision; of hearing whispers just over his shoulder; and of finding doors and cabinets randomly opened. Finally, I told him the same stories I've told you here. We both admitted to feeling a constant presence watching everything we did; how there always seemed to be another person in the room even when we were alone; and how at times we both felt violently angry for no reason at all.

    My aunt patiently listened to us purge ourselves of these dreaded recollections then, once we were finished, she asked us a simple question. "In all the time you two stayed there, did it never occur to you to tell the other what you felt and what you saw?"

    "No, it didn't," we said. Dad and I both explained that it always felt as if there was some reason not to speak about what had happened, almost like something had stayed our tongues. We said that we always found a logical way to explain what had happened, even though the logic never gave us any comfort.

Then my aunt told us, "It seems like whatever it was, it wanted you to feel isolated. As long as you never said anything, it had you where it wanted you—afraid. It kept you both separated and scared. I bet if you'd told each other about it then, made each other aware of your experiences, it would have stopped. It couldn't face you both at the same time."

We never really talked about the mobile home again and this is the first time since that night at my aunt's that I've gone into any detail about what I experienced there.

Every day, I can see the trailer from the main road as I'm driving to work and it always seems to loom creepily in the pale, early morning light. There are some days when I'll see something out of the corner of my eye or hear an unexplained noise and I'll think back to that mobile home. Those moments always make me wish my father was still alive, so that he and I could have another paranormal discussion, and properly settle once and for all: if we let our imaginations drive us to such a fearful state, or if we really did have our very own ghostly experience.

Anything Ghost Episode #162
September 18, 2012

The Haunted Victorian Home
Dave (Carlsbad, California)

In the summer of 2000 I received orders to report to Fort Drum in upstate New York. I was a newly promoted sergeant in the U.S. Army. Upon arrival, I excitedly discovered that due to my new rank I was able to live off-post "in town." This meant a lot to me, as living in the barracks was not an entirely pleasant experience. As I checked into my unit, I discovered a buddy of mine who I had met about six months prior while attending a military course. This friend of mine, Matt, was also assigned to the unit.

Matt had arrived to the Unit from a post in Colorado about two months before me. While talking to him and catching up, I learned that Matt was going through a divorce and that he had arrived to his new post alone. As Matt was a lower ranking enlisted person, he was obligated to living in the barracks. He also said that he was desperately looking for a roommate. Matt's plan was to keep his barracks room, but actually live off post—which he would be able to afford with the help of a roommate. I explained my situation to him, and we clicked. I figured, because he officially had a barracks room assigned to him, he would end up having different types of guard duties associated with living in the barracks; that meant I would have a lot more solo time in a luxury apartment that I also couldn't afford by myself. He said I could have the bedroom, and he'd take the couch. It sounded like a real good deal to me.

The largest town closest to Fort Drum was Watertown, New York. Watertown seemed to me to be a town that once thrived around the turn of the century, but kind of went to pot after that. The only industry that I was aware of, besides the U.S. Army, was a company that made those little pine tree air fresheners that people hang in their car. What I saw were large disintegrating Victorian mansions—places that a hundred years ago were the million dollar houses. This was weird to me, as I'm from the southwest where if a house has been around a hundred years, "it's really old." But here were these whole neighborhoods filled with them. Matt and I used to joke that the whole neighborhood was made up of houses from the movie "Psycho"—but were just a little more cheerful. It was no joke: every single house looked like a cliché haunted house from the movies. And it didn't help that this town was in the rust belt, and looked to have hit economic hard times, as the unmaintained condition of most of the houses attested to.

Well, my dreams of having a luxury apartment quickly faded with the reality of bills and a buck sergeant's paycheck. We did manage to find a cool little one-bedroom place, though, and the price was right—and it didn't hurt that the place was exactly one block from my new favorite pub either! And guess what? The house looked exactly like the others: a ghost movie cliché. The house where our new apartment was located had been separated into three individual apartment units. The entire first floor was its own apartment occupied by a somewhat grouchy old lady. I know this because the first day after moving in, I attempted a neighborly act of introducing myself and was quickly and briskly brushed off. Our apartment was on the second floor with the main entrance to our apartment through an added-on stairway to the rear of the house. This rear area was also where our apartment's parking lot was. Upon coming up the rear stairs from the parking lot, and immediately entering the back door was the third apartment unit (which sat unoccupied the entire time I lived there). A quick left, and twenty feet down a carpeted hallway, then lead to our apartment. There was also a front entrance that had an extremely heavy door that screeched when it opened, and then a set of sharply ascending stairs that led to my hallway and door.

The apartment living went well for about a month. Forays to the pub a couple of times a week, and a relatively short commute to the post, made it a pretty sweet deal.

At first nothing happened to me, only to Matt. A lot of times Matt would play the night owl role and stay up late watching movies on his couch. This didn't bother me because one of the first things you learn in the military is how to sleep anywhere and at anytime.

What Matt started telling me, though, honestly creeped me out. I'll be the first one to say how afraid of ghosts in the movies I am, but as I had never seen or had any sort of paranormal experience of my own, it's not something I think about often. Daily life is a lot more frightening and stressful to me. Matt said that on several occasions, sometimes three or four times a week, he would hear loud banging in my room—anywhere from one to three hours after I had gone to sleep. Matt said these banging noises would usually be in successions of five.

The apartment I shared with Matt was small, and the entrance to my bedroom was eight feet at the most from where Matt sat on the couch. He'd usually get up and see what the heck I was doing in my bedroom, and find me fast asleep. I remember specifically being angry on the numerous times when he woke me up asking if I had heard anything. He was incredulous at my sleeping through whatever had been making the noise. My room didn't have a proper door, it had one of the accordion type sliding things. It's very important to mention that this house, in which my apartment was located, was built entirely of wood. So any noise made was easily heard. Matt was able to replicate the noises he heard in my bedroom by literally jumping and stomping his feet on the floor of my room. This is what he said he heard. We both tried to think about possible reasons for these noises. Although Matt was a late night TV guy, he did try and be respectful of the old lady downstairs. I also knew that her bedroom was at the rear of the house, so I knew it was not her complaining about the noise. I think we finally wrote off the banging as possibly pipes settling or something like that. But what started happening next, honestly had me questioning my sanity.

About two months into our living there, the banging had subsided for about a week. Matt was up one night, when at about 1:30 a.m. he again heard the five quick bangs, and then heard whispering. Matt told me that the whispering was so faint that although he could identify it as whispering, he couldn't make out specific words or phrases. Matt said that he could identify at least two different voices: a male and a female. At that time Matt and I were in a U.S. Army communications unit, where our responsibilities included signal intercept. What that means is that we were basically tasked with listening in on the enemy. For this reason, I knew that if Matt said he heard voices, I trusted his judgment. I also felt that I knew Matt well enough at that point to know that he was a mature and sober minded individual. I trusted him and it freaked me out. A couple of days after that happened, Matt went on a two week leave to Minnesota to see his family. Since the time we moved into the place, I had only been alone overnight twice.

Because I had never experienced anything myself in the apartment, I wasn't entirely convinced that something was going on. Although I did trust Matt, I thought maybe I was talking in my sleep. Man, I have no idea. I just didn't want to think about it.

The first three nights that Matt was gone, my girlfriend slept over. We slept in my room and I didn't hear or notice anything. The fourth night, I remember quite well. I came home from work, and took a shower. I distinctly recall a strong feeling of being watched. In the shower I remember washing and rinsing my hair as fast as I could—feeling that as soon as I opened my eyes, I would see someone there. It was not comforting, but I remember feeling kind of excited that I could kick back on the couch with a beer watching movies and relaxing (Matt and I didn't have cable, so we owned a lot of movies). After showering, I sat down and watched my first movie, a comedy. I then watched a second movie that was some action flick we had seen about fifty times. After that movie, it was about 11:30 p.m. and I didn't quite feel like bed yet, so I decided to read and have a couple of cigarettes on the couch. I remember having a feeling like the air was being charged with electricity—and not in a good way. I heard what sounded like feet walking on dried leaves. It was a kind of a cracking or rustling noise, and it was coming from my room. That was followed by a loud bang. A single bang—just like how Matt had described it.

That was it! I got up, ran to my room and turned on the light...I saw nothing. The overhead light in the living room and the adjoining kitchen were also turned on. I was scared. I was a seven year veteran in the Army, there were not a whole lot of things that frightened me, but this did. I sat back down on the couch and said a prayer—trying to relax.

About five minutes later, I heard it: a low murmur; like people speaking softly in the next room. I couldn't make out words, I could just hear the rhythm of conversation. The voices didn't have any anger or emotion that I could notice, it sounded just like a normal conversation. This went on for maybe three minutes, and then ceased as I got enough courage to get off of the couch and go back into my room. I sat on my bed for about five minutes, wide-eyed and very scared. It didn't happen again.

By far the most frightening experience happened the next night. Again, I was sitting on the couch watching a movie. Our couch faced our apartment's front door. As our apartment was sectioned from a house, I didn't have a proper front door, as the door was more of an interior door—a bedroom door if you will. There was also a large, almost one inch gap beneath the door from where the hallway carpet was visible. As I was watching TV, I heard the front door open (the screech I mentioned earlier), this was followed by heavy footfalls that were coming up the stairs to my floor. Although the stairs and hallway were carpeted, the wooden house carried every noise. I started thinking, "My girlfriend was working, Matt was gone and the only other apartment on my floor was unoccupied. Who was this?"

I heard the footsteps approach my front door, and then I saw a shadow through the crack beneath my door. I watched as the shadow passed by my door. As soon as the shadow passed, the sound of the footsteps stopped. The wooden hallway was so loud that if whoever had just passed my door had kept walking, I would have heard them. I heard nothing. So my only conclusion was that a stranger was standing to the right of my front door. It scared the heck out of me, but if a possible burglar was about to break in, I could handle that. I grabbed a baseball bat that we kept by the door, and swung open the door.

No one was there.

I know what I experienced. I was sober, I was not hallucinating, it was real, and I have no explanation other than the paranormal.

I'm still in the Army; and since that night, I have been shot at, and spent time in combat both in Iraq and Afghanistan. Honestly, none of that compares to the fear I felt looking into that empty hallway.

Anything Ghost Episode #116
July 27, 2010

Room 212 in the Stanley Hotel
Jenna (Toledo, Ohio)

My boyfriend and I decided to take a spontaneous trip to Denver, Colorado. We didn't have any set-in-stone plans, so we played it by ear. We chose to visit Estes Park, Colorado that is about two hours northwest of Denver. While enroute to Estes Park, I was searching for cheap hotels to stay in. I came across the Stanley Hotel.

At first, I freaked (in a good way) because I thought it was where The Shining had been filmed. My boyfriend agreed that it would be a neat place to stay—even if it were more than we wanted to spend for one night. So we decided to check-in. Upon further research, we found that The Shining wasn't actually filmed there, instead it was where Stephen King got the inspiration to write the book, and that was still good enough for me.

We arrived at dusk and pulled into the parking lot. We proceeded to check in at the front desk where they gave us a key to room 212. Mind you, Stephen King stayed in room 217, five rooms away from us; this was bound to be an interesting night. According to rumors, the second floor is haunted by a little boy who roams the halls at night. It is said that you can hear him playing and running through the halls. I could go into much detail about the hotel, but that would take too long.

We explored the entire hotel: the most haunted rooms, the creepiest spots, etc. After exploring, we sat down at the bar in the downstairs lobby. I had a drink to try and calm my nerves. Nothing had happened as of yet, but I was on edge all night. We started chatting with another couple staying at the hotel. They told us about how they had brought along their two-year-old son, and two friends. They explained to us that earlier that evening, a diaper box had flown off their dresser, while the four of them were sitting around talking.

Following this, their two-year-old son turned to a corner, staring and pointing repeatedly, "Monster, monster," over and over. This just about set me over the edge. I was ready to run out of the hotel that second, even thought it didn't happen to me personally.

We retreated to our room and settled in for the night. I noticed the lamp to the right of my bed start flickering. This happened a few different times. I chalked this up to be that the light bulb needed replacing—anything to make myself feel a little better. After we had gone to sleep (or in my case, tried to sleep but barely slept), I randomly woke up at 5 a.m. and heard a very faint noise that sounded like it was coming outside our door.

It sounded as if a baby or a dog were crying. This lasted about ten minutes and then stopped. I eventually fell back to sleep. In the morning, I told my boyfriend about what I heard. He gave me a little smile and just laughed it off. I felt more at-ease in the morning, knowing it was daylight out. After we left the hotel, I was a bit bummed more paranormal experiences hadn't happened, yet glad at the same time.

If you ever get the chance to get to Estes Park, I highly recommend visiting The Stanley Hotel—whether it's just a ghost tour, or actually staying the night. It is very beautiful and creepy all in one.

Anything Ghost Episode #194
August 10, 2014

Haunted Hotels

Anything Ghost has shared many haunted hotel experiences over the years. Aside from the Bangkok, Thailand experience (previous page), here are some others that are included in this book:

- **Bangkok, Thailand Ghost Experiences**
    Anonymous (Minneapolis, Minnesota) - *Chapter 2*
- **Sidewalk Ghost**
    Roderick (Pas, Manitoba, Canada) - *Chapter 2*
- **Red Hill Hotel**
    Alice (Bendigo, Victoria, Australia) - *Chapter 6*
- **Mystery Man in a Hong Kong Hotel**
    Nick (Toronto, Canada) - *Chapter 6*

Peek-a-Boo, I See You!
Shannon (Tennessee, U.S.)

I feel I should start from the very beginning: when I first met my ex. I had recently befriended a new group of people through my employer. I spent a few evenings outside of work with them when one of the girls decided she needed to play match-maker and set me up with the only single guy in the group. I declined numerous times, before finally consenting and giving him a chance.

After a few dates, I finally agreed to see his house. Upon entering, I felt something was there. I couldn't place it, but there was a definite presence in that house. We did a tour of the house, and upon going down the hall to the back bedrooms, I nearly lost my breath because the presence was so strong. But as quickly as it had come, it was gone. The whole presence faded from the house, and I quickly dismissed that I had felt anything at all. I moved in over a period of time. I would often feel a presence there, but hadn't experienced anything else at that point—until I became pregnant with my son.

My ex had a 4-year-old son from a previous marriage, and I adored him greatly. He was a skinny, bright eyed, blonde haired boy. My ex got him every other weekend—although, occasionally his mom would drop him off on random days when she needed to run errands.

One morning, not long after I had found out I was pregnant, I was in the bathroom getting myself ready for work. I had left the bathroom door cracked open, and I was just putting on makeup. I had just looked back up into the mirror when I saw a little blonde haired boy smiling at me in the reflection of the mirror. Although it wasn't our weekend to have his son, I automatically assumed it was my ex's son, and turned around excitedly to say hi to him. I turned around and already had "Hey buddy!!!" out of my mouth, when I found myself facing an empty doorway.

His son wasn't the type to run and hide from me, he was usually hugging me tightly the minute he saw me, so I was naturally confused. Still, with half a smile on my face, I opened the door and peered out calling his name. No answer. I laughed a little to myself, and walked to the living room where my ex was watching TV. I asked where his son had gone. He looked at me quizzically and asked what I meant. His son wasn't there. I laughed and told him to knock it off, saying that I had just seen him while I was in the bathroom. He insisted his son was not at the house, and reminded me that it wasn't his weekend to be there. I got irritated with him as I knew I had seen him plain as day smiling at me in the mirror. So he called his ex wife and handed me the phone. When she answered, I asked if she had dropped their son off at the house, which she then informed me that she had just dropped him off at preschool 30 minutes ago.

Finally convinced their son was not at our house, I began to play over in my mind what had actually happened. I know I had seen a boy about the same age as their son, but as I thought upon the face, I realized the face was different. The smile wasn't even the same. I wasn't scared. I was just intrigued about this little boy who had shown himself to me.

After seeing the little boy, I started having more experiences, but most were minor. I was also preoccupied with my pregnancy—which had me in and out of the hospital. But after my son was born, the paranormal activity really picked up.

My son was given a toy rabbit that had long ears that covered its eyes. When the belly was squeezed, the ears would rise, expose the eyes, and then it would say, "Peek-a-boo! I see you!!" It was soft and fuzzy, but it required a hard push at just the right angle to get it to talk. My infant son and I were in the living room one afternoon, when I heard a loud thud in my son's nursery. I wasn't too alarmed, as I'd heard strange noises from his nursery before, but I still looked down the hall to see if I could tell what had made the noise. As I peered down the hall, I heard a voice. I immediately started down the hall, and about halfway down I heard his bunny, "Peek-a-boo, I see you! Peek-a-boo! I see you!"—repeatedly.

I stopped at the door and peered over to his crib in the far corner where the bunny sat. It continued: "Peek-a-boo! I see you! Peek-a-boo! I see you!..." I watched it sit unmoving, but continuing to play over and over. I finally walked into the room and picked it up. It fell silent. I looked it over for a minute—flipping it over and looking for an on/off area. Perhaps the batteries were finally dying and needed to be replaced. I couldn't find a hatch or Velcro area to remove batteries. Finally giving up, I flipped it over so it was facing me, and stared it over for a moment. I was about to place it back in the crib when suddenly, "Peek-a-boo! I see you!" Then it fell silent once more.

It had startled me, and without thinking I said out loud, "Well you're just being creepy." It remained silent. I placed it outside of the crib on the dresser, and it remained silent the remainder of the day.

I purchased a cheap digital camera shortly after my son was born to take a million pictures of our new pride and joy. I carried that little camera with me everywhere (this was before cell phones had cameras). At first I didn't notice anything out of the ordinary while looking over the photos, they were just a bunch of images of my little guy as he grew rapidly, like babies do. But as he grew, and started sitting up, the photos started to include more than the blank background of the room. I began to notice black motion type blurs occasionally showing up in the background. I initially chalked it up to it just being a cheap camera. I was very familiar of how cameras functioned, having had worked with film SLR's, darkrooms, and processing, and I knew the difference between a cheap point-and-click camera as opposed to a lens system camera with film. So, I assumed it translated over to digital as well. This was a cheap camera with a "whopping" 3 mega-pixels.

It didn't take long for me to notice though, that the black blur I was seeing in my pictures, was never there when I took pictures outside of the house (like I said, I carried it with me everywhere). At that point, I chalked it up to poor lighting in the house—perhaps causing a shadow or maybe dirt was getting on my flash. I tried to rationalize it as best I could.

By this point, I was feeling the presence more and more—so much in fact, that I was now making nearly daily calls to my best friend in another state to discuss the photos. Becoming a parent made me a bit overly protective—plus, the uneasiness was growing stronger in the house. I needed someone to bounce my ideas and thoughts off just so I didn't feel like I was going crazy. Now that I was staying home with my son, I heard things more and more often. My friend and I agreed that I just needed to speak out loud to the presence and tell it to leave me alone. I needed to do something. One afternoon, as my son was napping, I sucked up my pride about talking out loud in the empty house, and spoke to whatever it was. I told it something like, "I don't mind coexisting here with you. I don't know why you're here, or what you need, but this is my house now. I need you to stop trying to scare me and my son."

I felt absolutely silly saying anything out loud to something that I could not see, but I figured it couldn't hurt. Nothing seemed to happen immediately after I said my piece, but the energy in the house felt more calm and peaceful.

Later that night however, as my son was fighting sleep, I decided to rock him to sleep in the living room. I was standing in the living room rocking him, when I felt the uneasiness return. I tried to ignore it, but felt it in my gut and deep in my bones. I felt like I needed to run from the house and flee for my life. I told myself it was ridiculous, as I had nowhere to go. It was very late in the evening, and most people I knew had gone to bed. I tried to ignore it and just concentrate on getting my son to sleep, but it got stronger, and heavier. It was getting harder to breath. I started to panic. It was angry. And for the first time ever, I was frightened. I felt like it was behind me. I stopped rocking my son and I stood up straight. I planted my bare feet into the carpet, closed my eyes, and stood my ground.

I shouted "NO!" in my mind as loudly as I could. And I felt it back away. It didn't fade completely, almost as though it just took a few steps back and resigned to just watching me. I finished rocking my son, who quickly fell asleep after that, and I laid him down.

I decided to grab my camera and started snapping in random directions throughout the room. I didn't expect to catch anything. So, it was much to my surprise when I was reviewing the photos that I saw a tall black mass. It was clearly in the shape of a man, and was standing in the kitchen doorway. This showed up in not in one, but two separate photos. The first photo was taken with the kitchen doorway to the right side and only showed a portion of the interior of the kitchen. The mass was dark, but still mostly see-through. A head and a right shoulder were clearly leaning through the kitchen doorway ever so slightly. The second shot was of the front door that had a mirror hanging beside it. In the mirror's reflection, I could see directly into the kitchen, and in that reflection was the same black mass in the kitchen doorway—this time fully square shouldered and visible from the chest up (before the bottom of the mirror cut it off). If the mass was looking into the living room, he would have been looking directly at me. By measurements of the door for reference from the two photos, I would estimate the man to be about 6 feet tall. He had a short haircut, and was of medium build. I had taken about 50 photos but only caught something on those two photos.

Things didn't change after that day, but the uneasy feeling wasn't as strong for a while. We seemed to be co-existing better.

My favorite encounter happened when my son was just over a year old. Someone had bought him a few toys from a not-to-be-named series. The series contained figurines that had electronic chips in their feet, and when they were placed on certain platform scenes they would speak in the characters voice. There were about 60 or more different characters available in this series. My son loved them, and would play with them for hours. I had been looking at getting him a couple more characters to add to his little collection earlier in the day on eBay.

I had placed a few bids on a couple of them, but the auctions hadn't ended. So I was lying in my son's room with him, as we were in the process of transitioning him from the crib to a big boy bed. He was having a hard night that night, so I was lying with him until he fell asleep. As we were lying there, one of his characters started talking in the voice of one of his favorite characters. It was across the room and no one was near it. I figured the batteries were dying since my son played with it so often.

A few minutes later, it went off again, and shortly after it went off again. I finally got up and turned it off. I laid back down and went back to working on getting my son to sleep. Just after I climbed back into his bed, it went off again. Only this time, it was in the voice of a character we did not have. So, not only was it turned off, but now it was talking in a voice to a character we did not own. In fact, it was in the voice of a character I was bidding for on eBay. I got up and took the batteries out of it.

We moved out of that house shortly after that incident. Not because of that incident, just because my ex and I parted ways. My son visits his dad who still lives in that house.

Anything Ghost Episode #167
December 23, 2012

Is Emily a Ghost?
Alex (Utica, New York)

I currently live with my fiancée and her 5-year-old daughter, Gili. I have lived with them for the past 3-4 years. Prior to our current home, we lived in an apartment in another area close to where we live now. We never really thought much of the apartment, it seemed fairly modern to us and we never had any uneasy feelings while living there. However, after the first year, my fiancé's daughter (who was about 3 or 4 at the time) began talking to an imaginary friend named Emily. Since we both believe in the paranormal and how susceptible children are to it, we began to keep this in mind whenever Gili would talk about or play with Emily.

It soon got to the point that not a day would go by without Gili mentioning Emily. Finally, one night while we were driving, I asked Gili jokingly, "Alright Gili, I'm just going to throw it out there. Is Emily a ghost?"

She laughed and said, "Noooo! She's my friend!"

Immediately after her response a cow appeared in the middle of road causing me to violently jerk the wheel into the on-coming lane. Now this may have been just a coincidence and we ended up chalking it up to that, until we began noticing other strange things happen at the apartment.

One night while we were all asleep, I awoke to an icy, cold pressure press on the tip of my nose. I reached for my fiancée to see if she was playing a trick on me, but she was fast asleep. I even checked her hands to see if she may have accidentally touched me while moving, but her hands were warm.

Another night I was watching TV in the living room, when my fiancée nervously called me into the bedroom. I walked in and saw the TV on, but nothing out of the ordinary. She said she was sleeping when all of a sudden the TV turned on by itself. This began to happen quite often after that.

One time while I was sitting in the living room, out of the corner of my eye I saw who I thought was my fiancée walk into the bedroom, turn on the light and begin to put laundry away (or so I thought). After a while, I called to her and asked if she needed any help—since it seemed like it was taking longer than usual. She asked what I was talking about. However, her voice was not coming from the bedroom: my fiancée was in the kitchen, and said she had been in there the entire time.

Photo by Alex (Utica, New York)
Gili was three or four when she began talking to Emily.

    Perhaps the most interesting incident happened late one night when I heard Gili making a strange noise in her bedroom. I rushed into the room and found her crying, gasping for air and with a very unusual cough. She was crying and saying her chest was hurting. It turned out to be croup cough (which I had never heard of before this incident). That being said, I ran into my bedroom to wake up my fiancée and tell her that I needed help. After we calmed Gili down and put her back to bed, she told me that right before I burst through the door, she saw a little girl in a white dress with blonde hair open the door with a look of surprise and worry on her face. To this day we both believe that it was Emily trying to warn her friend that she was in trouble.

    After these incidents began occurring, I did a little research on the building. Though our apartment seemed to be very modern, the home itself was built in the late 1800's. Unfortunately this was the extent of my findings, however the history itself explains a lot.

    One last, quick story about Gili. This doesn't involve her ghostly counterpart, however it is still quite interesting. Last summer when she was about four and we were staying at a hotel on vacation. We'd just tucked her into bed, read her stories and said good night, to which she replied, "Okay! I'm going to go die now!"

    Shocked, we both told her that was not a nice thing to say and that she should not repeat it. In a nonchalant tone she replied, "Oh I was just joking! Besides I would just go up to heaven anyways!"

    Mind you we are not a religious family, and up until this point we had not really discussed such things with her. Nevertheless, her comment was both intriguing and freaky at the same time. We asked her how she knew this, and she continued, "Well that's what happened last time: Gerald came down and took the stone off my head —and then we both flew up to heaven!"

We began to ask about Gerald, and she answered, "Oh. He's the one that helped me get to heaven. He's got wings! I stayed up there for a while, then I decided to come back down here and live with you guys!"

After composing ourselves, we again said goodnight and all went to sleep.

On the way home we drove past a cemetery and Gili said excitedly, "That's one of the stones!" Pointing to a tombstone. "That's the kind of stone he helped get off my head!"

She would also talk about her "old family" and how she had children who did not want her and so they kicked her out. She also stated that she had to bury one of them as well as her mother.

Though the frequency of her comments about her past lives has diminished, she still occasionally will mention them.

Anything Ghost Episode #160
August 5, 2012

Types of Phenomenon Commonly Referred to as a Haunting

A Purpose Haunting
Similar to a Crisis Apparition (*see chapter 1*) without the trauma or stress factor.
- Always a reason for this occurrence; oftentimes to leave a message.
- Not confined to any one area or place.
- Sometimes communicated during a dream state, but not always.

Courtesy of Al Rauber. All rights reserved. Copyright 2016.

The stories that follow in Chapter 5 are not intended to be examples of the above described phenomenon.

Public Domain.
Castelli, Horace. 1825-1889.

5 | Chapter Five

- Dog Keeps an Eye on an Apparition
- Fourteen Floors Up
- Dan's Run in Henryville
- "Sing and Snore Ernie"
- Golden Gate Park Experience
- Waverly Hills Experience
- Noises in the Kentucky Woodlands
- The Tuxedo Man
- Haunted Home for the Elderly
- Haunted Auto Parts Store
- The Old Lady Who Lived Here
- The Little Yellow House in Redlands
- A Haunted Childhood Home
- Bronx, New York Ghost Stories
- The Haunted Evelyn Apartments
- Funeral Home Ghost
- A Small Boy Ghost in Fallujah, Iraq
- The Cobbler's Ghost in Merseyside
- The Notting Hill Flat
- The Forgotten Lodger

Dog Keeps an Eye on an Apparition
Ed (Washington, Pennsylvania)

Photo by Ed (Washington, Pennsylvania)
Ed's dogs on the couch—but there's "something" in the background that one dog doesn't like...

This photo was taken in my home on September 7, 2015. I wanted to take a picture of my two dogs lying on the couch. I decided to kneel down and take the picture at "dogs eye level." I was kneeling on the floor to the left of the black dog—and I was the only one in the house at the time.

When I loaded the picture on my laptop, the first thing I noticed was the reflection in the window. It appears to be a reflection of someone standing in the doorway between my living room and dining room. The "person" would have been standing approximately six feet behind and to the right of where I had been kneeling.

If you look at my dog on the right, his eyes are fixed on something or "someone." I have no explanation as to what this image is. It's not a flash from the camera, and it's not a reflection from the TV—and it's definitely not my reflection. Also, the window that shows the reflection is 15 feet above the outside ground, so it's not anyone standing outside.

Chapter 5 — Ghostly and Creepy Experiences

Photo by Ed (Washington, Pennsylvania)
A close up of the figure.

There's no history of a haunting and no one died in the home. At the time of the picture we had just finished gutting and remodeling the kitchen. I can say my one dog (the one staring) is very nervous when he's in that room, and is constantly looking around. He gets startled easily, as well.

05 July 2016

Fourteen Floors Up
Elly (New York, New York)

I was living on Roosevelt Island in New York City after attending school there for four years. I'd always lived in Manhattan, and actually never knew a thing about the island until my roommates and I found an ideal two-bedroom apartment in a nearly brand new, luxury apartment building. This was in the summer of 2004, and the housing market was still in a slump after the September 11th 2001 terror attack, so with rent split three ways, the place was a steal. I lived in a tiny room that was partitioned off from what had been a dining nook next to the balcony. My desk abutted the sliding glass door, and the foot of my bed was at the window beneath it. Despite a terrific view, the room was a nightmare during winter (as the windows and doors didn't have the best weatherproofing, and the wind would often whistle in). There wasn't anything remotely spooky about the room, in fact, what I'm sharing here happened outside of the apartment.

One winter's night a particularly noisy snowstorm was going on outside, and the dull sound of the highway and the wind came in faintly from the poorly sealed doors. I was watching TV from my armchair, when a strange sound caught my attention. The sound was emanating from the balcony. At first I assumed the wind was kicking up a notch, but I soon realized it was a shuffling sound (much like a person would make when muddling around in a large raincoat). I began to get very curious, so I peered out the window into the night. I knew from earlier in the day that there was about a half a foot of snow sitting on the balcony, so when I got up to look outside, I was expecting to find a bird making the noise. As I stood peering out into the blackness of the night—which seemed to swallow the bright, warm light thrown out my window by the lamp—I suddenly grew as still as a hare, because I began to hear a sucking, breathing noise join the slight shuffle sound. My nerves were straining with the feeling of another presence. Without a doubt, something was on the other side of the glass. I tried to dissuade myself with the fact it was the wind and the snow. But I'd grown very accustomed to the sounds the wind made. Something was hunkering on the ledge, and moving. I felt paralyzed, and could only avert my eyes from the window. I was afraid of acknowledging the presence, and for what must have been close to half an hour, I sat in terror of the sounds outside. The longer it went on, the more my rational explanations had trouble supporting them—and I was shaking. The balcony was 14 floors up, and the movement was large and heavy—not light and flitting like a bird's would have been. As I sat there, turned away from the window with my nerves raw and painful, the sounds finally passed. I did not dare go near the door the entire evening.

When morning came, nothing indicated anything had been there. There were no bird's footprints in the snow. However, the snow had been lightly falling all night long.

Perhaps this is not much, but I later found more details about the island's sordid history. It was well-known that an asylum had once been the dominating feature of the island. The asylum was known as the Octagon. The conditions at the Octagon were grim enough to have launched the book Ten Days in a Madhouse, an undercover report in 1887. The island had also housed a prison when it was still named Blackwell Island in the mid 1880s. At the time I experienced the visitor, the island still had the moldering shell of a ruined smallpox hospital at the far end—utterly overgrown and blocked off from public access. But at the time of my experience, I had known none of this.

Anything Ghost Episode #101
28 October 2009

Children Seeing Ghosts

Here are some other stories found in this book that involve children experiencing the paranormal while playing:

- **Basement Shadow Person**
  Noelle (Michigan, U.S.) - *Chapter 4*
- **Mr. Keen's Halloween Promise**
  Donna (Maine, U.S.) - *Chapter 4*
- **Haunted Birmingham Home**
  Erika (Birmingham, Alabama) - *Chapter 4*
- **Is Emily a Ghost?**
  Alex (Utica, New York - *Chapter 4*
- **Bronx, New York Ghost Stories**
  Errol (New York, U.S.) - *Chapter 5*
- **The Ghost of Llanrumney Hall**
  Gareth (South Wales, U.K.) - *Chapter 6*
- **The Shadow Man at Grandpa's House**
  Barbara (Monterey, California) - *Chapter 6*

Dan's Run in Henryville
Savannah (Indiana, U.S.)

This is a urban legend and a personal experience, all in one. It didn't happen to me, but to my boyfriend. He told me everything about it and I feel like I could have been there.

We live in Southern Indiana which isn't known for much outside of having a large old ammunition plant and the old Colgate Factory—that are both said to be haunted. Also, in Henryville (about ten minutes from where I live), there is the local legend of a gruesome murder that went undiscovered for over a year. Daniel Guthrie was murdered and placed in a shallow grave near a local cemetery. His body was discovered a year later and was given a proper burial in the same cemetery. The shallow grave he was found in is still an open hole that lies back in the woods just off the road. Since the murder, there have been numerous reports of sightings and other odd things reported that are believed to be associated with Daniel's untimely death.

My boyfriend, Zack (who considered himself an amateur paranormal investigator), got together with another friend, Leen, and planned a night of investigating the woods to see what they could find.

They started at the nearby cemetery, flashlights in hand, looking for Dan's grave. Zack was walking a few paces behind Leen, when he began to feel a chill in the air. Zack started to feel the edge of panic, but he stayed quiet for the moment. Suddenly, almost from right beside his ear, he heard a deep voice telling him to "get out." Not wasting any time, he took off for the car. Leen, having seen Zack running, joined him in the dash. They left immediately and headed straight home.

Sometime later, Zack recounted this story to me. He told me that it had been the scariest thing he'd ever experienced. After hearing this, curiosity overcame me, and I begged Zack to take me out to where it happened. After much talk, he finally relented.

We made our way out to the cemetery. It was a November night. I remember being excited until I saw the gate to the cemetery. A sudden feeling of terror came over me as I looked out into the darkness of the cemetery. The headlights of my car illuminated the first few graves, but after that was inky blackness and a dimly flashing light. I knew it was just my imagination taking over, but I'd heard countless stories of people seeing unexplained lights in cemeteries, and that halted any thought whatsoever I had of entering that cemetery. My boyfriend laughed at my fear. But I knew he didn't want to get out of the car either. I finally got up the strength to drive away.

As we drove back down the country road (laughing at the situation), a deer jumped out of the woods and onto the road in front of me. I swerved and just missed hitting the deer with the front of my car. The deer sprinted off into a cornfield off the side of the road. As I slowed, the steering wheel gripped tightly in my hands, my boyfriend pointed out that where we were was eerily close to the bridge that takes you to the spot of Daniel's original shallow grave.

Blocking out that thought, I sped all the way home.

Anything Ghost Episode #101
October 28, 2009

"Sing and Snore Ernie"
Savannah (Mississippi, U.S.)

When I was nine years old, my two-year-old brother drowned in our backyard pool. We kept his favorite toys and his pacifiers on a shelf in the living room. One of these toys was a Sing & Snore Ernie. Every couple of days for the first few months after Kasey died, Ernie would "snore" for a couple minutes, wake and then announce that he "felt great." We figured it was a battery problem but Ernie didn't do it often enough to bother anyone—plus it reminded us of Kasey, so we let it go. For 11 years, Ernie sat on the shelf, finally quiet.

My grandpa had been in the hospital for eight months, struggling to breathe with a disease called COPD. He could barely speak, opting to nod shakily and then go back to his TV. We visited him as often as we could, but work and school took up a lot of time. He slowly grew worse and worse, until he finally passed away.

In the week that followed his death (busy with the wake and funeral), my mother walked around the house acting strong—even though her father had died. We were all in the living room talking about grandpa and our memories of him, when suddenly Ernie, who had been silent for 11 years, suddenly started snoring. We all stopped talking—listening in mixed awe and confusion as Ernie "woke up" and announced to us all that he "felt great." No one had touched Ernie, changed his batteries or even picked him up and dusted him off for years. He repeated it a couple times in the next hour. We all took it as Grandpa letting us know that he was finally in peace.

Anything Ghost Episode #101
October 28, 2009

Golden Gate Park Experience
Audri (San Francisco, California)

I spend a lot of time in Golden Gate Park (given that I live right next to it and have an active toddler to keep entertained). Even on the gloomiest of days, the park is a cheerful place with its great playgrounds, museums, and hidden away gardens that make you forget you're in the middle of a city. My son and I pass a lot of our afternoons in one of the busiest and most cheerful playgrounds—as do most of the parents in this area. But I have yet to muster the courage to talk to anyone I know about the strange experiences I've had right on the edge of this popular playground.

Right at the edge of this playground is a tiny barn looking structure that is always padlocked shut (I'm assuming the park employees use as a storage shed or something), and a picnic area right next to it. This spot is particularly cheerful and cute, and I see lots of birthday parties and other activities going on here when the weather is nice. We've even considered having our own son's birthday there next year! Only problem is that I get a terrible sensation of oppressive fear whenever I am near that area. The closer I am to the shed, the more I get an overwhelming sense of something being very wrong. The hairs on the back of my neck stand up, I feel a constant sense of someone (or something?) standing right over my shoulder, and a little voice in my head screams, "RUN! Get out of here fast! Go!"

I'm not new to experiencing the paranormal. Its been a part of my life since I was very young, and I've had my share of strange occurrences, but I'm used to them happening in the home, and its not often that I feel such menace in an outdoor place.

Once, very recently, I was near this structure chasing after my son who was chasing pigeons, and from the corner of my eye I saw a figure standing in the small archway of the little shed. This was in broad daylight, so at first I didn't think anything of it, until I realized the figure I was seeing in my periphery was watching me. Still not thinking anything strange, my Spidey sense told me to get a good look, because this person seemed to be lingering in one spot for an awfully long time. When you have a kid you start to notice things like that. When I turned to look there was no one there.

I keep wondering if its an overactive imagination, or if there really is something bad lingering near such a happy place. I've tried to do research on the area, but so far have come up empty handed. I find only the same urban legends repeated again and again on multiple websites.

Anything Ghost Episode #194
August 10, 2014

Waverly Hills Experience
Walt (Kentucky, U.S.)

As someone who has been interested in the paranormal since I was a little tyke, it might surprise some to know I am a true skeptic. In my years of searching for the unknown there have only been two instances in which I cannot explain away what happened to me. Hope you enjoy them.

Waverly Hills Shadow Person

Being from Kentucky I had always been interested in the Waverly Hills Sanatorium in Louisville, Kentucky. For those who aren't aware, Waverly was a tuberculosis hospital in the first half of the 20th century. Before the discovery of a cure, tuberculosis was often a death sentence for all those diagnosed with the "white plague." With an estimated 56,000 deaths in Waverly Hills it is often considered one of the most haunted places in the U.S.. It is also the location of the infamous Death Tunnel (which was used to carry the dead out of the hospital, so the living patients wouldn't see them).

I've been to Waverly only once in the fall of 2007. We took a paranormal tour of the hospital that was after dark, and did not end till just after midnight. Floor by floor we trekked through the darkness with only our flashlights to guide us.

- The renowned room 502: where a young nurse hanged herself while the mentally ill patients watched.
- The "shadow people" of the 4th floor: which I explained away as the process of one's eyes becoming adjusted to the low light. I had seen or heard nothing the entire time I was there.

When we entered the 3rd floor, I rolled my eyes at the tour guide's story of people seeing a little girl without eyes on this floor, and to not tempt the spirits as they mess with nonbelievers the most.

We left the middle of the 4th floor and headed toward the end of the hall where the operating room was located. I was looking into each room on the left and right of the hall as I passed each doorway. When I reached the 45-degree bend in the hallway, I looked into the room on the left and turned my head to look into the room on the right. As I turned my head there was a figure of a full sized person moving in front of the doorway. I stopped in my tracks so fast that my cousin's wife, who was behind me, ran into me. I ran into the room as I assumed that someone was messing with us. Inside the room there was no one. There were no doors in or out of the room other than the one I had come in. Outside the window there was a 3-story drop to pavement. I know what I saw that night in Waverly Hills, but I still have no idea what it was.

Noises in the Kentucky Woodlands
(Story 2)

My second story comes from when I was a younger man, and at a time when multi-day camping trips were a normal thing for me. My friend and I were deep in the Kentucky woodlands one humid August night, on day two of a three day excursion. The fire roared from the overly dry fuel. We fed it, which lit up the forest at least two dozen feet into the darkness. As the fire died down we decided to retire for the evening and climbed into each of our tents. For those who have never camped before, there is an overwhelming calm that overcomes the woods at night. It starts as dull loudness of animals, insects, and woodland rodents; and over several hours this reduces to a whisper. For some this calm is the entire point of camping and for others it can be eerie. I was one of the former, but I was about to have a change of heart.

I had just drifted off to sleep, when I was awakened by a noise outside of the tents. It sounded like a small animal rustling through the leaves so I didn't think much about it. The forest noises had calmed again for a short time when loudest thud I had ever heard came from forest. I could tell it wasn't close to the tents and first assumed that a dead tree had fallen. I laughed to myself pondering the old question of whether a tree makes a noise in the forest. But my whimsy was short lived as another, albeit it less loud, thud came from the woods, followed by another and another. It did not sound like it was getting close to our campsite but the thuds continued. I tore out of my tent to find my friend standing outside his tent with a look of terror in his eyes. He had gotten out of his tent so quickly that all he hadn't even taken the time to get dressed wearing only his flip-flops and his lightweight fleece sleeping bag wrapped around his waist. Only afterward did I realize I had done almost the same.

The thuds continued steadily, but slowly reduced in noise—leading us to believe that whatever it was, it was moving away from our location. After ten long minutes from the moment we left the confines of our tents, the noise had faded off into nothing. Not knowing what was going to happen next, we took the respite to build up a huge fire and to quickly get dressed. We sat back to back next to the huge fire, scanning the forest, and hoping that our firewood would last till morning. Although it was a humid August night, and we were drenched in sweat from the heat being thrown off the fire, neither of us moved a muscle for hours. The noise never returned.

Anything Ghost Episode #131
April 9, 2011

The Tuxedo Man
Travis (Upland, California)

I have to admit I am quite the skeptic and do not believe in ghosts, but I enjoy ghost stories very much and absolutely love your podcast. My sister, however, is quite the believer and I thought I'd share a story of hers.

My sister is in her forties now. She has three children and is a school counselor. Given her degree in psychology and how much knowledge she has of all the tricks the human brain can play on people, one would expect her to be a skeptic. However, she's had multiple ghostly encounters and insists on their reality. Her resolve that she is not mistaken has been unshaken for years and, to her credit, I can't find much of a logical explanation for one of her stories.

On multiple occasions my sister claimed to see a handsome man dressed in a tuxedo walking back and forth along our house's lone hallway. The tuxedo man never did anything other than walk back and forth along the hall. Sometimes she'd see him through a crack in the door, other times her door would be wide open. He'd occasionally glance in, as if watching her, but in a kind way. She often referred to him as her guardian angel. The rest of the family assumed she was dreaming, because all of these events occurred late at night and nobody else experienced it.

One night she was up late studying. Her room was well lit and her door was closed. There were no shadows to play tricks on her eyes. The tuxedo man appeared. However, this time he was not in the hallway, he was in her room. She looked up and saw him staring at her. He did not speak, he did not move. My sister froze with shock. She had been somewhat comfortable with the tuxedo man and he didn't frighten her before, but this time he had a frown on his face as if he were disappointed in her. My sister did not dare remove her eyes from the man who was standing in the center of her room. After a moment of him silently watching her with disapproving eyes, he vanished. She never saw him again.

I've never known what to make of the story. I like to insist that, even though the circumstances of her story have her wide awake in a well lit room, she may have been dreaming and simply not realized it. Yet I admit that even that is a stretch. Whether the tuxedo man was a disappointed angel or an upset ghost, it is eerie to me that her story isn't like the others I hear so frequently. It wasn't something she glimpsed in the darkness at the corner of her eye; it wasn't some feeling she had that she was simply so sure was of a supernatural nature; it was just a man in a tuxedo that she could see as plain as day, and he was there for her to look at for a full minute or so before he vanished without a trace.

Though I am a skeptic, I find these stories fascinating and would have researched the history of our house if I could. But our house was brand new when my family moved in—being newly built on what used to be a lemon grove in Southern California. If ghosts are real, then I have absolutely no idea where the tuxedo man could have even come from. But until the day I die I will always wonder if he is a machination of the mind, or a lonely spirit who enjoyed traveling.

Anything Ghost Episode #161
September 1, 2012

Clicks at the Freedom Mausoleum - by Lex Wahl

As I said in an earlier story, in my early 20's I worked at Forest Lawn Cemetery. My job was mostly delivering flowers to graves. Forest Lawn Glendale has two large mausoleums: the seven-floor Great Mausoleum (of which I spoke of in an earlier story), and the smaller and more modern Freedom Mausoleum (which is open to the public). Both mausoleums have many celebrities buried within. The Freedom Mausoleum houses the remains of three of the Marx Brothers, Nat King Cole, Gracie and George Burns, etc.

There was something strange about that place, though. The Freedom Mausoleum was open to the public (I read that at present the staff is more strict about visitors, though), so it wasn't like I felt alone there—plus, it was very well lit with ample sunshine pouring in through high windows. But whenever I was there placing flowers, a clicking sound would follow me from room to room. I'd pull the flower cart in front of a room, look at an order and then walk toward the room…"click…click…" Then I would finish my work and roll the cart a few rooms down…"click…click…" This went on the whole time I worked in the Freedom Mausoleum. Sometimes, it seemed to predict where I was headed next: I'd hear a "click…click." a few rooms down as I headed that way. These clicks were always there while I worked—upstairs and downstairs.

Another scary part of working there lied in a particular area of the mausoleum. It was in the northwest area of the lower floor near the flower room (in the back corner). Whenever I was working back there, I had a feeling of something not wanting me to be there—it was dark, and full of hate and violence. It seemed to be mostly in the flower room, or just near it. So I avoided that room as much as possible. In fact, if my co-worker and I showed up to work there together, I always made sure to do the upper portion of the mausoleum—just to avoid that back area. This always confused him, because the upper floor had most of the celebrities, and as such required more work. "Are you sure?" He'd ask.

During my last year at that job, something very strange happened in that back area of the Freedom Mausoleum. You can read about that experience by reading "Halloween at the Freedom Mausoleum (in the following pages)."

Haunted Home for the Elderly
Spring (Texas, U.S.)

For about a year, I worked at an assisted living facility for elderly people suffering with Alzheimer's and other dementias. I can recall three experiences I had within the year that I worked there.

The first experience was in regards to a man who was perfectly healthy for his condition: he would go for walks, get himself dressed, and make his own coffee. The last time I saw him there I noticed no difference in his condition. But one morning, after he was given a second cup of coffee, he just suddenly stopped breathing and passed away.

About a month after the man passed away, I was on an overnight shift. While I was looking around to make sure everyone was safe in his or her room, I saw a solid black shadow of a head peek around the corner of the hallway (this was the hallway that lead to the residence of the aforementioned man). The shadow was solid enough that it made me think someone was there. So I got up and walked over to look around that corner, but no one was there. If one of the residents had come out of his or her room and gone back in, I would have heard a door open and then close. But I heard no such sound.

My second experience was of a white figure I saw. There was an elderly woman who we knew was near the end of her life. A couple of nights before she passed, I was sitting in the employee office in the center of the two hallways where the residents' rooms were located. Through one of the windows, I saw a white shrouded figure walk down the hallway. I then saw the same figure walk across the other window of the office towards the ailing woman's room. Then I saw the figure move across the same window towards the ailing woman's room a second time. That was the last I saw of the figure.

My last experience was during dusting duties we had when working overnight. While I was dusting around a TV in the living and activity room, I saw someone move across the reflection in the blank TV screen like they were walking along the area behind the couches. I turned around to speak to my coworker (whom I assumed it was I saw in the reflection), but when I turned my head, no one was there.

Anything Ghost Episode #164
October 25, 2012

Haunted Auto Parts Store
Jake (Raleigh, Mississippi)

About a year ago, I worked at an auto parts store in Raleigh, Mississippi. Raleigh is a small town in a very rural county with lots of history. My cousin was a former employee at the store, and he told me about the weird things he experienced while working there. However, this didn't bother me about working there.

The first month or so, I didn't have anything weird happen and I began to doubt my cousin's stories. After my training was done, I began to work by myself at the store from time to time in the evenings.

One evening it was about time to close up, so I began to clean and do the financial paper work for the day. The first computer and cash register were lined up with the front door, and that was where I was sitting. I then heard the front door open (this door had a bell on it, and the hinges always made a creaking sound when opened). As soon as I heard it open, I looked up: the door was shut and not moving, but it was still making the creaking sound. The bell on the door also rang, but it didn't move either. Then I heard footsteps walking straight towards me. This didn't bother me at the time, I was just shocked and in awe of what was happening. The footsteps stopped about five feet in front of me. I didn't hear anything else after that.

That was not the only experience I had there. One day I was stocking the shelves on the other side of the store, and my boss (who was sitting at a desk on the opposite side of the store), was talking to me. The desk was built into the wall and it was made out of a wood platform, so you had to step up to get to the desk. A few minutes later I heard a very loud sound coming from the desk. It sounded like someone stomping their feet very violently. I thought it was my boss doing it, and I looked up and saw that she wasn't there. As soon as I began to walk over to the desk, the stomping sound stopped. When I made it to the desk, I looked, and found no one around.

Over the next year I heard plenty: voices, doors slamming, and other unexplainable things.

Anything Ghost Episode #138
August 7, 2011

The Old Lady Who Lived Here
Dee (Los Angeles, California)

In 2001, my family and I moved into a new house. It was a small four bedroom, two bathroom home. I was the first to claim which room was mine. I picked the last room down the hall to the left.

From the moment we moved in, things didn't feel right but we ignored it—thinking it was just us needing to warm up to a new home.

My first night in the room was normal—aside from it being really cold. It was so cold that I used five thick blankets and when I breathed I can see the cold air coming out of my mouth. I just thought it was the winter weather and nothing more.

A week later, my mom asked me how I was sleeping in the new house. I told her it was okay, but that it was really cold. I took advantage of that moment to ask for a heater in my room. But she disagreed with me, and said I was crazy, adding that it was not cold in the house. It was then that I realized the rest of the house was pretty warm. Keep in mind that I live in L.A. and our winters are not that cold.

Some time later, I woke up in the middle of the night and saw a black figure in the corner of my room. I was so freaked that I tried to run out of my room, but on my way out I hit my head on the corner of a shelf. This landed me on the floor, passed out. I found myself on the floor when I was awakened by my alarm at 6 a.m. (that was set to get me up for work). I remembered the shadow person that I had seen the night before, and decided that it had been my imagination going wild, or my eyes playing tricks on me.

While I was at my mirror getting ready for work, I felt a spot of freezing air behind my neck. I looked in my mirror, and to my horror I saw a lady sitting on my bed! I stood frozen and shook it off, saying to myself (in still half asleep or groggy from being conked on the head), "I'm just seeing things."

A week later a neighbor across the street came and welcomed me to the neighborhood. We got into the conversation about the previous owner of the house. She told me the previous owner was a nice old lady who had been sick.

I asked what had happened to the old lady. She told me that the lady had a mental condition in which she would run up and down the street screaming—constantly causing a scene in the neighborhood. She then told me that the lady's daughter was trying to take her to a home so she could be properly managed by doctors, but before the daughter was able to move her, the lady passed away—she died in the room that I had picked as mine!

I then asked my neighbor to describe the lady. She described the lady that I saw sitting on my bed while I was looking into my mirror!

After hearing all of this, I bribed my little brother to switch rooms with me. I didn't tell him anything about the hauntings I had experienced.

The next day he told me the room was too cold to sleep in and he felt uncomfortable. Being that I was older, I told him, "Tough luck! It's your room now."

We moved to a bigger house four years later. That was when my family and I talked about that other house. I told them what I had seen, and what happened to me—as well as the things I heard. My brother added that he heard and felt the same things as I did.

But what surprised me the most was when my mom told us what she had witnessed: she'd heard the cupboards opening and closing in the kitchen; someone walking up and down the hallway; and the doorknobs twisting and shaking like someone was trying to get in.

Anything Ghost Episode #200
December 22, 2014

Halloween at the Freedom Mausoleum - by Lex Wahl

I spoke earlier of clicking noises I heard while I was doing work in the Forest Lawn Glendale Freedom Mausoleum. Well, there was another strange occurrence at this mausoleum—but this one happened to my co-worker.

It was a Friday; an hour before closing time (4 p.m.); and it was Halloween. I was looking forward to the Halloween weekend, and was chatting happily with the florists in the office. In my peripheral vision, I noticed my co-worker (Jim) walk over to the front counter, and look over the weekend work-orders (we each worked every other weekend, and it was his turn to come in that weekend). Not one to like idle time, he grabbed the work-orders and suggested we get as many done as possible. I sighed. We put together the flower orders, and headed out.

After placing most of the orders, our last stop was the Freedom Mausoleum—the one I hated, because I felt there was something angry there. When we got inside, I told Jim that I would work the top floor (the top floor was much more work because there were more celebrities, but I couldn't stand the idea of working in that creepy back corner of the lower floor). Jim happily agreed.

I scrambled up the marble stairs and began my work. When I was almost done, my co-worker called out to me, and asked me to come see when I was done. I headed back downstairs, and he said, "Hey, you gotta hear this."

He lead me down the marble halls to that dreaded "angry" flower room area. My stomach sank. As we approached the area, I heard it: a low, creepy, howling noise coming from the roof vent—it was straight out of a ghost movie! There was no wind; we'd never heard it before. We stood and listened, but were unable to come up with a reason for the howl. We headed back to the flower shop in the van, and tried to convince each other that it was some sort of Halloween prank.

The Little Yellow House in Redlands
Kathy (Ventura, California)

My sister rented a cute yellow and white house in Redlands California. For the first few months nothing happened—or nothing that they really noticed. But things slowly started to change. At night they could hear doors open and close; all the lights would turn on; the cabinet doors in the kitchen started opening. Then they started getting phone calls. Sometimes it was static; while other times it was an old woman saying, "Hello?"—after which time the phone would go dead.

It was the day after my nephew's birthday and he had a Mylar balloon with "Happy Birthday" on it. The balloon was in my nephew's bedroom while we were sitting in the den watching TV. As we sat there, the balloon came floating out from the bedroom, into the den and then floated to the ceiling. The balloon kept floating down just a little and then back up to the ceiling again. We figured the balloon was losing air, and eventually my sister put it back in my nephew's bedroom.

She came back to the den and we all start watching TV again. It didn't seem that long before the balloon came floating back out to the den. This time, it kind of hovered around five feet from the ground and just kind of slowly floated out to the den. I was in the recliner and my nephew and his mom (my sister) were on the couch. The balloon floated over to the couch near to where my nephew was sitting and stopped. We were all looking at it wondering what was going on. Then, the balloon slowly turned around until the "Happy Birthday" was facing my nephew. We pretty much left the house after that.

My sister told me that one day when she walking from the bedroom to the kitchen, she saw an old lady standing in the kitchen. She said the lady was just standing there holding what looked like an old handbag from the 1940's, and was just watching my sister. She freaked out and left the house.

When she did move out, our brother-in-law who is cop said, "Did I ever tell you I got a call to do a welfare check on that house about one year before you moved in? The old lady who lived there passed away in her bedroom."

Needless to say, my sister wasn't pleased with him not telling her until after she moved out.

Anything Ghost Episode #209
July 25, 2015

A Haunted Childhood Home
Julie (Pittsburgh, Pennsylvania)

We had moved into what is now my parent's house when I was only 13, it was only my mother my father and myself. It was a very nice house, though a little bit old. I know in my heart that we were not really alone in the house, though I never was able to find out if anyone had passed away there—or if it had been built on grounds that were haunted. Anyways, I have a few stories to share that all took place at different times in the house.

Before we moved in, I had been having a recurring dream that I would come home from school and go into the house alone. The house in the dream was not the house I had lived in, but in the dream I recognized it as my own. As I went inside, I came to a hallway connected to a living room and looked up a set of stairs. I froze in fear, staring up at a man dressed completely from head to toe in black. I would wake up right after that—usually breathing hard out of fear. I never really thought much about the dreams until we had moved into a house that had a staircase just like the one in my dreams. At the top of the staircase there were two rooms, one of which was mine and the other a guest room. When I began high school, I came home before my mom and waited for about an hour in the empty house. That dream always came to mind and I was always afraid to go to the steps until she got home.

One of those high school days, while waiting for my mom to get home, I was in the bathroom. It was before I had turned the television on, so the house was quiet. That was until I had heard, loud and clear, the basement door handle jiggling as if someone was playing around with it instead of turning it. The only thing I could think to do was to crack the bathroom door open just slightly to look across to the basement door. Sure enough, the door handle was jiggling around and making noise. The top lock was still in place, so I was pretty sure no one could open the door. I didn't know what to do, so as quickly as I could, I ran past and through the living room and out the front door. As soon as my mom came home I had told her what had happened. She was worried that someone was in the house, because I didn't see anyone leave out the front, and the garage didn't open to let anyone out the back. With help from a neighbor, who was a police officer, they searched the whole house. No one was there.

When I was in my early 20's, my husband ended up moving right into that house with me until we could save up enough money for a down payment on a house of our own. It was nice because we had the whole upstairs to ourselves. My mom would constantly wake up in the middle of the night—she always has and probably always will. One night, my husband and I were out with some friends but decided to call it an early night because we were tired. We ended up coming home around 11:00 p.m. The next morning my mom asked how late we were out—as if getting ready to scold us for staying out all night. When I told her 11 p.m., she asked me to repeat myself. She got a strange look on her face and began telling us that around 2:30 a.m., she woke up to go to the bathroom and looked into the living room (that was connected to the set of stairs that led to our room). She saw the three hanging flower baskets that she keeps filled, swinging back and forth as if someone had walked past them in a hurry—or as if someone had hit them while walking past. She didn't think anything of it at the time because she had thought that we had just come home.

On a different evening, my mom woke up in the middle of the night and went to the steps calling up for me and my husband. She was yelling so loud that she woke us both up from pretty deep sleep. She asked us what was wrong, and why we were running up and down the steps and making such noise. She was wondering if one of us might be sick. Apparently, we had been keeping her up for some time while we made stomping noises going up and down the steps, and she wanted us to quiet down. But neither me nor my husband were awake, since we had fallen asleep many hours before that.

Anything Ghost Episode #170
March 2, 2013

Bronx, New York Ghost Stories
Errol (New York, U.S.)

My first encounter with the afterlife was when I was about seven or eight. I was living in the Bronx with my great grandmother and she lived in co-op city.

My friend and I would go on the roof of the building and try and throw little rocks in to the lake that was behind the building. We both knew that we were not supposed to be up there, but boys will be boys. One day when we went up there, it was windy, so we placed a cinder block in the door so it wouldn't not slam shut (as it can't be opened from the outside). The door was in front of where we were, so it was not possible for someone to sneak up on us. We were tossing rocks in the wind, when from out of nowhere an older man tapped my friend and I on the shoulders. We were scared out of our minds, because as I said we could see the door from where we were, and with the cinder block there the door would have slammed—or made a noise of some sort. The man was standing in front of us. He looked very dusty—something like a carpenter would look. He told us that we knew we should not be up there and that he was going to report us. We started to cry, and pleaded him not to tell anyone. Then he told us that he knew where we lived—he told us our apartment numbers that we lived in. He told my friend that he was going to tell his mother, and that he was going to tell my great gran. After a while, he got us to stop crying, and told us to go back downstairs and move the cinder block on our way out. He said wouldn't report us.

After moving the cinder block, we ran down those stairs—this was no ten story building, it had at least 23 floors, give or take. When we got around the 18th floor, I started wonder how the old man was going to get off the roof (as the door cannot be opened from the outside). I told my friend this, and he was just as puzzled as me. He suggested, "Maybe we should go back up and open the door?"

We started to make or way back up the stairs, when we heard a very deep bellowing voice say, "Go back!"

Well let me tell you we went from the 20th floor to the 14th floor faster than anything. To this day, I don't think that I have ever moved that fast.

When we got to my friend's apartment on the 14th floor, he was too shaken up to be around, so I went to my apartment on the 13th floor. My grandma noticed that I had been crying, and being that I have never lied to her, I told her everything. She scolded me for going up there, but added that no maintenance was being done on the building. She then asked me what the man looked like. After I described him, she asked me if I was sure that was what I saw. I found out later, that while the building was being constructed, numerous workers had died, and he was apparently one of them.

The building that I was living in had a closed circuit television system so if some one rang your buzzer, you were able to see who you were letting in. As a kid, when the cartoons went off, I would turn on the closed circuit screen and watch.

One night, I could not sleep and I turned it on (it must have been around two or three in the morning). I just happened to look at the screen, and I could make out a figure by the buzzers. The screen was in black and white, so I didn't really give it much thought. But whatever it was, stopped in front of the main door and looked at the camera. It looked as if it were looking right at me through the screen. I did not think much of it until our buzzer started ringing. Once the buzzer was going off it woke my grandmother. She told me, "Don't bother, it'll go away."

I did not realize until I was older, that this was a reoccurring thing that my grandmother knew about.

The hallways of my building were like regular hallways, in that if someone got off the elevator and was walking around, you could hear it. Sometimes, late at night, when I would be up with my gran, we could hear someone wandering the halls.

One evening I had to take out the garbage (I was a shy kid who did not feel comfortable with people seeing me in my pjs). This night, just before I walked out, I heard someone walking past the door. I waited until they passed so I could take out the trash. The footsteps passed, and then I opened the door. I didn't pay any mind to the fact that the sound of the footsteps continued, I just figured someone was going to the elevator. But after I exited the apartment, I looked around and saw no one—except, I kept hearing the footsteps. But now the footsteps sounded like they were heading towards me from behind! I ran back into the apartment and locked the door.

I looked through the peep hole, and heard the footsteps approach the door. I heard them pass but there was no one there. After that incident, I would never take out the garbage unless my gran was standing right at the door.

Anything Ghost Episode #134
May 29, 2011

The Haunted Evelyn Apartments
Mindy (Grand Rapids, Michigan)

I guess I should start by saying that personally, I experienced none of this. I'd like to think it's because the ghost in my apartment was fine with me living there. Although, it's most likely because I'm just not sensitive to those things.

At the time of these incidents, I was an art student in Grand Rapids, Michigan. The school I went to had no dorms and students generally rented apartments in the old houses that occupied the nearby historic district called Heritage Hill. My roommate Jessie and I lived in an apartment on the upper floor of a building called "the Evelyn." The building itself was a little creepy, but it was liquor store adjacent, it was big and it was cheap—so Jessie and I were happy. Not long after moving in, however, Jessie began to feel a little weird about the place.

The first incident happened one night some months after we'd moved in. Jessie and her boyfriend were asleep in her room when all of a sudden he sat bolt upright, and started urging her to wake up—never taking his eyes off the door.

"What..." She grumbled.

"There's something outside your bedroom" he said, staring at the door that was slightly ajar, so that a bit of the dark hallway outside it could be seen.

"What are you talking about" she said, sleepily, "go back to sleep"

"Listen to me!" He insisted, "There is a little girl outside your door right now! She was just playing with your cats! I could hear her."

This got Jessie up, but she was still fairly certain he had been dreaming. She got up and opened the door. In the hallway outside sat our two cats, but no little girl. The only thing odd about the situation was that the basement door, which was always locked, was slightly open. She closed it, but both she and her boyfriend were just a little too spooked to go back to bed, so they stayed up the rest of the night watching TV with the lights on.

They told me about this the next morning. I told them I'd heard nothing, and my bedroom was right next to theirs. I agreed with Jessie that he was most likely dreaming. Although, I do admit that he was usually a logical guy, and did appear genuinely scared. Jessie was uneasy after that night, as she'd had an inkling that the place was a little weird before that. After a while she eased up, though.

About a month later, I was busy studying for a final with a friend from school (whom, I should add, had never met Jessie's boyfriend, nor had she been told the previous story). It was late at night and we were memorizing slides for an art history test. I excused myself to go to the bathroom, and when I came back I found her staring, unblinking, at the kitchen table about ten feet away.

"How haunted is this apartment?" She asked me.

"Uhh... maybe a little?" I offered.

"I swear to you I just saw a little girl sitting at your kitchen table." She said. "She was there, and just as quickly she was gone. But I know I saw it."

Photo by Mindy (Grand Rapids, Michigan)
The Evelyn building

I looked at the table and saw nothing, but my friend was visibly shaken. She left not long afterward, and from then on always offered a public place to study.

Jessie and I never saw anything ourselves, but the fact that two visitors of ours said they saw something, made us curious about the history of the building. We were a little embarrassed to ask our landlord about this, so we didn't; but we soon recalled that when we first moved in, the landlord asked if we had any children. We were two college girls, so we thought his question was a little odd.

He told us, "I don't rent the upper units to people with kids—that's all." He added, "They can fall from the balconies."

Anything Ghost Episode #101
October 28, 2009

Funeral Home Ghost
Ethan (U.S.)

This is a brief recollection of a story told to me by my aunt, who worked in a small funeral home in our town. It was a few years ago on a day when my aunt was working by herself.

Being a very small operation, the funeral home only had a handful of employees, and on this particular day she was the only one in the building. It was around lunchtime, and her daughter, my cousin, had stopped by to bring her something to eat and to keep her company during her break. Also at this time, there was an elderly man whose body was in the process of being prepared for his funeral services the following day. To my understanding, the embalming process had already been completed a few hours prior, and the body was being kept in a small area in the back of the building.

My aunt and cousin ate lunch together and talked for a while. When it was time for my cousin to leave, my aunt walked with her outside the building to her car. As they stood only a few feet from the front entrance to the building (which was a large glass door), my aunt noticed my cousin staring at something with a perplexed look on her face.

"What is it?" My aunt asked.

"I thought you were here by yourself." My cousin said with confusion in her voice.

My aunt explained that she was indeed alone that day, since two of her coworkers were away on a business trip for the funeral home, and the other was out sick.

"How strange. Because, I swear I just saw an old man standing there in the entrance." My cousin explained.

My aunt said she felt a chill run down her spine as she shot a glance towards the doors to look into the small foyer behind the glass door—unable to see anyone.

My cousin further explained that the old man she saw had been wearing a green striped shirt with dark brown trousers and black shoes. Upon hearing this, my aunt recalled that when the body of the old man had been brought into the funeral home the day prior, he had been dressed in clothing that perfectly fit what my cousin had described. My aunt later found out he had died rather suddenly of an aneurysm while at home.

After seeing my cousin off, my aunt quickly finished her work for the day, and since business was slow for the time being, left earlier than normal. She hasn't told of anything similar happening since, but she won't soon forget the feeling she had when my cousin told her of what she saw that day.

Anything Ghost Episode #194
August 10, 2014

Haunted Hotel in Carmel-by-the-Sea - by Lex Wahl

On a visit to Carmel-by-the-Sea, California we booked a room at an old but stylish and comfortable hotel. We had just checked in, and I was removing the luggage from the trunk when I heard a woman call out, "Hello Mr. Wahl. Your room is ready. If the heat is on, go ahead and turn it off—I may have left it on."

I found this odd because it was fairly warm spring day. I waved and thanked her. We loaded our luggage into the old wooden floor hotel, and headed out to walk the dogs.

The room was located on the third floor, and there was either a long ramp that we could walk up, or we could use the stairs on the other side. On the way back from the walk, we decided to take the ramp, but as we approached it our larger dog (normally a very brave and fearless boy) stopped in his tracks and refused to go up the ramp. This happened the entire visit; so if we had the dogs with us—which was always—we had to walk up the stairs.

The first night there, we were watching television. I was entrenched in an old movie and my wife went to sleep. At midnight, I shut off the TV and the lights, and went to sleep.

"Creeeeeeeeek..." Within seconds of turning off the TV, the bathroom door moved what sounded like a several inches (it was dark, so I couldn't tell if it had closed or opened).

That night was chilly so we had the heater on. The room was quite warm, so before bed I got up and turned it off. In the middle of the night I heard my wife get up because the room was roasting—even though I had turned off the heater before bed. She turned it off, and went back to bed. I woke up at 6 a.m. and the room was once again so hot it was unbearable. I got up and once again turned off the heater—and opened a window to cool the room down. At that moment, it hit me: the housekeeper told me she had turned on the heat (on a warm day)...the heater was turning itself on during the night...we heard the bathroom door move by itself...our dog was afraid to go up the ramp...

We had a ghost.

My wife went out the next day and came back with a book about ghosts in Carmel-by-the-Sea. It was little more than local legends, and I didn't find anything about our hotel.

At that time "ghost hunting" was not yet an established hobby, and I was several years away from creating Anything Ghost, so on our departure I didn't have the nerve to ask the front desk about any history of ghosts in our room.

I left with a ghost story that I have never been able to verify.

We've stayed there a couple times since that experience, but not in the same room, and nothing unusual ever happened.

A Small Boy Ghost in Fallujah, Iraq
Kevin (U.S.)

I have a story for you that me and many other Marines experienced. In 2008 I was deployed to Fallujah, and as many know, there was a lot of blood shed there. At night we would stand post and look over a certain area of the city, these posts had names: I was on "Boulevard."

About a month in, I had a rotation with my buddy on Boulevard, and it was there that we began to see a small boy. He would stand in the middle of the street looking at us from about 100 feet away (at night it seemed faint). We would radio in to the Central Operation Command and ask if they could see what we were seeing by using their G-BOSS (the G-BOSS was an inferred camera mounted on a pole about 50 feet high). They radioed back that they saw nothing.

Eventually, everyone had seen this little boy. So one day me and my buddy decided to set out a patrol. When we left the wire we had eyes on the boy with guys on the post, and our team moved around the alleys in case it was an ambush. So, with eyes above we moved on.

When we got to the corner to where the boy should have been standing, we found he was not there, so we radioed in. However, we got no response, and the radio began making a strange high-pitched white noise. Each time we pressed the button it would make the same loud noise. So in fear of giving away our position, we stopped messing with the radio.

Photo by Kevin (U.S.)
Kevin and his Marine Regiment in Fallujah, Iraq.

We patrolled around for another hour to see if we could find the boy, but we found nothing. That night, the section of the city we patrolled was very quiet and eerie, and although there was a nine o'clock curfew in place, there still should have been people out. But that night, no one was out.

We quietly and smoothly made it back to our Forward Operating Base, and talked about what we experienced—feeling disappointed and foolish because we'd made a big deal of searching for the boy.

When the post was relieved from his post, he came down to talk to us about something. As he approached us, my first thought was that his face looked, I'd hate to say it but, as if he'd seen a ghost. The post told us that he had radioed in to us over and over but that his radio was making strange noises. He then added that when we got near the corner the little boy disappeared. But stranger yet was that when we patrolled away from the corner, he would come back—this cycle repeated as we patrolled the corner. It was as if the boy were playing a game with us.

I would like to dedicate this to my Brothers in Arms fighting, fallen and severed.

Anything Ghost Episode #161
September 1, 2012

The Cobbler's Ghost in Merseyside
Nicholas (U.K.)

I'm not a particularly religious person. I would even go as far as saying I'm an atheist. But I have had many experiences that some would describe as paranormal. The first story I'm going to tell you didn't happen to me, but to a friend's wife and daughter.

(Story 1)

I met my friend Jim while teaching art at a college in Merseyside, England in the early 1990's. We both taught the same subject but on different courses. After I'd known him for about a year, he bought a small Victorian semi-detached house that was in great need of renovation and modernization. The house had been owned by his great uncle who had just passed away. His uncle and his wife had been cobblers (shoe makers) all their lives; so while helping Jim clear the house, we came across a lot of shoe making ephemera such as tools, cast iron foot templates and leather cutters.

I moved on from my teaching post and moved out of the area in the mid nineties and lost contact with Jim. But in 1998, we met after both ending up working once again together in the same department—but this time at Liverpool University. Jim had met a girl in the period between and married and had a daughter. He was still living in the same house but now with his new wife and daughter. One night, Megan (his three-year-old daughter) was upstairs with her mother playing with a doll on her parents' bed. Megan had been preoccupied with her doll for some time but suddenly stopped playing, sat bolt upright and stared out of the bedroom to the stairs out on the landing. Megan's mother noticed the sudden distraction from her game and asked Megan, "What are you looking at Megan?"

Megan replied, "The lady on the stairs!"

Slightly alarmed at this response, but clearly able to see nobody on the stairs her mother asked, "What is the lady doing?"

Megan responded in a matter-of-fact manner without hesitation, "Making shoes!" The reply sent an icy shiver through her mother.

Photo by Nicholas (U.K.)
Nicholas' friend bought this small Victorian house that was haunted by the ghost of a cobbler.

The Notting Hill Flat
(Story 2)

The next story also happened in the 1990's while I was living in the Notting Hill area of West London. I was living with my girlfriend of the time in a flat above an antiques shop; the building was well over a hundred and fifty years old and prone to random noises—especially at night. I never felt uncomfortable in the flat, even when alone; but sometimes I would get strange feelings of what I can only describe as nostalgia. I have never really been a nostalgic person; in fact, looking back for me has never been a pleasurable thing—as I have suffered with anxiety and depression as a result of abuse during my time at boarding school. My girlfriend, however, would refuse to stay in the flat alone, and would give me a hard time if I ever had to go away. I always found this strange as she was a little bit witchy, and would often do tarot card readings.

One night in late September we had just gone to bed and switched the lights out, when the bedroom door swung slowly open. Like I said, it was an old building so I got up closed the door. I returned to bed but a couple of minutes later the door opened again. Thinking nothing of it, I once again got up and closed the door. Before I'd managed to settle down into bed the door swung open once again. My girlfriend voiced her anxiety of the place being haunted, but after closing the door for the third time my attention wasn't on my girlfriend bemoaning that the flat was haunted, it was on a barely audible cracking noise. I scanned the room for possible sources of the noise and my eyes finally came to a small, very delicate glass vase sitting on the shelf. I approached the vase; slightly turning my head to make sense of the noise; but on reaching the vase the noise faded. I lifted my hand and gently gripped the vase, and as I did so it fell into about five pieces. My girlfriend was by now in a state of some distress, but I played the whole thing down so not to freak her out even more—although, inside I too was in a state of alarm over the events of the previous few minutes.

My girlfriend moved out shortly after this, our relationship ended too after I found out she had been cheating. I think her fear of being alone in the flat was a reflection of her negative and dishonest attitude to life.

I think we experience way more paranormal activity than we care to believe; I recently was walking through a back street of Liverpool with my dog, Alfie. Alfie has a habit of suddenly stopping; when he stopped this time, I expected him to be sniffing like he usually does, but this time he was staring back at an old lady heading in the opposite direction. We hadn't passed anyone and there were no building exits on either side of the road, just twelve foot high walls.

Anything Ghost Episode #168
January 25, 2013

The Forgotten Lodger
Chris (Dublin, Ireland)

Before beginning it is absolutely imperative to this story that I provide some context for the kind of man my grandfather was. He was first and foremost a provider, and that is largely all he saw himself as. In forty-plus years of his working life, he never once voluntarily took a day off. As you might imagine, this is a man who had little or no time for games or stories, and was furthermore a brutally honest man who had even less time for lies and fabrications.

Photo by Chris (Dublin, Ireland)
Chris' grandfather stayed on the top floor of this building. While there, he experienced footsteps and knockings on the door.

Now the story. In his early twenties my grandfather was living in Dublin, and had been for a few years by this stage. He had been shipped off to the big city at fourteen years of age due to his family's inability to continue feeding and clothing him. He had found a job at that young age in a pub, and by his twenties was still earning the barest minimum to survive in a city already brimming with unfortunate souls. As a result of his meager income, he was forced to take lodging in a run-down hostel. Architecturally, the city of Dublin is a fascinating place—especially with regard to poorer areas. A city that was once the second city of the British Empire, swiftly fell out of favour amongst the elite in the early 19th century due to the revocation of certain privileges (self-governance being one), and resulted in a mass exodus of the wealthy upper classes of the country. Without the money to maintain their opulent properties, many became dilapidated and subsequently slums; and it was in one of these historic, but quasi-ruinous houses, that my grandfather found himself a bed on one fateful night.

Despite the unpleasant weather, the house was far from full and my grandfather was given a choice of rooms. As he was a light sleeper, and not overly keep to spend any significant amount of time with the other down-and-outs who might look for deliverance there, he chose the top floor room. This was not quite an attic room but, due to the particular design of the house, was a single room with its own staircase. My grandfather found the room adequate, and as it was only a place to dump his belongings and rest his head for the night (he spent very little time getting to know the place before laying down to sleep).

At some point, in the pitch black night, the silence of the building was shattered by a thumping on his stairs. The heavy, even footsteps ascended to his door and paused. Ever a logical man, my grandfather reasoned that he was not aware of the time and that the landlady, for whatever reason, may be checking the house before turning in herself. Although not fully convinced by this, my grandfather lay back once more to sleep. It was then that the footsteps began the descent from his room and he agreed that it must indeed have been the landlady after all. Before even being allowed to complete this thought however, the footsteps once again beat their thumping methodical tattoo upward towards his door once more, and paused... and knocked. Knocked is perhaps too polite a word for the action that reverberated his door in its frame. My grandfather by this point was absolutely livid with this drunkard or prankster that refused to let him rest—but decided to let the person move on again in the hopes that would be the end of it. Upon hearing the upward march for the third time, my grandfather threw back the sheets of his bed and padded to the door. If this person was so keen to get his attention he would give it face-to-face. When he heard the final stamp a foot from where he stood he threw open the door...to blackness. There wasn't a single living soul on that staircase. Whether through lack of funds or lack of a superstitious mind, my grandfather then made a decision that sends shivers down my spine: he closed the door and began to return to bed. Before he had walked half way across the room however, he received a blow right between his shoulder blades that was enough to send him sprawling the rest of the distance. The door had been closed. Not a sound had been heard after that last footstep. Whatever had walked up those stairs had entered the room when he opened the door. Once again my grandfather was left with no choice but to pull the blankets up to his chin and make the best of a bad situation. Whether he returned to sleep or not is unknown, but whatever happened, he never heard those footsteps again.

In the morning he sought out the landlady before leaving the house, and ran the events by her. She appeared ashen after the tale, but offered no explanation for the enigmatic footsteps.

A few years later, in a pub not far from the scene of this story, my grandfather struck up a conversation with an elderly man propping up the bar. While discussing local events, the story of his time in a nearby hostel returned to my grandfather and he recounted it to the man. In response, the elderly man confirmed the house in question and was, unlike the landlady, willing to offer some background; for the first time my grandfather felt a chilly unease. The old man informed him that during the Irish war of independence, the house in question had been the lodging of several Black and Tans (a brutal auxiliary British army unit infamous for various atrocities in Ireland at this time). At some point during their stay, an IRA unit entered the house and assassinated every one of its occupants.

My grandfather was a simple man, and this story was told once, and once only to my father in complete sincerity.

Anything Ghost Episode #200
December 22, 2014

Types of Phenomenon Commonly Referred to as a Haunting

A True Haunting

A True Haunting by an earthbound spirit will display both energy and consciousness. This means there will often be some type of response from the spirit when addressed. Some are here by choice. They realize they should not be here but they refuse to go on. This type of spirit will make itself known especially when upset with someone or something. They can be here to watch over a loved one, or because they refuse to leave what they consider to be theirs (possessions).

There are also those here because they are confused. Having been stripped of all physical attributes, they still maintain their mental capacities but in a confused state. They often find themselves replaying some habitual function that they performed while living. Usually this is a boring or mundane task which is now an obsession for the entity caught up in this cycle. This type of entity is normally oblivious to those in the physical world that it is intruding upon, although sometimes they appear to be conscious of the living. This entity is unable or unwilling to deliver any message.

Courtesy of Al Rauber. All rights reserved. Copyright 2016.

The stories that follow in Chapter 6 are not intended to be examples of the above described phenomenon.

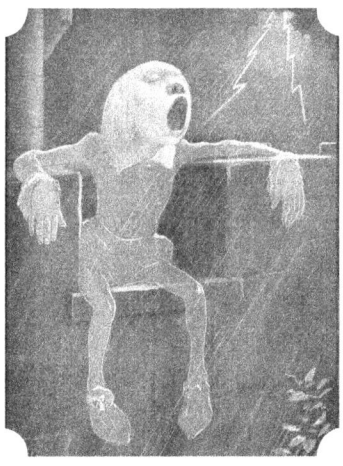

Public Domain.
Newell, Peter. 1862-1924.

6 | Chapter Six

- The Ghost of Llanrumney Hall
- Haunted Club
- The Ghosts of 39 Gordon Street
- The World War II Ghost
- The Haunted Projection Room
- A Hospital Ghost
- Mystery Man in a Hong Kong Hotel
- Red Hill Hotel
- A Ghost at Uncle's House

- Haunting at Silverwater Prison
- Unexplained Experiences
- The Shadow Man at Grandpa's House
- Haunted Family Summer Cottage
- The Breathing Dead
- A Haunted House in Nebraska
- Uncle Makes One Last Visit
- The Walking Lady of Auburn
- Loyola Marymount University
- She Followed Us Down from the Attic

The Ghost of Llanrumney Hall
Gareth (South Wales, U.K.)

When I was nine years old, I lived at and attended primary school in a small suburb of east Cardiff called Llanrumney in South Wales. It was a pleasant school, nice teachers but not a lot of students (being a village and all). In my class there were about fourteen students that were an even mix of boys and girls. The school didn't have an awful lot of money, so our class trips mainly consisted of visiting various sites around Cardiff (the Capital of Wales), and other landmarks of historic significance. This worked well for us as there were many really old and interesting places in South Wales that were within a reasonable distance to our school. I remember one morning our teacher told us we were going to visit a place called Llanrumney Hall.

The hall, now a pub, was built just before the 16th century. At that time it belonged to a Mr. Thomas Morgan. Thomas was a close relation to the famous Captain Henry Morgan who was a 17th century buccaneer and adventurer who battled the Spanish for control of the Caribbean. Henry, like Thomas, was born in Llanrumney and spent a lot of time at the hall during his life. To this day, many people have said that Llanrumney Hall is one of the most haunted places in the U.K., and that one of its most frequent deceased visitors is that of old Captain Morgan.

I remember it was a hot July afternoon, as our school's small white minivan pulled up at the grounds of the hall. I wanted nothing better than to jump out of the van and into the cool breeze. Our teacher and driver, Miss Brown, pulled open the side door of the van and took a step back—because she was almost knocked down by a group of over-excited kids tumbling out of the van. Once she and another teacher got us all under control, they decided to pair us up. I remember being upset that I wasn't paired up with my friend Darren—and even worse, I was paired with a classmate named Gemma. I was still at that age when girls weren't yet on my radar.

When we entered the hall, I was instantly taken back with just how old the place looked. Inside, a sunny L-shaped bar lead to an antique looking lounge that our teacher told us retained the original, ancient looking fireplace and a 300 year old Morgans table. I remember not really paying attention to her, and instead looking up at all the old paintings high up on the walls of people long gone—and wondering why nobody in olden times seemed to smile when being painted.

The central bar was built in mahogany and had a staircase behind that lead to B&B accommodation upstairs. This is where me and my classmates were put to relax and chat whilst our two teachers, accompanied by the owner of the hall, would take two pairs of kids and give them the tour. I guess they figured there was more chance of us paying attention in smaller groups.

I can recall playing on my digital Nintendo watch (that was a watch but also let you play a very basic version of Super Mario Brothers on it). Frequently, I would look up to see pairs of kids leave and then return looking completely disinterested by their experience. When it finally came to me and Gemma's turn, we realized it was only going to be me and her because we were the last—everyone else was waiting to go back to the school.

We were taken through the old corridors of the hall. Even as a child, I remember how narrow the halls felt; and there seemed to be different levels at every turn (which made us climb up and down plenty of stairs). At one point, the owner mentioned that there was a cellar on the grounds that we were heading toward, and it was where all the alcohol was kept (due to the cellar being naturally cold). Climbing down the ladder into the dark cellar felt like walking down into a freezer. The temperature change was very dramatic, and Miss Brown asked if we were alright. I nodded and slowly looked around. Small lamps dotted the big stone cellar that looked more like a tunnel. I looked at the ceiling, and to my surprise icicles were hanging down like pale white teeth between the old bricks.

As we continued slowly down the corridor, I looked back to see Gemma was now holding Miss Brown's hand, as the owner was going on about how they stored beer.

I walked into a room at the end of the tunnel. It was just as dark and just as cold. It was also completely empty except for one small candle on a chair in the corner. I remember Gemma's voice behind me saying, "Aren't you scared Gareth?"

I turned around and smiled amusingly. "Na," I said.

Miss Brown smiled and looked down at Gemma. "He's very brave," she said. I remember feeling good at this comment to the point that I started walking around obnoxiously showing how brave I was.

From there everything happened fairly quickly, and even now it's still a little fuzzy. Gemma started screaming loudly. I looked up and she had a look of complete terror on her face. What was worse was that she was pointing behind me. I looked over to the teachers who looked confused and concerned for Gemma. I turned around and to see what Gemma was pointing at and...I don't recall anything after that.

Whatever it was I saw down there nineteen years ago, I seemed to have blanked from my memory, because the next thing I recall was being escorted out of the cellar—clutching Miss Brown so tight, and screaming in a tone I've never heard myself scream before or since. I only remember Miss Brown in a panicky voice saying, "You're both so brave," as she tried to comfort me.

I don't remember the trip back to school, and I didn't really speak to Gemma about what happened. When I left the school to attend high school, I never saw Gemma again.

That is, until last year when I met Gemma on a Works' night out in the city. It was funny seeing her again. I have lived in South Wales all my life, so one would think I would have bumped into her in those nineteen years. She recognized me straight away as I approached her. She gave me a friendly hug, and I hugged her back. The rest of that night was spent reminiscing about school and all kinds of nostalgia. I couldn't bring myself to ask her about that day at Llanrumney Hall, because it would have felt too out of place to bring it up.

A couple of days later Gemma had added me as a Facebook friend, and we started to chat more. About a week later we were discussing the Paranormal Activity 2 movie, and I mentioned the corridor. To my surprise, she said, "I did wonder if you had forgotten."

I told her how much I remembered—up until when my mind blanked out—and to my surprise, she was able to fill in the rest.

She told me that as I was walking around the room, a mist started to appear right above the candle on the chair behind me. This was when she started to scream. Then she said a face slowly started to appear in the mist. This apparently was when I turned around to come face to face with whatever it was. She said that I stood perfectly still and just screamed. At that point Miss Brown ran over and pulled me back. That's when I turned and clutched her as hard as I could.

So that's my story. Me and Gemma are good friends now, we often meet up for coffee as we both work in the city. From time to time we will talk about what we think it was in that cellar, but I think I'm fine with not knowing. Maybe blanking out what I saw in that corridor has been a blessing.

Anything Ghost Episode #161
September 1, 2012

Haunted Club
Elizabeth (U.K.)

I worked in a live music venue for six years while I was 18-24; and while I was there, people reported a lot of strange happenings. The promoter would feel his hair being ruffled while standing watching bands; a female performer said someone pinched her behind while she watched alone from offstage during an instrumental number; and on one occasion a roadie went back to get something he had forgotten, and came back out very pale—saying he would come back in the morning. While working there alone during the day (cashing up, cleaning, etc.), the atmosphere would suddenly change and become very tense—and I felt like I was being watched. I wasn't the only person to experience this.

Two particular incidents stick out for me though. One of the girls who worked there once reported seeing a person walk across the venue and into a glass cabinet. This didn't make much sense to me as there was a thirty foot drop to the pavement at the other side, and therefore would never have been a door there in the past—so it didn't make sense that, with all their reputation for walking through walls where doors had once been, this would be what was happening. I put it out of my mind. A few weeks or months later, a colleague was in the staff area of the barber's shop downstairs, and reported that there was a beautiful spiral staircase that had been blocked off, and that ended in a ceiling. After some careful calculations about the layout of the building, we worked out where the staircase would have come out: in the cabinet where my colleague had seen the figure disappear.

The other story happened over a period of months or even years. It started, for me at least, one afternoon when I was on my own in the building; the manager, my boyfriend at the time, had nipped out to do the banking. I was sitting just out of view of the door as I polished the brass kick rail on the L-shaped bar. I heard someone walking towards me on the wooden floor, so I stuck my head around the corner of the bar to tell them that, unfortunately, we were closed. As I moved, I saw the bottom of someone's legs, wearing cream trousers and workman's brown boots walking towards me, but they disappeared as soon as I saw them. I put it down as an over-active imagination and carried on with my cleaning. I soon forgot about it, and because of that, never mentioned it.

I'm not sure precisely how long later, but at least a few weeks, my ex was in the office, cashing up and heard someone in the greenroom. He put his head around the office door to see who it was, as he had the safe open. He saw who he assumed was the promoter walk back into the main part of the venue; so he locked up, and went to say hello. On getting into the venue he couldn't find anyone, and the place was locked up. On phoning the promoter, my ex discovered he was still at home. I asked him what he had seen, only to be told "just the bottom of the legs as they walked out into the venue." Neither of us mentioned it to anyone.

A few months further on still, while talking around the bar one night after hours, one of the sound engineers, known as Fester (because of his resemblance to the guy from the Addams family), was telling us that one day he was moving some equipment in the cellars; and every time he walked past a particular sofa, he would see someone sitting on it out of the corner of his eye. Eventually he got fed up and told it to go (or words to that effect); and the next time he walked past, there was nothing there. I asked him what, exactly, he had seen. He replied that it was just someone's legs, out of the corner of his eye; and when I asked if he had seen what he or she was wearing, all he said he recalled seeing were pale trousers and dark brown boots. My ex and I just looked at each other. All three of us had seen the same thing: just legs, wearing the same thing. None of us had the impression of them being dismembered, just that we hadn't seen the rest of the figure.

We never did find out who it was, or why we only saw the legs.

Anything Ghost Episode #168
January 25, 2013

The Ghosts of 39 Gordon Street
Lee (Newport, Wales, U.K.)

This story is a recollection of my introduction to the other side and takes place over a number of years.

I live in Newport, in South Wales, U.K. The house where I grew up was a simple terraced house on Gordon Street. It dates back to around 1920. The first incident I can recall took place when I was about ten years old. I was a typical boy and my bedroom was very messy, with books and comics strewn all over the floor. One night, whilst lying in bed, I heard what sounded like paper rustling, as though somebody had stood on one of my comics. The footsteps continued, got closer to my bed, and finally stopped inches away. I froze in terror, unable to move. It took a few hours to sleep after that.

But the incidents really began piling up when I moved to the bedroom at the back of the house. Almost instantly, I would hear knocking coming from around the room. This culminated in one of the most terrifying moments of my life. One day, it sounded as though my bedroom door was being knocked on every hour or so. This continued even when the door was open. That evening, the door knocked as I was walking though the open doorway. Not taking it too seriously,

I knocked back and continued my journey towards the stairs. I stopped in my tracks when the door knocked again—this time louder. I don't know why I did it but I knocked back once more. Five seconds later, the door gave an almighty bang—as though somebody had thumped it with all their might. The door itself didn't move in the slightest, however. I ran down the stairs without looking back.

A few days later, I was in my room when I heard a voice calling my name. It was a quiet whisper at first—but it gradually got louder, then stopped as quickly as it started.

These incidents continued for about a year: objects being moved; loud noises coming from inside wardrobes, etc. What I found scariest, however, was the often intimidating atmosphere that would manifest itself. I could be in any mood, not necessarily thinking of ghosts, but I would freeze at the bottom of the stairs. However much I wanted to go upstairs, I couldn't bring myself to do it. I knew that something bad was waiting. It was at this time that I began to experience two different atmospheres: sometimes, when there was activity the room felt calm; at other times the room felt "evil." I don't like using the word evil, but it felt hateful—as though something despised my presence.

One morning, I decided I'd had enough and with tears streaming down my face, told my parents everything that had happened. I was now about thirteen, and felt like I had been haunted for three years of my young life. I told them that there were times I felt hated in my own bedroom by something that I couldn't even see. I told them about the night when somebody walked across my bed whilst I was lying in it—able to feel the mattress sink with each step. They dismissed it, and put it down to my overactive imagination. My father's face wasn't as convincing as his words however.

I also told my friends, David and Matthew, about what was happening; neither one believed me. But one summer changed their minds. We were enjoying our summer holidays, and spent a lot of time at each other's houses playing video games and board games. One day, David was at my house, and we were playing Streets of Rage in my room. When it was time for lunch, we turned the console and TV off, and went downstairs. When we returned 30 minutes later, both TV and console were turned on again. David began to believe me that day. The following week, David, myself and my brother played a mean trick on Matthew. My younger brother hid under my bed. David and I were telling Matthew about what had happened with the TV and Matthew was telling us how it couldn't be true. At that point, my brother grabbed his leg and made him scream. At the time, we found this amusing; but it would also add a chilling aspect to the next day's events—one that almost cost me two friends.

David and Matthew returned the next day and we were sat downstairs playing Monopoly. I had warned them both that it had been a morning of increased activity, and to try to ignore anything they heard. We were the only three people in the house, as my parents and brother had popped out shopping. About 20 minutes into our game, we heard the distinct sound of somebody walking upstairs. David and I looked at each other; Matthew laughed and said he wasn't falling for our tricks again. We assured him there were no tricks being played this time; He didn't believe us. The footsteps then walked down the stairs. At the bottom of the stairs was the bathroom, and a door leading to the living room (where we were playing). There was nowhere else to go. Matthew laughed again, and told my brother to just come in because he wasn't scared. I said to Matthew, "If that is my brother, he'll be on the other side of that door or in the bathroom. Why not have a look?"

He did, and found nobody. Neither of my friends ever returned to my house. It wasn't so easy for me to get away of course. But at least I was now coming to terms with the noises. That's what I thought anyway.

When I was 16 or 17 years old, things became more intense. Around this time, I would lie in bed and hear doors being slammed, and things being moved downstairs when everybody was sleeping. There was more anger now, too. It was also around this time that I first saw "them." One night, I awoke and found myself looking into the eyes of a young girl who was on the bed next to me. About twenty seconds later, she vanished. I didn't feel scared at the time—which seems odd now. A few nights later, I awoke and saw a man in a brown suit standing at the end of my bed, glaring at me. This time I felt fear: a fear that stayed with me a long time after he disappeared.

When I was eighteen, I moved out of the Gordon Street house to go to a university. I would still occasionally think about the things that happened to me whilst growing up there; and one day, over a few beers, I told my father of my experiences, again. I knew that he really believed me, as I was now aware that things had happened to him as well. He would never tell me what had happened because I was young, but now that I was an adult, he told me everything. His stories would make a great e-mail for this podcast. He told me about the young girl he would see around the house—especially in my room. He described her perfectly—his description matched the girl I had woken up next to. Then he told me that from time to time, he also saw a man in a brown suit; a man he described as being horrible. This reassured me that I wasn't just crazy, and that I had seen those things.

I put the incidents out of my mind. But a few years ago, things took a twist that I could NEVER have expected. I'm beginning to get goosebumps just typing this.

By that time of my life, 39 Gordon Street was owned by a different family. I had been having a recurring dream that I went back to that house to tell the new owners that they had a ghost. I had this dream every night for about two weeks. At that point, I became fascinated again and decided I had to do some research. I had to find out if that girl had ever lived in that house. I went to the Newport reference library and scoured local Kelly's Directories (for non-Brits: a Kelly's directory was released each year in each town, and lists ever house in that town, along with details of the house's owner—such as occupation). I found 39 Gordon Street, and found the house's owners. After searching through many copies from the 1930s and onwards, I realized that I was getting nowhere. As the young girl would not have owned the house—these books would not help me.

Taking a break, I picked up a random ghost story book called "Ghosts of Gwent" (Gwent being the county where Newport is situated) by Alan Roderick. I opened to a random page and dropped the book. Every hair on my body stood up and I was covered in goosebumps. The librarian even asked if I was okay. I nodded, but didn't feel okay. I read the first line in that story, again. The random story in the random book I picked up, read: "Gordon Street looks like a typical terraced street." I read the story, almost in tears of shock. I couldn't believe my eyes. The story told how in 1933, a man named Will Stephens had been visited by the ghost of a young girl. No prizes for guessing that the young girl's description matched what I had seen. Then I had a thought: I picked up the Kelly's directory for 1933; I looked at Gordon Street and found W. Stephens—he had lived in 40 Gordon Street, right next door; Our bedrooms were separated by one wall.

That same day, by coincidence, I saw my neighbour (a guy I hadn't seen for a few years) and I excitedly told him everything. He looked at me and told me that for the last few years, his young nieces and nephews had also seen a young girl in their house.

I hope you enjoyed my story as much as I enjoyed sharing it. I'll send some more as soon as I have permission from those involved. I hope to join a paranormal research group soon and would love to return to that house. If it happens, I'll let you know.

Anything Ghost Episode #135
June 12, 2011

The World War II Ghost
Steve (Kent, England)

I live in Kent, England. I'm married and am a very proud dad to a three-year-old girl. About 4 months ago, my wife was out late with friends, and my daughter was in bed; I was watching TV. Around 11.30 p.m., my daughter screamed and began to cry—I ran upstairs, and when I reached her, she said, "Dora screamed at me!"

I guessed it was a bad dream, and that Dora the Explorer (which all the little kids watched) was responsible. After a battle to get her to sleep again, all went quiet.

In the morning, I went to work, and later that day my wife called my phone to say our daughter was talking to the front door. When I asked who she was talking to, my wife replied, "Dora."

That give me a chill, and I began looking into what Dora was. I contacted a local historic website that gave a tiny bit of info, and left them some questions. The next day there was a reply waiting for me: a lady had read my inquiry and was concerned. We struck up a correspondence. She asked bits and bobs, and I would give her information as I knew it.

Time moved on, a week maybe. By this time, my two-year-old daughter would keep getting scared, and would always want to be carried all over the house. I would be the typical grown-up and tell her there was no one there. My daughter would reply, "She is there!"

One Sunday I was sitting at the top step of our staircase, and my daughter was at the bottom looking at something. She moved her eyes from mid staircase and followed something up towards me. When her eyes reached me there was a little icy breeze that moved up my left side.

I had kept correspondence with the online historians, and they eventually found a golden nugget: it was a letter that read: "1944. The Germans knew the war was going to be over, and Hitler decided to damage as much as he could. So a relentless shelling of Dover started." From a photograph they emailed me, I could see our semi-detached house had taken a direct hit from a shell. It was an aerial photo that I was sent, and the roof was smashed to bits. The letter continued: "Otherwise, there were injuries to my house, but the adjoining house had serious injury. Dora Smith, age 33."

That put the biggest chill ever all over me: my daughter was being shouted at by a spirit.

Anything Ghost Episode #145
December 11, 2011

The Haunted Projection Room
Matt (Suffolk, England)

First things first, I want to let you know that I'm a bit of a skeptic of the paranormal. But after having discussions with my girlfriend and my mum, I thought I would share some strange things that have happened to me.

For five years I worked as a projectionist at a cinema in Suffolk. Working in a small team of about six people and the long hours we would have to work, we often found ourselves working on our own for long periods of time—isolated from the rest of the cinema staff (who worked in the front of house, downstairs).

The projection booth was in an eight screen cinema, and the booth was just one long corridor with the projectors lined up on both sides. These were old 35mm projectors, so there was a lot of reflected light and noise from the film being pulled through the projector. The projection booth light was always kept low, so as to not disrupt the lighting in the actual theaters.

I would often draw the short straw, and would have to work the 5 p.m. to midnight shift—although, I would often not get out until closer to 1 a.m.

There have been many stories from many people that have worked there about hearing strange things, but not so much of seeing anything. That was about to change.

It must have been about 10:30 p.m. as all the projectors were running. I was sitting at the desk in the middle of the corridor filling out some paper work, when all of a sudden I heard a strange noise coming from one end of the booth. It was a strange clicking sound, but much too deep of a sound to be from the film. Like I said earlier, it was always noisy up there, so I didn't think much of it; I just leaned back in my chair and looked up. I didn't see anything out of the ordinary, so I went back to my paper work. Five minuets later, I heard the noise again from the same place. This time I got up and walked up the booth, to have a closer look.

Screen 5 (where the noise was coming from) was our only digital projector at the time—next to a 35mm. But it was the 35 that was running at that moment.

I had a look around; checked all the film paths; but everything was running fine, so I walked back to my desk. While walking back I heard the noise again, so I swung around to have a look. I must have been about five meters away when I saw something that will be burned into my brain until the day I pass. There was a figure of a man standing between the two protectors leaning out and looking at straight at me. It was like a shadow, but dense; I couldn't see through it; It was just black with no features; but I could feel it looking at me, and I somehow knew it was a man. As I said, he was behind the projector leaning out looking at me. I could see his leg his arm hanging down at his side, as well as his head. He didn't move, he just stood there. I just looked back at him paralyzed with fear. I snapped out of it and I ran as fast as I could out of the projection door (which was just to my right), down the long flight of stairs, and bolted for the manager's office downstairs.

Photo by Matt (Suffolk, England)
Projection room at the theater where Matt saw an apparition.

I opened the door and the manager, Dan (with whom I was friends), asked me what was wrong. I couldn't say anything at first; I had to catch my breath and compose myself. I told him, and naturally he thought I was just imagining it. I told him I was not going back up there alone. But even though I didn't want to, I knew I had to go up there at some point to shut everything down.

I was the butt end of Dan's jokes for the next few weeks, until something else happened—and Dan was there to witness it.

As projectionists, we had to check all the films before they went on to be shown to the public. One morning, I was going to preview a film and Dan came to watch them as well (this wasn't uncommon, depending on how much work he had). I started the film and went down with my clipboard to sit in the screening room and check the film. Really, we used to just like watching the films before they went on the main release. Me and Dan were sitting in the screen just chatting while the adverts ran through—as those needed to be check as well. When the trailers came on, we sat watching. When one trailer ended, there would be black on the screen for a few seconds before the next trailer started. Being that it was on film, we would sometimes see scratches and flickers on the screen, as well as darker patches where the emulsion on the film had worn—this created an ever so slightly brighter black mark on the screen. We were watching the black screen, when I saw something in the blackness between the trailers: it was a face—looking out at us. It was not a human face, rather a devil looking face. I sat there in shock not saying a word (thinking it was just a weird coincidence such as a lucky mix-up of odd patches from the film being arranged on the screen). But the odd thing was that this image wasn't moving—it wasn't flickering at all. As the images would sometimes do, the film would shift tiny amounts through the film trap on the projector, making the image flicker ever so slightly on the screen. But whatever we were looking at was perfectly still. I sat in stunned silence.

Suddenly Dan turned to me with a pale face, and said, "What the hell was that!?"

"You saw that!?" I said

"Yes!" He replied

We didn't say another word to each other until the end of the film. We agreed to come back in the screen when it was running to the public to see if we could see it again. As you can probably guess, there was nothing there.

These were the only two incidents I ever had at the cinema in the five years I worked there—I just feel it's strange that they happened so close together.

I remember hearing in one of your older podcasts about someone talking about shadow men. Hearing that it kind of prompted me to share this story.

As for the devil face, I have no idea. It was just something really strange that I saw, but I'm just happy someone else saw it as well—to rule out the idea of me going crazy.

I also remember a story that one of the supervisors told me about an old lady that lived in a house over-looking where the cinema is (before the cinema was built). They were planning to build the cinema, but had to make sure there were no strong oppositions. Everyone was happy for it to go ahead except for this one old lady—and that's what held back the cinema being built for so long (or so the story goes). She died and there were no longer any objections to the cinemas being built, and so it was constructed.

Anything Ghost Episode #168
January 25, 2013

A Hospital Ghost
Darren (U.K.)

I've worked in various hospital areas over the years, mostly as a cleaner. I've had odd experiences in many of them, but one building in particular stood out.

Judging from the architecture, this building dated from around 1910. It looked like it had once been a large house. But at the time the hospital had been acquired, it was a retirement home. The interior was a mix of old and new: some new additions had been added, but some impressive old features still remained—most notably a sweeping grand staircase near reception.

The first time I felt anything odd there, was my first evening. The physiotherapy department was at one end of the building, and it comprised of several rooms. Two of the "physio" rooms were separate and at the end of a narrow L-shaped corridor. The whole department had an unsettling atmosphere, but it was particularly strong in those two rooms. I felt I was being watched with disapproval, as if I had ventured somewhere I was not welcome. Still, I gradually got used to this feeling.

The first actual event was when I was cleaning one of the rooms at the end of the L-shaped corridor. It had a full-length mirror in it. I was alone, but when I happened to catch sight of myself in the mirror, I saw a woman standing behind me. She was staring right back at me from the reflection. I knew immediately she was the one who had been watching me. Her face was pale, her eyes were large and dark, but the striking thing was her hair: it was the deepest black—as if it sucked in all the light from around her. She seemed quite passive, not a threat exactly, but still disapproving of someone uninvited being in her room. When I glanced back, she was gone.

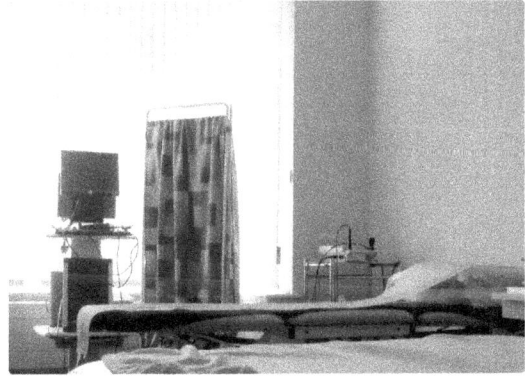

Photo by Darren (U.K.)
The room with the mirror. The mirror is not visible here.

The next time I saw her was bizarre. I was walking down the corridor to physiotherapy, when I saw a black form at head height gliding across. After a moment, I recognized it as hair—the deep black flowing hair of the woman I'd seen before; but this time without a head or a body. This disembodied hair seemed to go from the fire exit to the L-shaped corridor.

Photo by Darren (U.K.)
The L-shaped corridor going toward physiotherapy. The ghost glided across at the far end of this hall.

Another odd occurrence was the knocking noise in the basement. Nobody worked down there; it was used for storage. The elevator mechanism was down there too, but when I was alone in the building, that would have been dormant and silent. At first I attributed the knocking sound to heating pipes; but it sounded much more like someone banging on the floor from below—as if they were trying to get attention. Eventually, I noticed the noise started when I was upstairs and headed towards the back stairwell; it would get more frantic once I was down by physiotherapy. It started to creep me out a bit, and one day I asked aloud, for it to stop. It did—at least for a while. On a couple of occasions, I even got the courage to go down to the basement and look, but the knocking stopped while I was there.

I wasn't the only person to experience things in the building. Others had noticed the strange knocking; and some of the nurses spoke of seeing a man they called "the butler" around the grand stairs—and I think one also claimed to have seen a ghostly woman upstairs. Whether this was the same one I saw, I don't know.

Eventually the hospital sold off the building for redevelopment. Just before it was pulled down, I had a dream that still makes me feel uneasy. I dreamed I was in the building, but it was about 1920, and all the later modifications were gone. The place was empty. I wandered through the rooms, and saw a door I hadn't seen before. I could hear a weird metallic noise coming from it. I opened it, and it was a bathroom. The noise was coming from a washbasin. I approached, and listened. The sound was a distant baby crying, echoing through the pipes. I woke up with that noise still in my ears. It disturbed me. Perhaps I'm being overly romantic, but somehow I felt it was the voice of the building itself, crying out that it was dying too soon.

Photo by Darren (U.K.)
The grounds of the hospital after its demolition.

I watched some of the demolition, and the subsequent building on the site. The atmosphere had gone. I wonder if the people living there now ever see anything, but I doubt it. I get the feeling the building took its spirits with it.

Anything Ghost Episode #169
February 9, 2013

Mystery Man in a Hong Kong Hotel
Nick (Toronto, Canada)

This event happened in 1996. My parents and I vacationed in Hong Kong for a few weeks and stayed at the Excelsior Hotel in Causeway Bay (I do not remember the room number). One night, after a long day of trekking around Hong Kong, we all got ready for bed at around midnight. We stayed in a room that had one double bed and one single bed. My mom and I slept on the double and my dad slept alone in the single near the window. Since we had such a frantic day, my parents were immediately out cold. My dad is a big snorer, so he was as loud as a train once the lights went out. I had difficulty sleeping so I reached for my cassette player and played some music loudly into my headphones to drone out his noise.

> As of 2015, the Excelsior Hotel appears to be set for redevelopment into a commercial building.

Time passed and I still couldn't sleep. I checked the clock on the night stand and the time was showing 2 a.m. I was on my back and continued to look up at the ceiling with my music playing when I noticed at the corner of my eyes that my dad started to move. I didn't have direct sight of my dad cause my mom was sleeping beside me. So I had to lift my head up and turn slightly to look over at my dad on the other bed. At the time I was thinking he was probably up for a late night bathroom visit. But this felt different—eerily different. As I watched him get up from his bed, he moved in such slow-motion, that there seemed to be something off about it. The room was dark but there was enough light gleaming through the curtains for me to see his silhouette, but too dark to see any features on his face. He finally got to a sitting position on the bed and turned and faced me. He sat up and walked slowly between our beds and towards the window instead of the washroom. At this point I was worried because I thought he would be headed in my direction and to the bathroom. I took off my headphones and was about to say something to him, when suddenly I noticed that my dad's snoring was still loud and persistent. I looked over at his bed and I could still see my dad sleeping in his bed! At this point I was in full panic. I looked over to the mystery silhouette, and he was looking out the window. But when I looked at him, he started turning towards me again. I threw the sheet over my head and tried to wake up my mom by kicking her, but she did not budge. As I was under the sheets, I felt frozen and couldn't move.

I did not end up sleeping at all that night, and waited for the sun to come up before I found the courage to peer out from under the sheets. The mystery man was gone.

I told the story to my parents when we went for breakfast that morning. I didn't want to say anything while we were still in the room. We talked to the manager, and he said he had never heard of any paranormal disturbance in the hotel. He apologized and offered us another room. We ended up going to another hotel the next day.

Anything Ghost Episode #195
September 5, 2014

Haunted Hotels

Anything Ghost has shared many haunted hotel experiences over the years. Aside from the Bangkok, Thailand experience (previous page), here are some others that are included in this book:

- **Bangkok, Thailand Ghost Experiences**
    Anonymous (Minneapolis, Minnesota) - *Chapter 2*
- **Sidewalk Ghost**
    Roderick (Pas, Manitoba, Canada) - *Chapter 2*
- **Room 212 in the Stanley Hotel**
    Jenna (Toledo, Ohio) - *Chapter 4*
- **Red Hill Hotel**
    Alice (Bendigo, Victoria, Australia) - *Chapter 6*

Red Hill Hotel
Alice (Bendigo, Victoria, Australia)

This happened in 2002. I was running a pub when I was 23 in Chewton, just outside Castlemaine, Victoria Australia. By Australian standards it was a very old pub that was built in 1853 (so it was 149 years old at the time of my story). The cellar was divided into catacombs, and during the gold rush they were used as holding cells, and as a morgue; the pub itself was used as a courthouse for some time. The property had an old well out in the back that is filled in now, but still has the brickwork around it. It also had an old stable out the back, and if someone came though the town at dusk riding a horse, we had obligations by law to put them up for the night. It had so much history and character. I just loved it!

While cleaning up the office, when I first got the job there, I had a 16 year old girl helping me out. The office was in the first of the catacombs. The floor was dirt, and the walls were stone. As we were cleaning up, a heavy cold rush of air came in though the door. It felt like it just clung to your skin—I have never felt anything like it. The hair on the back of my neck stood on end. I looked over at the girl and asked, "Do you feel that?"

Photo by Alice (Bendigo, Victoria, Australia)
Carlton Pub in Chewton, Victoria Australia (built in 1853).

She just looked at me white as a ghost, and nodded her head.

I said, "Smoke time."

She agreed. So we walked up back to the bar near the old fireplace and had a smoke. She refused to go back in the office after that. I went in about an hour later, and it felt the like the room was back to normal.

Another time, I was up cleaning the kitchen and humming to myself. I said out loud, "I'd like to hear some music." I talk to myself out loud every now and again, just so I can hear something—because most of the time I was by myself for hours. Then, the radio on top of one of the refrigerators turned on. It was not tuned in to any station; it was just static, or white noise. I thought it was weird but didn't think much of it—I assumed it was faulty wiring as it was a very old place. So I walked over to the radio and had a look—it wasn't even plugged in! That freaked me out. As I picked up the cord, the static sort of faded away—it had only been going for about 30 seconds. I stood there a minute, then plugged it in, tuned it to a station, and went back to cleaning. I know I wouldn't believe it if someone told me that story, but it's true never the less—it happened to me.

I did have to stay the night at the pub one night, but never again. I had always felt uneasy in the resident's area—even during the day. There was a heavy feeling there, and a feeling of being watched. We had an event that day that was going to be running until late at night. So knowing this, and thinking I might have a drink after the night winded down, I brought my sleeping bag and pillows. I knew the beds in the residents would be taken up, so decided to sleep on the floor. That was the worst night I have ever had. I didn't sleep a wink. I just kept my eyes open and stared into the dark room, feeling like someone, or something, was watching me—not only in front of me, but behind me as well. I did not feel welcome there, at all!

One night, I had closed up the pub, and it was about 11.30 p.m. I was waiting for my brother to come and get me, and I found the bar was too cold. There was a fire dying down in the bar room, so I walked into the pool room and sat on the stairs to keep warm while and I looked out the window and into the street. The street was dark because there were no streetlights. When in the pool room, if you're standing next to the pool table, you can't see over the bricks to look through the window, so that's why I was sitting on the stairs waiting to see my brother's car headlights. As I was looking out, I got a really cold feeling—the same cold I was talking about earlier. I didn't turn around, but I looked at my reflection in the window. Behind me there was a tall man who was wearing a hat. I didn't take much note of what else he was wearing, but to me he appeared to also be looking out the window. I stood up slowly, walked down the staircase and out of the pool room. As I was leaving, I took a slow look over my shoulder toward the top of the stairs, but there was no one there.

I waited in the cold bar until my brother showed up.

Alice pointed out that this photo appears to contain a shadow standing in the room above the stairs (where she saw the man standing behind her).

Photo by Alice (Bendigo, Victoria, Australia)
Left: Looking through the door down into the cellar.
Right: the stairs where Alice saw a man behind her.

I never really told anybody about this until about two years after it happened. I was scanning some photos into my computer, and came across some of the ones I had taken in the pub. One photo was a shot looking down into the cellar. In the photo, you can see the stairs that I was sitting on while waiting for my brother; and that was where I saw the man in a hat standing behind me. In that photo, you can see a black shadow in the back.

Anything Ghost Episode #211
September 5, 2015

A Ghost at Uncle's House
Claire (Sydney, Australia)

When I was a little girl, from about the age of five until maybe twelve, I used to spend a lot of time sleeping over at my uncle's house while my parents traveled on business. My uncle was unmarried and had no children, so it was just he and I in the house during these visits.

The house was old, built at the turn of last century, and had creaking wooden floorboards and very ornate (but heavy) glass sliding doors. It sat on a very large block of land, so the backyard was enormous. Sort of to the left of the yard (behind the main house) sat an old, very small cottage. My uncle used the cottage as an office, but he told me that originally it had been built as a lodging for the housemaid that looked after the property back around the 1900's. The house was absolutely gorgeous during the day. Sunlight would stream through the many large windows and birds would chirp in the backyard trees. At night, however, the vibe was completely different.

A couple of times my uncle would leave me alone in the house while he visited his elderly next door neighbour. He went every day at around 5 or 6 p.m.—just when the sun was setting or had just set—to check on her and to make sure there wasn't anything she needed. He was never gone for more than 10 minutes at the most. Whenever he left the house though, I would immediately get a sense of dread. I felt like I could feel something in the house…some sort of creepy or eerie presence…and it was watching me. My mind didn't immediately go to ghosts—I'm not even sure I knew what they were at that age—instead, I always suspected that someone was watching my uncle leave in the evening (like they were hiding in the bushes or something), and that they were trying to break into the house to steal things while he was gone.

I'd hear odd noises: like someone was walking up and down on the wooden floors, or rustling around in the kitchen; and sometimes, if I was feeling brave, I'd yell out, "I know there's someone here. Stop it!"

Then the noises would stop. No matter what though, I still felt that sense of being watched.

When my uncle returned home (as I said, he was usually only gone for ten minutes), I'd immediately relax and the sense of dread would ease. We'd have dinner, maybe watch a little TV and then he'd put me to bed and read me a bedtime story. The room I slept in was very large. It was in fact the master bedroom. I remember asking my uncle why he didn't sleep in it himself. He told me that he felt comfortable in the smaller bedroom, because he liked the huge picture-window in there that faced the front garden.

I never felt comfortable sleeping in that room. My uncle had a small portable radio, and often when he put me to bed he'd let me have the radio under my pillow, playing a little soft music. I found that it helped me sleep and it made me less afraid of the dark. Other times he'd leave the hallway light on for me (which illuminated my room slightly if I left my door open), and this was on a timer that would switch the bulb off after twenty or so minutes—usually after I'd fallen asleep.

One night, when I was about eleven, I was lying in bed and just could not fall asleep. I didn't have my radio and I had to keep getting up out of bed to switch the hallway light back on whenever the timer ran out. After about the third or fourth time I got up to switch the light back on, I decided to just leave it off—sure that I would soon be able to fall asleep. What happened next was very strange. I remember lying in bed, still no closer to sleep, when I heard very distinct footsteps walking up the hallway in the direction of my bedroom. I could hear the creak of the wooden floors and a rustling noise—like the kind people wearing jeans make when they walk. I lay frozen in my bed for a few minutes. The footsteps seemed to go on and on, and got louder and louder, but they kept going as if the hallway was a mile long and the person—or thing—never actually reached my doorway.

After listening to this noise for a few minutes, I decided to get out of bed and go into my uncle's room (his was directly opposite mine) to see if it was him making the noises. I turned on my bedroom light and crept towards the hallway. The noises stopped when I got about halfway to the door. I looked down the hallway. Nobody was there. I opened the door to my uncle's room and saw that he was in bed, fast asleep, so he wasn't the one making the noise.

Convinced now that burglars were in the house, I shook my uncle awake and told him what I'd heard. He got out of bed and checked all the doors and windows. They were locked. We looked under furniture, in closets, anywhere someone might be able to hide, but there was nothing. He told me that I must have been dreaming and that I should go back to bed. I said that I didn't want to sleep in that room; so he pulled out a mattress for me, and let me spend the rest of that night on the floor of his bedroom. I continued to hear weird noises—the sound of the glass doors sliding on their tracks, and footsteps—but felt more secure in this bedroom, where at least I thought my uncle could protect me.

The next day I went around the house checking for anything that could have made the original noise that I'd heard. I turned on ceiling fans, walked over the exposed floorboards, looked for any secret entrances where someone might have been able to break in. I didn't find anything, and I couldn't recreate the noise that I'd heard.

Later that day I went with my uncle as he visited his neighbour. Thankfully my parents came that night to pick me up. I told them what I'd heard, and their reaction was a little puzzling. They didn't completely dismiss that I'd heard something, but they did say that children have overactive imaginations and that I must have been dreaming.

I stayed a few more times in that house and every time I did, I refused to sleep in my room or to be left alone. When I was 12, my father got a new job, meaning that I no longer had to sleep over at my uncle's, and things calmed down.

Years later, when I was about 20, my mother told me that there was a rumor that my uncle's house was haunted, and that that's why the previous owners before him had moved out. They had never told me this as a child because they didn't want to scare me, and because my uncle didn't believe in the legend at all. My mom said that the ghost was a woman who'd built the house—a widowed piano teacher—and the legend was that she'd only show herself to women. By coincidence, my mother's hairdresser (a good friend of ours), told me that she'd once stayed in the house when it was owned by someone else, and one night while she was sleeping in the master bedroom, she saw the ghost of a woman standing near her bed. She said the woman watched her for a moment, smiled and then faded. Then she claims she heard footsteps walking up and down the hallway.

I never saw the ghost in that house, and I hope that I never do. I do hope, though, that she's a good, kind spirit. I'd like to think that she's just watching over things and making sure my uncle takes care of the home that so she so loved.

Anything Ghost Episode #159
July 15, 2012

Haunting at Silverwater Prison
Edwina (Sydney, Australia)

This story comes from a friend of mine who recently got out of jail for a petty crime (I won't go into the details of the crime). He told me a story about what happened to him when he was "inside" that I thought I would share with you. As part of his sentence, he was to serve out his time in the Silverwater prison. In the early settlement days, Silverwater prison used to have hangings of both aborigines and convicts. Unfortunately, he was assigned to a cell in the exact location where the hangings occurred.

The prison itself was known to be haunted, and this was often spoken of between cell mates and guards. Many of the cell mates would complain to each other of loud thumping noises in the night that sounded like a heavy man running up and down cell blocks. There was also the sound of keys shaking (keys were no longer used to open the cells).

The footsteps running across the flooring outside the cells were a regular occurrence—and the sound would end right at my friend's cell. This sound was followed by a falling sound, then a loud thump. He believed it was the spirits of deceased prisoners who were hanged at the prison; and the thumping sound was the body hitting the ground of the pit where the bodies would fall (this pit was where his cell was located).

One evening, my friend was lying in bed. He shared the cell with a blonde haired, quiet Irishman who would snore heavily in his sleep. He was nearly asleep himself, when out of the corner of in his eye he saw what appeared to be an elderly aboriginal man with a heavy beard. The spirit was sitting next to him (my friend was on the lower bunk). He automatically responded by turning his body towards the unknown visitor to get a proper look. Acting in panic, after seeing what it was, he forced his fist toward whatever or whoever it was. As his fist met the spirit's face, its expression turned to shock—its eyes widened and mouth opened. The head lifted back as to avoid my friends strike, and upon meeting its face the spirit almost appeared to be sucked back—as if the fist had met its face and then simply disappeared in a backward fashion into thin air.

One of the guards was speaking with him about all the different strange phenomena that took place at Silverwater prison; the guard told him a story about one day when he was in the changeover period of the shifts. The guard walked out and said "see ya" to one of his colleagues who was there to take over his shift. He noticed his fellow guard was dressed in uniform, but it was that of an era from a long time ago. He later confirmed it to be of the 1950-60's, and was presumably the spirit of one of the guards who died there while on duty. After realizing something odd about the uniform, the guard said he looked back after passing him, and watched as he began disappearing about 5 to 10 meters behind him. Perhaps it was the same spirit who was jiggling his keys: making sure everything remained in order in the prison he once worked in, and finally passed away in.

Anything Ghost Episode #166
December 6, 2012

Unexplained Experiences
Desmond (Tasmania, Australia)

I grew up in a small tin-roofed house deep in the bush of Tasmania. While living there I experienced phenomena I can't explain. Not unexplainable, just unexplained. Our house didn't have a particular paranormal feel to it. I didn't get cold chills or feel like I was being watched—well, at least not most of the time.

My first story begins when I was ten. It was a chilly evening and I was comfortably snuggled in my bed reading a book. My parents were out shopping in town. Now just for logistics, my bedroom was nearly adjacent to the front door of my house. I was deep into my book, when I suddenly I heard voices from outside.

"Great," I thought, "mum and dad must be home!"

I can still remember the voices, and in retrospect, I can remember why I thought they belonged to my parents. One voice was extremely low, almost guttural, and the other was shrill and annoying. I couldn't hear what they were saying but I could clearly make out syllables. So there I sat in bed waiting for my parents to come through the front door any second.

My parents arrived home an hour later.

My second story occurred later that year. It was a summer evening, and I was fast asleep. I was having the most wonderful dream, which unfortunately I can't remember now. I abruptly woke halfway through this dream. I scanned my room and standing at the foot of my bed was the figure of a man. I remember describing it to one of friends later on as a gray shadow. The figure stood there silently watching me with neither good nor bad intent. As I was only ten, I was terrified so I pulled the cover of my bed and closed my eyes—forcing myself to fall asleep. The next morning I told no one.

My third account isn't really a specific story but rather a menagerie of stories from ages ten to twelve.

I remember at twelve, hearing footsteps outside every weekend. It was a constant and terrifying factor to me: every weekend I would hear audible human footsteps coming up my gravel driveway or walking around the deck. This always occurred at around midnight when the rest of my family was fast asleep. I also remember a story when I was nearly thirteen. It may not qualify as a ghost story but I still found the ordeal creepy. I was a at the end section of my house where the television was. Just to give you a mental picture, this room was large; at the end of the room there was a vast array of windows for sunlight to flood in. It was night and I was alone in the room watching a game show. Suddenly, I heard a tremendously loud sound. It sounded exactly like a jet plane flying. Then even more bizarrely the room filled with green light. I was terrified. I ran out of that room faster then a bullet. I kept running until I met the rest of my family in the living room. I plunked myself down on a couch and stared at my family. They were all just staring at the television like nothing had happened at all. That was the eeriest bit. I still haven't told them what happened to this day.

These experiences may sound strange, but compared to where I live, these are standard. In Tasmania we have a long gory history of pain and bloodshed. Everybody has a story, and these were mine.

Anything Ghost Episode #181
September 23, 2013

The Shadow Man at Grandpa's House
Barbara (Monterey, California)

When I was growing up, my grandparents lived in a rambling, old Victorian house in Montgomery, Alabama. It was a house that had grown over the years with its occupants. I can still picture the house. If you conjure up a stereotypical southern Victorian haunted house, this is the house that would appear. It was white with big windows and a large front porch and rocking chairs. Walking in, you find yourself in the center hallway, which bisected the house neatly with three rooms on either side of it. The ceilings were very high and domed in the hallway. Interestingly, the ceiling was a painted mural of a landscape done in a classic style. The doors off of the hall were very tall, with transom windows over the top to circulate air on hot summer days.

During the Great Depression, each of the six rooms had been a separate apartment, but it was all one habitation now. The original house, built in the 1800s, had no indoor plumbing, so the two bathrooms, with their classic claw foot tubs had been tacked on to the side of the house. There had been a screened-in porch that wrapped around the back of the house (at some point the screens had been replaced with windows, which turned it into an indoor room with the feel of a porch). The opening into the adjoining dining room still had a door that belonged on a back door, with a window and lacy curtains. The kitchen, off of the other side of the porch-room, was large and had an old fashioned stove and a corner closet with mirrored doors.

I loved my grandparents very much, but I dreaded our twice-yearly trips to Alabama to visit them, because of the house. I never mentioned how I felt to my grandparents, because I didn't want to hurt their feelings, but I used to try to convince my parents of what I saw and felt in there. They didn't believe me.

From the time that I was very young, I remember being afraid of "the man."

We would walk through the front door into that domed hallway, and I would catch the shadow of a man at the end of the hall. I sometimes saw or felt a female presence, but the man radiated possessiveness.

At night, I slept on a sofabed right next to the door that lead to the porch room. I was afraid of the dark, so my parents would leave the light on in the bathroom that was just off of the porch area; its light would filter through the lacy curtain over the back porch window. It was certainly creepy: I would watch the curtain move in unfelt breezes; and watch the shadows shift, while footsteps moved restlessly across the porch. I knew everyone else was asleep.

Soon, I would duck my head under the covers—even when it was August and 90 degrees out—to avoid the eyes I felt watching me. While under the covers, I would sometimes feel a depression in the bed—as if a body sat down on the edge—then the whisper of fingers would run across my head. This was not the man, I was certain about that. This felt like a mother seeing to her nervous child. I wouldn't look to see who was touching me because I couldn't decide whether it was worse to see someone there, or not to see someone there.

The house had lots of little hidden corners, and my brother and I were always finding some hidden treasure or other. A real jackpot was finding a box of old comic books that we would read sprawled on the floor on the porch during rainy summer afternoons. Sometimes we found relics from past inhabitants such as old glass bottles and paintbrushes. I never knew anything about the people who used to live in that house, but that changed when I was eight.

Right around that time, the city built a freeway right next to my grandparent's house. I think that caused the possessive spirit of the man to become more active. I had felt him and saw his shadow as soon as we entered the house during that visit. At night, the footsteps became relentless. One night, I held my breath in fear as I felt the man hovering over me oppressively close (this was not the mother figure I was used to), until eventually, the feeling dissipated.

The next morning, I was eating breakfast alone in the kitchen when a man walked out of the porch area and crossed the room—as I stared open-mouthed. He opened the mirrored door to the closet in the corner, and finally looked at me warningly, before he disappeared into the closet, closing the door behind him.

He was tall and gaunt with gray hair, and wore old-fashioned clothes. He was very real and yet a watercolor version of reality—a solid mist. When he looked at me, I knew that this was him—the man, in the flesh, so to speak.

My grandmother returned to the kitchen, and I decided to ask her some questions.

"Grandma Pat, what's in that closet?" I asked curiously.

"Oh, just some jackets and the like. I try to keep it clear in case I want to use the passageway."

"Passageway? What passageway?" I asked.

"Why, back there, under the shed, there's a room. It hasn't been used much since the painter lived here."

My grandmother proceeded to tell me about a painter who lived in the house. He was the one who painted the front hall, and he had kept his painting supplies out in the secret room under the old shed in the backyard. The room had probably been built for another purpose, originally, such as for the Underground Railroad.

I had many other experiences in that house before my grandparents died and the house was demolished. Somehow, having an identity for the ghost made it less frightening. It was very sad to think about that beautifully imposing house being demolished. I still wonder what happened to the man once his home was gone.

Anything Ghost Episode #194
August 10, 2014

Haunted Family Summer Cottage
Christine D. (Gatineau, Quebec, Canada)

The following are two of my sister's experiences that occurred in our haunted childhood home. She would have been between the ages of five and twelve. The bedrooms in the home were located on the lower floor and were the most active areas, in regards to the supernatural—my sister's room was definitely no exception.

Many nights my sister would hear the sound of invisible heavy footfalls pacing back and forth along the side of her bed. She sensed the presence was that of a man that meant her harm—and she could feel him intensely staring at her as he paced. All she could do was stay hidden in fear under her blankets.

One night, she became so tired and frustrated that she told it out loud to go away. Only moments after she said this, she felt this "thing" leap onto her body. She struggled with the heavy evil energy that began to squeeze the air out of her lungs. After some time, she managed to squeal out a noise to call out for help. My parent's room was not far, and often my mother left her bedroom door open. This proved useful because my mother heard my sister and got up to see what was the matter.

When she entered the room, my sister recalled that the energy swiftly jumped off of her. However, she still had to catch her breath so she could explain to my mother what had happened. Luckily, she never had this specific thing happen to her again—although, the pacing around the bed occasionally happened from time to time.

Another time, my sister was sitting on the side of her bed tying the laces of her running shoes. She suddenly felt drawn to the dresser mirror over to her left. When she turned her head, she saw a disembodied face of our deceased grandmother (of whom my sister had been very fond). Initially, the expression on the face was gentle and kind, but in a matter of seconds the face began to twist, and turn, and transform into something else—something that she knew was not our grandmother. She quickly ran out of her room without looking back.

The Breathing Dead
(Story 2)

I have had many experiences that can be classified as supernatural. With the exception of a few, most have not been frightening. The following experience is one of the exceptions.

When I was in high school, I would often hang out at a best friend's house. One night, I decided to sleep on her comfortable family room sofa situated in the home's finished basement/family room. I had a restful night's sleep since I was the only one in the room. The door closed so it was dark and quiet—just as I like it. At 7:00 a.m. I was awoken when her mother made some noises upstairs before leaving for work. After her mother was gone, I turned over to face the inside of the sofa to prepare for a few more hours of sleep. It was now extremely quiet in the home since it was just me and my friend (my friend was in her bedroom with her door closed in another part of the house). I had my eyes shut, and was thinking about things.

Then I heard a faint sound. The noise started to get progressively louder and closer to me; perhaps a foot or two from me now, the sound loomed over my head. I soon realized it was the sound of heavy, labored breathing. I knew there wasn't an actual living person in the room since that would not be possible. I could, however, strongly sense that this "breather" was an elderly male presence that was extremely angry with me, and I had no idea as to why. As his breathing intensified, I practically stopped my own breathing out of fear. I slowly slid the blanket over my head in hopes he would go away. Nevertheless, I continued to endure minutes more of this presence that seemed to be struggling to breath—all the while it continued a piercing gaze down on me. In my mind, I began to pray for it to leave. The breathing did not stop suddenly, but rather it faded until it was finally gone.

I stayed frozen in my position on the sofa for some time, until I felt it was safe to come out from under the blankets. I then quickly turned on all the lights and the television to make myself feel better.

My friend woke up and joined me about an hour or so later. I told her what had happened. She nonchalantly said, "Oh ya, it might have been my dead grandfather. He had breathing problems before he died."

Apparently, her grandfather had problems with senility as well. He died when he fell out of his bed and hit his head on the bedside table. My friend owned that very same bed, bedside table, and much of his living room furniture—including the sofa I had been sleeping on.

Anything Ghost Episode #194 & #195
August 10, 2014 & September 5, 2014

A Haunted House in Nebraska
Michael (Lincoln, Nebraska)

Many members of my family and myself have had experiences with the paranormal. I've often wondered if we were susceptible to this, or if we were simply lucky or unlucky to be seeing and hearing what we've seen.

I am just going to go with one example of what I personally experienced in an apartment house near Weslyan College in Lincoln. It was 1987 and I was 11 years old. My brother and I shared a bedroom and the bed. We always took turns sleeping on either side of the bed, so one could be near the fan that ran all night. On this particular night, I remember being restless and seemingly excited for something the next day (my birthday or Christmas, or something). My brother was a heavy sleeper, and its was very difficult to wake him.

As I was lying in bed, I saw a woman walk through the bedroom door from the living room. She resembled my mother very much: long dark hair, about 5' 3" and wearing what looked like one of the novelty night-shirts my mother used to wear. As she walked into my room, I sat up and said out loud, "Mom?"

No response.

I don't actually think she was making her way towards me, until I said again "Mother?"

Then she turned and headed her way towards me. As she got no less than two feet away from my bed, she simply vanished. At that point I screamed for my mother, who came in and convinced me that I was dreaming—but I knew I was not.

I won't go into everything that happened in that house. But just one more thing. My mother would have a recurring nightmare in which she would wake up and the kitchen would be on fire. Well, we later found that the house burned down no sooner than two weeks after we moved. The landlord told us that the only part of the upstairs that had any damage was the kitchen.

I later did some research and found that the house was once a hospice building.

I still find myself going back to the spot where the house once stood, and I always feel a presence there. I've never asked anybody living in the new apartments if they've had any experiences. Maybe someday I will.

Anything Ghost Episode #164
October 25, 2012

Uncle Makes One Last Visit
Shannon (Layton, Utah)

This isn't a story that happened to me, but to my younger sister in West Jordan, Utah. It occurred two years ago, last January, about a week after my uncle had killed himself.

My uncle Brent had struggled with drug addiction and alcoholism for most of his adult life—and had overdosed many, many times before he died. He had become increasingly depressed over the last couple of years before his death, and although he had been doing well at times, his improvement slowly began to slip.

After his overdoses and subsequent hospitalizations, he had stayed with my grandmother for a while. Even after moving in with her he tried twice more to kill himself with prescription meds. A couple of months after he moved in with my grandmother, he decided he was feeling good enough to move into an apartment of his own. My grandmother, still being very worried about his mental state, would go visit him every day. However, one morning, after uncle Brent had been living on his own for about a month, my grandmother entered his apartment to find he had hung himself.

Me and my sister were still living with my parents at that time. My parent's bedroom was on the main level, and my sister had a bedroom in the basement—which was very large and fully furnished. My parents were the only people living in the house at the time.

The staircase that lead down to the basement was on one side of the basement, and my sister's room was on the opposite side of the basement; so it was quite a long walk from one side to the other.

On the night of the incident, my sister was asleep in her room with her West Highland Terrier named Cooper sleeping at the foot of her bed. She was awakened by the sound of footsteps in the basement. My parents had just put new, very shaggy carpet throughout the basement that made a distinctive crunch noise when walked on. My sister, half-asleep, didn't think much of the noise and assumed it is my mother walking around cleaning up, or getting something out of one of the other basement bedrooms. It was still dark outside, but being January, this wasn't unusual for the morning hours. My sister then noticed that Cooper had also been awakened by the noise and was looking towards the door as if listening. My sister then listened carefully to the footsteps for a few minutes more. The footsteps seemed to be walking very close to her room. She was expecting our mother to enter her room to talk to her or peak her head in the door, but suddenly the footsteps stopped. Silence.

My sister checked the time by grabbing her cell phone from the bedside table. She flipped the phone on and noticed it was only 3 a.m. At that moment she had an intense feeling that our uncle Brent was standing outside her bedroom door. She laid quietly in her bed terrified for the next few hours. Eventually, she heard my parents walking around upstairs.

She asked my parents if they had come downstairs that night, but was told they had been asleep the entire night.

We discussed it, and believe that it was our uncle coming by for one last visit before he passed on to the other side.

Anything Ghost Episode #162
September 18, 2012

The Walking Lady of Auburn
Brandon (Auburn, New York)

In my hometown of Auburn, New York, almost everyone is familiar with "the Walking Lady." Rumor has it that if you go down Beech Tree Road late at night, and if you're lucky, you'll see the ghost of an elderly lady walking along the side of the road carrying an old oil lantern and an umbrella.

The road itself is already creepy, being a connecting route between towns, and very set back between wide open fields and thick forests. One night, my friends and I were going down Beech Tree at about midnight when we saw the lady walking alongside the road toward our car. We sped by her, all astonished to have actually seen her. Forever the skeptic, the driver of the car insisted we turn around, so he could get another look, and convince us that she was a normal, human lady.

We pulled into the very next driveway, only a few hundred yards down the road, turned around, and drove back down the road and she was gone. Completely gone. We went on for a few miles and saw nothing.

A few weeks after, my girlfriend and I were walking down the same road at night, when we saw the lady walking toward us—maybe 300 or so yards away.

We freaked out and ran back to the house we were walking from. When we looked back down the road she was only maybe twenty feet from us—a distance she covered in a matter of maybe ten seconds. Too scared to even try to walk again, we ran back to my friend's house where we wound up spending the night.

Anything Ghost Episode #194
August 10, 2014

Loyola Marymount University
Ed (Bellflower, California)

My experience happened a long time ago while I was a student at Loyola Marymount University in Los Angeles. It was during Christmas break, and at Loyola, our Christmas breaks were of an unusually long duration. I lived in an on-campus apartment complex with three other guys. Our apartment was in the middle of three floors, with the bottom floor dug below ground level.

I had come back from break early and was set to have a couple of weeks to myself there before everyone else returned. The first night I got there it was a cold and windy night, so I decided just to stay in and have a quiet evening. I decided to make myself some dinner so I went to the kitchen and started frying up some food. To fully appreciate what happened next, you must know that the kitchen was to the left of the front door. If you were at the stove, your right side would be facing the door; if you were at the sink, your back would be to the door. Immediately in front of the door was the living room that led to the two bedrooms, which were placed side-by-side.

I was at the stove looking down at what I was cooking, when all of a sudden, I heard the front door open and close; this was followed by the sound of footsteps walking across the living room, and into the left hand bedroom. Taken completely by surprise that one of my roommates returned early, and didn't have the nerve to not even say hello, I left the food and went to see who was there. I saw that both bedrooms were still dark—and even the closet lights were out. I called out the names of my roommates who occupied that room, but there was no answer. Shrugging it off, I went back to the kitchen to finish cooking my dinner. About ten minutes later, I was finished cooking; I had plated the food, and was in the process of putting the frying pan in the sink, when once again I heard the front door open and close, and heard those same footsteps go across the living room and into the same bedroom. Once more, I called out my roommates' names, and as before, heard nothing. I decided to do a little more investigating, so I went outside and went to the apartments above and below ours. Without exception, all of the apartments were unoccupied. I walked around the complex, thinking that this may have been some sort of acoustical trick, but the only other apartment that was occupied at that time, was on the other side of the complex.

Starting to wonder if I was I was losing it, I went back to my apartment and sat down to eat on the living room couch. Sure enough, a few minutes later, the same thing happened: only this time I was in the living room when it occurred. Though the door didn't open, the sound of it opening and closing was audible, and I could follow the sounds of the footsteps as they passed right in front of me. This time, I bolted off the couch and actually followed the footsteps (i.e.: I was following the footsteps as they were making their way across the living room and into the same bedroom). Once we (that is, me and the footsteps) got passed the threshold of the bedroom, the footsteps suddenly stopped, and I found myself in the middle of a dead silent, darkened bedroom. I made an immediate dash for the closet to turn on the light—just to see if it was some sort of prank...but no one was there.

Badly shaken, I made my way back to the living room, where I sat down and waited for it to happen again. It did not, but I was not able to finish my dinner, which was just as well—knowing my culinary skills. I spent the rest of the evening reflecting on what had happened.

I never felt like I was in any danger, or whatever was there was trying to force me out; maybe it was just trying to let me know that I was not as alone as I thought. What I found particularly interesting about this experience was that these were brand new apartments—freshly built. In fact, we were the first occupants in this complex (this happened in the Hannon apartments, should any L-M-U'ers be listening). They certainly did not look like you would expect a haunting to occur; and we had not heard of any construction workers dying during construction of the building—and as Loyola was (at that time anyway) a small community, any unusual happenings would have spread around.

Nothing else happened for the rest of the time I lived there; but I've often wondered if any students who have lived there since, experienced anything in the Hannon apartments.

Anything Ghost Episode #81
January 10, 2009

She Followed Us Down from the Attic
Marié (Sweden)

In December of 2005, me, my husband and our two-and-a-half year old daughter moved in to a large 121 square meter apartment in Svaneholm (south of Borås), Sweden. It was next to an old rubber factory that was very well known to that area. The apartment had once been two units but was reconfigured into one; so we had two exterior doors leading from the staircase.

We didn't have enough curtain rods for all the windows but I got a tip from a neighbor that earlier residents had left some things in the attic, and that I might find something of interest there. So one day I went up to the attic, and brought my daughter Michelle with me. Sure enough, I found abandoned junk in some of the corners and open storerooms that were up there. I searched for curtain rods without success, and then went into one of the open storerooms at the end of the attic (it was just above the second staircase). All in all, there were almost 40 storerooms up there. As I went into the little area, and stretched to look in the corner behind some boxes, my daughter startled me, "Mom. Girl dance."

I just said, "Yeah okay," and tried to peek into the dark corner.

She got annoyed and said firmly, "Mom look! The girl dance!"

I turned at her and asked, "Okay where?"

"THERE!" She pointed to the dark corner where I had just tried to see behind the boxes (and which was now behind me as I had turned to face her). I got scared and backed out of the storeroom. We went quickly down to our apartment...just below the attic.

After that day nothing felt the same again in a particular part of the apartment. It was the area where our bedroom, our daughters room, the dining room and one of the hallways connecting the other three rooms were. In the other half of the apartment there was never a bad feeling: I could sit in the dark with only one lamp reading without a problem. But the other part, well, it gave me chills even in the daytime.

At first it was only a feeling of sadness, malice, and a feeling that someone was very annoyed with me. But when my young daughter went from talking to toys as she played (which was nothing strange), to conversing with someone who was clearly sitting beside her—I got creeped out.

In the days that followed, I began having problems falling asleep. I never saw anyone, but I could feel someone standing in the doorway looking at me. I could not see her with my eyes, but I knew it was a girl (since I could see her in my mind standing there...looking at me). After a while, she came closer and began standing by my side of the bed...watching me. I had to keep the lights on in the hallway so I could see with my eyes that no one was actually there. But I felt it so clearly.

Things continued to get more terrifying.

Something inside of me said I had to close the door to the dining room every night to prevent the visits. But this task wasn't as easy as just leaning in, turning off the lights and then closing the door behind me. No. I had to grab the door, reach in to turn off the lightswitch and slam the door hard—this gave me only a fraction of a second to reach in and turn of the light before slamming the door. I did it this way because I felt there was a face right in front of me each time I approached the door—and it was a nasty, angry face.

I was beginning to think I was crazy and that it was all in my head—because I had never actually seen anything.

One day I was telling my experiences to a neighbor who lived in the apartment below us; her eleven-year-old daughter overheard our conversation and afterward she came over to talk to me. She she assured me I was not imagining anything—even though her mother did not believe in the paranormal. She went on to say that she knew who came to visit me because the girl visited her, as well. She added that this girl was not nice. She had visited to show her awful stuff— one time she brought a bloody knife with her. She said the girl had blue eyes, long dark hair and was not a typical Swedish girl.

"The girl looks like me but with blue eyes. She wears a white nightgown with blue flowers and has long dark, almost black hair. She's about my age, so I would guess ten. She scares me."

I can't remember all she told me, but I left the conversation knowing that it was a malicious little girl who was visiting us.

What does one do? I had no idea what to do to help her. It had been escalating and I was getting scared that something bad was going to happen—and what about the bloody knife she told me about?

A few weeks went by and nothing changed. I got almost no sleep in my bedroom and I had to sleep on the sofa.

In February of 2006, my cousin came to visit. I told her all about the events, but she had been sleeping in the "safe side" of the apartment, so she wasn't affected by the haunting. So, my cousin and me decided to ask my daughter about the girl.

Being that my daughter was too young to speak fluently, and hadn't yet learned colors, we were not able to ask questions that would lead her on such as, "is the girl's hair long and dark?" Because she probably would answer yes, no matter what the question was. So we chose to ask questions in a way that she could not answer yes or no.

She was laying in my bed under the blanket when we talked to her.

"Have you seen the girl lately?"

"Yes."

"Can you describe her? Her hair?

She sat up and touched my hair and then my cousin's hair—both dark at the time and half long, and said, "Like mum, like Jojja (my cousin's name is Ronja)."

"She has her hair like us?"

"Yes!"

"Okay. Can you remember her clothes?"

"Yes. A dress."

"What color is the dress?"

She looked around and saw that I was wearing a white shirt. She grabbed my arm and said, "This!"

"You mean white?"

"Yes!"

"Does she ever speak to you?"

"Yes."

"What does she say?" This was one of the creepiest moments ever; I get chills every time I think or speak about it, and I tear up.

My daughter brought the blanket up to her face so it was covering her mouth; staring in to my eyes, she said, with a whispering, monotonous, raucous voice, "Come with me. Come with me."

I am actually crying as I write this down now, as it terrified me so bad. I got so scared—this girl tried to lure away my child somewhere. But where? Thank God she had not followed.

My cousin and me stared at each other, and at that point I decided I had to get help.

I talked to my mother-in-law who gave me the name of a medium who had helped her once. I had to go through the phone book and call those in the area with the same name until I found to the right person. When I finally found her, I told her we needed help with ghosts. She immediately interrupted me. She said I was not allowed to tell her anything, as that would prevent an open mind and could disrupt her. She asked for nothing in return—no money or anything, She was just happy if she could help.

The night before her arrival, I woke up from the sound of wet feet running from the foot of the bed up to my bedside table. Fast, back and forth. Thump thump thump thump…over and over. I followed the sound with my eyes, but didn't see anything. But it was loud and clear, and I could tell by the sound that the feet were wet or muddy. It was not a dream or sleep paralysis, as I could move my head. I finally woke my husband, but the sound went silent.

When the medium came over the next day, I started to tell where she could find the issue; she interrupted me again, and told me she needed an open mind. She walked from the safe side of the apartment and immediately went into the dining room. She looked around and said, "Here. You have something, here."

Using those metal sticks that some can use to find water (divining rods), she raised and lowered her arms in front of the door—the dining room door where I'd always felt the face before closing it.

"It's a female and she's about this tall." She showed about shoulder height to me. The height of an average ten-year old.

Then she said, "She's going somewhere." She walked straight into our bedroom, and stopped at the side of my bed.

"She's here. She likes to stand here."

My husband had up until that point believed I was imagining everything. He did not believe in ghosts. I looked at him when the lady said that and the look on his face showed he knew that I was not crazy: we lived in an apartment of five rooms, two hallways, two bathrooms, a kitchen in 121 square meters—and the two spots that I pointed out as my problem places, this woman found in seconds. He could no longer deny something was going on.

She also asked if we had an attic. She felt that we had the energy of several spirits, and she felt the dining room was like a portal from a floor above (such as an attic). She added that these souls were not actually in the home, but through the portal we could feel them: a sadness.

We went up there and she stood still for a few seconds with her closed eyes and just breathing. Then she opened her eyes, turned around and walked straight across the whole attic and into the storeroom where my daughter first saw the girl. Once there she said, "Here. She was murdered here."

We all froze. Then stared back and forth at each other. My cousin and I, whom I showed that room to before, did not know what to do.

After we got down to the apartment the woman told me I was well protected. I had two spirits of my own with me—my guardian angels, as it were. One was a man I had with me from birth; another was a relative that chose to follow me after her passing (I know this was my grandmother, Ann-Marie, from whom I got my name); there was also a third, but this one wasn't for me, rather, he was protecting the child in my womb. I had not even a week before found out that I was pregnant. I asked her about the sex of the child, and she told me it was a boy.

Unfortunately, the medium was not able to help the girl cross over. After a few months of living there, we moved out.

Before we moved, a friend of mine came over to visit. When she walked in she asked me where the girl went. I asked her what girl she was referring to. She said that as she was walking up the stairs that lead to our front door, she saw a girl walking up ahead of her (the stairs zig-zagged); the girl went up to our door, but was gone before my friend reached the top.

I knew what she meant and asked, "A white dress with blue flowers?"

"Yes! Where did she go? I would have seen if she kept going up the stairs."

"She's dead," I told her.

She just stared at me. Then she laughed, and said she could have reached out her arm grabbing the girl's ankle if she wanted to—she was just as real as any of us.

"No, I'm not joking. The girl you saw is dead." Then I told her the story.

She had been a non-believer up until that moment. She had to ask my husband later just to be sure; and when he confirmed, she looked as if she was going to faint. She said over and over again, "I saw her! I really saw her! I could have grabbed her—she was there! I saw her!"

My mother in law still lives in the house next door, and she told me that everyone that has stayed there talks about the girl. We brought her down from the attic and she still stays in the apartment. I wish one day someone would be able to help her before her anger turns into something worse.

As a little note: I can tell that those houses were built for all the Greek, Yugoslav and Finn people who came to Sweden in the 1950's to work. The rubber factory next to these houses took a lot of lives, and the ones that did not die from accidents, knife fights or other violence, died in lung diseases caused by the toxic fumes in the factory. The immigrant laborers got the dirty work and the death rate was high. We think the girl was from Greece or Yugoslavia due to her looks. But we can't be sure, because we haven't found any information about a little girl being killed (my guess is she was killed with a knife up in that attic).

Was she even registered? Was her family here and she got lured up there? Or was she an illegal immigrant that was later dumped like garbage? I really would like to know as that could help me to give her the peace she needs. It's no wonder she's not a nice girl: she was taken from this life with violence, and with no one to give her redress.

One thing is for certain: I am not going back there until I know, because she still freaks the heck out of me.

I have told the story many times—and I have also told to my son, who was born in September 2006.

I hope some residents down in Svaneholm read this story and now know they are not alone.

Anything Ghost Episode #226
August 21, 2016

The End.

Take care...

Artist Unknown. Public Domain.
"Folk and Fairy Tales" c. 1883

Chapter 7

Index of Names

Alex (Central New York, U.S.) 138
Alex (Utica, New York) 166
Alice (Bendigo, Victoria, Australia) 224
Angel (Paramount, California) 21
Anonymous (Minneapolis, Minnesota) 52
Audri (San Francisco, California) 179
Barbara (Monterey, California) 232
Bekah (California, US) 59
Ben (Fort Smith, Arkansas) 117
Beth (Salem, Massachusetts) 79
Brandon (Auburn, New York) 238
Briana (Virginia, U.S.) 101
Briana (Virginia, U.S.) 105
Cari (Willington, Connecticut) 50
Carro (Stockholm, Sweden) 35
Celia (Cincinnati, Ohio) 81
Chris (Dublin, Ireland) 200
Christian - (Donna, Texas, US) 61
Christine D. (Gatineau, Quebec, Canada) . 234
Christine (San Francisco, California) 41
Claire (Sydney, Australia) 227
Claire (U.S.) 134
Darren (U.K.) 219
Dave (Carlsbad, California) 156
Dee (Los Angeles, California) 186
Desmond (Tasmania, Australia) 231
Donna (Maine, U.S.) 144
Donna (Plymouth, Michigan) 32
Ed (Bellflower, California) 239
Ed (Washington, Pennsylvania) 173
Edwina (Sydney, Australia) 229
Elizabeth (U.K.) 210
Elly (New York, New York) 175
Emily (North East of England) 49
Erika (Birmingham, Alabama) 148
Errol (New York, U.S.) 190
Ethan (U.S.) 194
Gareth (South Wales, U.K.) 207
George (South Wales, Swansea) 47
Helena (Stockholm, Sweden) 23
Isidro (Salt Lake City, Utah) 136
Jake (Raleigh, Mississippi) 185
Jenna (Toledo, Ohio) 160
Joevanny (Puerto Rico) 19
J. Steven (Texas, U.S.) 109
Julie (Pittsburgh, Pennsylvania) 189
Juliette (Paris, France) 13
Karli (Boise, Idaho) 39
Kathy (Ventura, California) 188
Kel (Seattle, US) 18
Kevin (U.S.) 196
Kia (Arkansas, U.S.) 152
Kong (Eau Claire, Wisconsin) 114
Krista (Phoenix, Arizona) 64
Kristina (New Jersey, US) 56
Lane (Boston, Massachusetts) 70
Lauren (Ventura, California) 40
Lee (Newport, Wales, U.K.) 211
Lemon (Texas, U.S.) 111
Liz (Glen Cove, New York) 100
Lora (Louisiana, U.S.) 127
Lucas (New England, U.S.) 72
Lynn (Orlando, Florida) 68
Maggie (Rochester, New York) 98
Marco (San Jose, California) 54
Marco (San Jose, California) 94
Marié (Sweden) 241
Matt (Suffolk, England) 216
Michael (Lincoln, Nebraska) 236
Michael (Queretaro, Mexico) 22
Mike (Manoa, Honolulu, Hawaii) 116
Mindy (Grand Rapids, Michigan) 192

Minnie (Korea) 82
Naomi (El Monte, California) 96
Natarsha (Massachusetts, U.S.) 120
Nicholas (U.K.) 197
Nick (Connecticut, U.S.) 150
Nick (Toronto, Canada) 222
Noelle (Michigan, U.S.) 140
Priscilla (California, U.S.) 146
Randy (New York, U.S.) 131
Rita (Queensland, Australia) 24
Robb (U.K.) 15
Rob (California, U.S.) 130
Robert (Texas, U.S.) 108
Roderick (Pas, Manitoba, Canada) 66
Ryan (New Orleans, Louisiana) 89
Sandi (Stauffer, Alberta, Canada) 97
Sara (Apex, North Carolina) 99
Savannah (Indiana, U.S.) 177
Savannah (Mississippi, U.S.) 178
Shannon (Layton, Utah) 142
Shannon (Layton, Utah) 237
Shannon (Tennessee, U.S.) 162
Spring (Texas, U.S.) 184
Stephanie (Green Bay, Wisconsin) 75
Steve (Kent, England) 215
Steve (Manchester, UK) 26
Tracey (Mountain Grove, Missouri) 27
Travis (Upland, California) 182
Valerie (Bakersfield, California) 37
Vicki (Bulacan, Philippines) 25
Victoria (New Zealand) 95
Walt (Kentucky, U.S.) 180

Chapter 8

Index of Extra Material

The Crisis Apparition - by Al Rauber. 9
Haunted Apartments 14
The Great Mausoleum - Lex Wahl 18
Milo Says Goodbye - Lex Wahl 20
Booms in the Basement - Lex Wahl .34
Haunted Guest House - Lex Wahl 38
A Place Memory or Residual Haunting - by Al Rauber 43
Haunted Hotels 53
Ghostly Knocks. 69
War Ghosts 74
Children Seeing Ghosts. 83
Transient Spirits - by Al Rauber. 85
The Mirror at Myrtles Plantation 93
Sleep and Snore Ernie Stories 97
War Ghosts 113
Poltergeist Activity - by Al Rauber 123
Haunted Office Spaces 133
Children Seeing Ghosts. 145
Haunted Hotels 161
A Purpose Haunting - by Al Rauber 169
Children Seeing Ghosts. 176
Clicks at the Freedom Mausoleum - by Lex Wahl 183
Halloween at the Freedom Mausoleum - by Lex Wahl. 187
Haunted Hotel in Carmel-by-the-Sea - by Lex Wahl 195
A True Haunting - by Al Rauber 203
Haunted Hotels 223

www.ingramcontent.com/pod-product-compliance
Lightning Source LLC
Chambersburg PA
CBHW070548050426
42450CB00011B/2762